Going Abroad

Going Abroad

EUROPEAN TRAVEL IN

NINETEENTH-CENTURY

AMERICAN CULTURE

William W. Stowe

PRINCETON UNIVERSITY PRESS · PRINCETON, NEW JERSEY

Copyright © 1994 by Princeton University Press
Published by Princeton University Press, 41 William Street,
Princeton, New Jersey 08540
In the United Kingdom: Princeton University Press,
Chichester, West Sussex

Library of Congress Cataloging-in-Publication Data
Stowe, William W., 1946–
Going abroad : European travel in nineteenth-century
American culture / William W. Stowe
p.   cm.
Includes bibliographical references and index.
ISBN 0-691-03364-1
1. American prose literature—19th century—History and
criticism.   2. Travelers' writings, American—History and criticism.
3. Americans—Travel—Europe—History—19th century.
4. American literature—European influences.   5. Europe in literature.
6. Travel in literature.   I. Title
PS366.T73S76   1994   818'.30809355—dc20   94-1365   CIP

This book has been composed in Adobe Garamond

Princeton University Press books are
printed on acid-free paper and meet the guidelines
for permanence and durability of the Committee
on Production Guidelines for Book Longevity
of the Council on Library Resources

Printed in the United States of America

1   3   5   7   9   10   8   6   4   2

FOR KARIN

Contents

Preface

HENRY JAMES'S "'Europe'" is the story of four women who live in a "square white house" at the end of a "straight brick walk" in a "good Boston suburb." It is a mild house, a quiet house, above all a "cultured" house; indeed, the narrator thinks it "must have been the house, in all the world, in which 'culture' first came to the aid of morning calls."[1] Its air of distinction depends in large degree upon its inhabitants' special relation to something known as "Europe." Mrs. Rimmle had been one of the first post-Napoleonic American tourists: "[She] was understood to have made . . . the tour of Europe at a date not immensely removed from that of the battle of Waterloo" (10:37). Her three daughters—still known, despite their advancing age, as "the young ladies" (10:38)—have been raised in the hope of "going" one day themselves.

But a lifetime of suburban exile has put the object of their common desire in quotation marks. "Europe" has become for them not so much a real place as a very commodious signifier. To Mrs. Rimmle it stands for the social and intellectual advantages provided by her own glamorous past and promised by her daughters' longed-for "European" future. "There's a duty that calls them to those wonderful countries," she says, "if it be only that of laying up for the years to come the same store of remarkable impressions, the same wealth of knowledge and food for conversation as, since my return, I have found myself so happy to possess" (10:40–41). To the "young ladies" it signifies some vague combination of freedom, danger, and fulfillment, embodying for Jane "the lifelong, secret, passionate ache of her little rebellious desire" (10:40) and raising for them all "the oddest vibration of dread," "as if they had been in the presence of danger" (10:42).

As it turns out, only Jane actually "goes," and the use she makes of Europe is very different from her mother's assiduous accumulation of cultural capital. Not content to acquire a gingerly sampling of European life and art to bring back home to Boston, Jane plunges in, "tastes blood" (10:53), and declines to return at all. Witnesses report that she has "appeared . . . in a new character" (10:53), that she is "rather strange and free and obstreperous" (10:53) and "has taken to flirting" (10:54). This news is apparently more than old Mrs. Rimmle can handle, and she takes it into her head that Jane is dead.

"Jane's dead. We've heard," said Mrs. Rimmle. "We've heard from—
where is it we've heard from?" She had quite revived—she appealed to her
daughter.

The poor old girl, crimson, rallied to her duty. "From Europe." (10:59)

James's story provides a knowing, ironic summary of some of the uses
upper-middle-class Americans made of Europe from the close of the Napoleonic Wars to the turn of the twentieth century. Mrs. Rimmle, who
could have met Washington Irving on her youthful tour, uses Europe
decades later as a sign for another time, a proof to herself and others that
she has lived, and a token of social and cultural distinction. Her homebound daughters, the contemporaries, roughly speaking, of Bayard Taylor, Margaret Fuller, and William Wells Brown, use it to embody the
vague object of their ill-defined but powerful desires, the dangerous fulfillment of their unacknowledged wishes. Jane uses it as a stage to act out
her newfound social and sexual freedom. The narrator, a fin-de-siècle
Jamesian dilettante, uses it as a literal retreat and a sign of his own distance from narrow lives and small rectilinear towns near Boston. All of
James's characters use Europe to stand for some combination of social
distinction, high culture, eroticism, and freedom, construing it variously
as alluring, threatening, elegant, artful, and wicked. James himself uses it
in all these ways too, and, notoriously, as a subject for his fiction.

This book is about the uses that travelers and writers from Washington
Irving to Henry Adams made of Europe and of European travel. The
question of Europe's meaning for North American culture and experience
has been debated since colonial times. One need only mention Benjamin
Franklin, John Adams, Thomas Jefferson, Benjamin West and John Sin-
gleton Copley, Emerson, Thoreau, Fuller, Douglass, Hosmer, Story,
Hawthorne, Howells, James, and Wharton among politicians, writers,
and artists and Van Wyck Brooks, Henry Seidel Canby, Cushing Strout,
and Robert Weisbuch among literary critics and cultural historians to get
some sense of the range and the duration of the debate. The purpose of
the chapters that follow is to intervene in this debate from a new angle,
not to attempt once again to define the meaning that nineteenth-century
U.S. culture assigned to Europe but rather to provide an account of the
ways in which that culture and a number of its writers, little known as
well as famous, used European travel and travel writing. My method has
been to ask what nineteenth-century American classes, groups, and individuals got out of the expensive, time-consuming, even dangerous, but

extraordinarily popular practice of European travel. Several answers to this question have emerged in the course of my study. I present them here in a summary, schematic way and invite the reader to explore them in more detail in the rest of the book.

One way nineteenth-century Americans used European travel was to help construct and claim identities variously defined by gender, class, race, and nationality. The connection between travel and the construction of identity has a long history. Early American travelers such as Thomas Jefferson and John Adams were eager to define themselves in transnational terms as ex-Europeans with a special relation to European culture, whereas their successors in midcentury—Fuller, Greeley, and Twain, for example—were more concerned with asserting a uniquely American identity. The whole enterprise of European travel by nineteenth-century Americans was intimately associated, furthermore, with the construction of a privileged bourgeoisie in the context of an ostensibly classless society. And American travelers used the experience of Europe to help them think about questions of race and gender, about ways of relating to their country, their compatriots, and the wider world as African Americans, former or current slaves, slaveholders, abolitionists, independent or dependent women, and marginalized or actively engaged men.

Much of the best work on the intersections of questions of race, class, gender, and nationality with the experience and the writing of travel has been done by feminist scholars, who have seen travel as a site both of female empowerment and contestatory discourse and of the definition and assertion of power by dominant races, classes, and nationalities. Although the most suggestive work in this field has concerned travel by Europeans to actual and potential colonies,[2] the sense that it conveys of the traveler as both assuming and constructing a "natural" superiority based on class, race, gender, and national identity is directly applicable to American travel in Europe. In addition to explicitly feminist works, the arguments of such theorists of class and power as Veblen, Weber, Bourdieu, and Baudrillard and the impressive body of American social and cultural history that includes the work of Ann Douglas, Alan Trachtenberg, Nancy Cott, Carroll Smith-Rosenberg, Lawrence Levine, Jackson Lears, and Jonathan Freedman have influenced my thinking in this area.

Of course, travelers were motivated by personal as well as cultural and social agendas. James's Mrs. Rimmle may have used her European trip to claim or affirm membership in a genteel New England elite, but her daughter Jane seems to have had something else in mind. Her European experiences remind us that Americans also used Europe as a setting for personal liberation and the fulfillment of desire, whether erotic, as in the case of Margaret Fuller, sociosexual, as in the case of David Dorr, or sublimated and aesthetic, as in Adams, James, and a large number of ordinary tourists. This complex of erotic desire and sublimated fantasy was best formulated by Proust's Marcel, whom the very names of distant places could instantly suffuse with sweet desire.

> Even in spring, to come upon the name Balbec in a book sufficed to awaken in me the desire for storms at sea and for Norman Gothic; even on a stormy day the name Florence or Venice would awaken the desire for sunshine, for lilies, for the Palace of the Doges and for Santa Maria del Fiore.[3]

In James's life and in his fiction, in the minds of the young Margaret Fuller, the aging Henry Adams, and the tourists whom Twain satirized and Emerson earnestly criticized, Europe played the part of Proust's Venice, and such unlikely names as Chester, Kenilworth, and Vevey raised associations comparable in their allure to the Norman and the Oriental charms of Balbec.[4]

Finally, if most nineteenth-century American travelers used Europe for both social and personal purposes, a large minority also exploited it for professional ends, using their tours as occasions and subjects for writing. For reasons I will explore in detail in chapter 1, the nineteenth-century American traveling class was also a writing class: bourgeois travelers often used the production of texts to justify what might otherwise have seemed the sinful self-indulgence of travel, aspiring writers crafted apprentice work, and established writers kept the pot boiling using the available form of the travelogue and the abundant material provided by a European tour.

In the course of this book, I will show how European travel and travel writing were used by Americans in general and by variously defined groups of Americans to forward their personal and collective agendas. I will also show how European travel and travel writing helped Lydia Sigourney and Bayard Taylor, David F. Dorr and William Wells Brown, Ralph Waldo Emerson, Margaret Fuller, Mark Twain, Henry James, and Henry Adams to construct lives and careers for themselves in the context of the cultures and the societies they were helping to shape.

I begin by describing the importance of travel and of writing in nineteenth-century U.S. culture, outlining their social and historical settings and the literary and cultural conventions that they followed, criticized, modified, or rejected. I then discuss the ways in which writers used these conventions to do their work and the work of their class, race, gender, and nationality. The sections on Dorr and Brown, Emerson, Fuller, Twain, James, and Adams have arguments of their own, dictated by their subjects' very different origins, material and cultural circumstances, ambitions, and personalities. They all depend, however, on the historical and conceptual context provided by the opening chapters, and their conclusions reaffirm the more general view of cultural activities like travel and travel writing as partly prefabricated settings for advancing the multiple simultaneous agendas of individuals and the groups to which they belong.[5] Readers interested in any one of these figures can read the section devoted to him or her as a freestanding essay. Anyone reading the whole book will find a few key ideas repeated in more than one chapter, but I have done my best to keep such repetition to the absolute minimum consistent with each section's coherence.

Acknowledgments

THIS BOOK would never have been completed without the help and encouragement of more friends and colleagues than I can mention here. Peter Brooks presided over my early studies of James; Fran Bartkowski, Karen Lawrence, and Dennis Porter helped shape my early thinking about travel literature; Richard Brodhead and Richard Slotkin helped me move from comparative literature to something akin to American studies. Christina Crosby, Ann duCille, Joan Hedrick, Gertrude Hughes, and Joe Reed read, commented on, and greatly improved parts of the manuscript. Bill Marling helped me find out what little there is to know about David Dorr. I continue to profit enormously from my conversations and collaboration with Andrew Szegedy-Maszak and Khachig Tölölyan.

I have also been cheered and instructed by a large number of Wesleyan colleagues, especially those in the English Department and the Center for the Humanities, who have been extraordinarily generous with advice and encouragement. For all this I am grateful to Nancy Armstrong, Annie Dillard, Paul Fisher, Indira Karamcheti, Bob Richardson, Phyllis Rose, and Len Tennenhouse, among many others.

Wesleyan University has provided time and money to help complete this project. Librarians at Wesleyan and Yale have provided invaluable help. Bob Brown, of Princeton University Press, has encouraged my work for several years. The Press's anonymous readers guided my revisions. Dalia Geffen has helped tone up my prose and tighten my argument.

A version of chapter 6 appeared in *American Literature* 63 (1991); a version of chapter 9 was published in *New England Quarterly* 64 (1991). I am grateful to the editors of these journals for permission to reprint this material.

This list could go on and on, but it ends now, as it has before, with the name of my closest friend, reader, and traveling companion, Karin Trainer.

Going Abroad

CHAPTER ONE

Americans Abroad

THE AMERICAN is a migratory animal," wrote Robert Tomes in *Harper's New Monthly Magazine* in 1865. "He walks the streets of London, Paris, St. Petersburg, Berlin, Vienna, Naples, Rome, Constantinople, Canton, and even the causeways of Japan, with as confident a step as he treads the pavements of Broadway."[1] East and west, north and south, for business or pleasure, exploration or rediscovery, many nineteenth-century Americans traveled, and many more participated vicariously in the experience of travel by reading travel letters, sketches, and narratives in newspapers, magazines, and published volumes.

Europe was by far the most popular destination for nineteenth-century American travelers; accounts of European travel were a standard feature of many newspapers. In the late 1840s Horace Greeley's *New-York Tribune* published Margaret Fuller's letters from Europe and Bayard Taylor's "Glances at Modern Germany." In the early 1860s Greeley went to Europe himself, and his foreign correspondence appeared in the paper's columns. Not ten years later Henry Adams was breaking into public print with his account of his travels in Germany and Italy in the Boston *Courier*. And the most popular travel book of the century, Twain's *The Innocents Abroad,* began as a series of letters commissioned by the San Francisco *Alta California*.

By 1875 so many people were sending accounts of their travels to newspapers that the guidebook author M. F. Sweetser saw fit to warn his readers that "among the thousands of our people who visit Europe every summer, many scores are afflicted by the *cacoethes scribendi* and our newspaper men consign the average proposals for a foreign correspondence to the limbo of spring poems."[2] His own burlesque of "the average letter from Europe (which generally goes into the editor's basket, but sometimes strays into print)" seems exaggerated today but would in fact be hard to distinguish from many of the more breathless published accounts.

To the editor of the "Battle Cry."

At last I am in the Eternal City!!!!!!!! About me are the temples!! and palaces!! of Rome!! once the mighty mistress of the world!!!!!!!!!!!! The pres-

ence of the Venerable Past!!! is brooding over her ancient hills and ruined
shrines!!!! and inspires my soul with a strange and reverential awe !!!!!!!!!
Mystic and wondrous city!!!!!!! (108–9)

And newspapers were not the only outlets for travelers' prose. Magazines, too, were full of travel articles and reviews, usually soberer and
more polished than newspaper pieces but catering to a similar appetite for
the foreign. Early in the century the *Port Folio* printed travel essays
cribbed from London journals, the *North American Review* and the *American Quarterly Review* ran long review articles with copious excerpts from
current travel books, and even the austere *Dial* published "Voyage to Ja-
maica" (July–October 1843), "Discoveries in the Nubian Pyramids" (January 1843), and a number of other travel-related pieces. By midcentury
Godey's was running many short reviews, and the new *Harper's* and *Atlantic* were publishing both reviews and original accounts, preparing the
ground for Howells, James, Woolson, and Wharton.

And then there were travel books, some privately printed, but many
brought out by commercial publishers. Harold F. Smith lists 1,822 travel
books published by Americans before 1900,[3] of which the vast majority
appeared in the nineteenth century; Mary-Suzanne Schriber counts 691
American books of travel between 1800 and 1868, of which 152 described
travel to England.[4] Ahmed Metwalli reports that "all kinds of books of
travel, a large number of which were mere hasty collections of unedited
letters or article serials, sold by the tens of thousands," the most popular
making their writers' reputations, if not always their fortunes.[5]

A quick glance at the biographies and collected works of the canonical
figures in nineteenth-century American literature will show that all but
Whitman, Thoreau, and Dickinson went to Europe, and most wrote
about it. Irving went and began his popular series of travel books with
The Sketch Book of Geoffrey Crayon (1820–21). Cooper traveled extensively
and produced a series of *Gleanings in Europe* (1837–38). Longfellow went
and wrote *Outre-Mer* (1846); Hawthorne recorded his experiences in *Our
Old Home* (1863). Margaret Fuller went at last, after years of yearning, and
sent letters back to the *New-York Tribune* (1846–50); Harriet Beecher
Stowe recorded her grand tour in *Sunny Memories of Foreign Lands* (1854).
The popular writers Grace Greenwood (Sara Jane Lippincott), Fanny
Fern (Sara P. Willis), and Lydia H. Sigourney, "the Sweet Singer of Hartford," all weighed in with contributions. Frederick Douglass recorded his
European experiences briefly in *My Bondage and My Freedom* (1855); William Wells Brown traveled to the Paris Peace Conference of 1849 and
wrote *The American Fugitive in Europe* (1855).

In addition, many otherwise unknown Americans offered accounts of their European travels to the public. Zachariah Allen toured the farms and factories of England, France, and Holland and reported on his findings in *The Practical Tourist; or, Sketches of the State of the Useful Arts, and of Society, Scenery, &c. &c.* (1832). Fanny W. Hall took the grand tour in 1836 and published her *Rambles in Europe* two years later. David F. Dorr went to Europe as a slave, escaped to the North on his return, and published *A Colored Man Round the World* in 1858.

A wide variety of nineteenth-century Americans traveled and many of them wrote up their journeys. Among them they produced a few memorable texts and a large number of very similar accounts of nearly identical trips containing predictable comments on predictable sights and experiences.[6] What explains the appeal of the conventional European tour and the success of such a repetitive form of writing in the literary marketplace? What was there about nineteenth-century American culture that made European travel, travel writing, and the reading of travel literature so attractive to a certain segment of the population?[7]

The most obvious answer is still in many ways the most important. Until very late in the century the United States was widely believed to lack almost every element that made up what Henry James called "the denser, richer, warmer European spectacle." James's famous list of lacks ("No sovereign, no court . . . no museums, no pictures . . . no Epsom nor Ascot!")[8] suggested a general lack of traditions, glamour, polish, and culture. To obtain these desirable elements of a gracious and refined way of life one naturally had to travel to Europe.

The desire for high culture and distinguished society could not by itself have created the nineteenth-century tourist boom, however. Claiming a tradition and espousing a style of living were also ways of defining oneself and the social groups to which one belonged. For traveler after traveler, as we will see, Europe served as a stage for independent self-definition, for establishing personal relations with culture and society that did not necessarily fit the conventional patterns prescribed by hometown and family standards. In addition, European travel was a way of affirming the respectability of one's race, class, or gender. Through travel newly rich Americans could simultaneously claim membership in a superior social class and justify the privileges of that class by demonstrating its "inherent" sensitivity and refinement. Similarly, poor men like Bayard Taylor, African Americans like David Dorr and William Wells Brown, and especially women could use the European tour and their written reports of it to claim the attention and the respect of an American audience.

Furthermore, economic and social conditions for travel grew more and more propitious as the nineteenth century went on. Many eighteenth-century Americans doubtless aspired to European grace and refinement, and some few, mainly from the cities of the Atlantic seaboard and the slave-run Southern plantations, traveled to Europe to acquire them, but the vast majority of their compatriots were using all the time and resources at their command to set up and run their farms, mills, homes, and businesses. By the end of the Napoleonic Wars, the relatively steady rise of a leisured class of property owners and capitalists and the growing ability of the economy to support a class of educated professionals were creating a pool of privileged individuals who could act on their desire for the social and cultural distinction that Europe offered. These same developments, furthermore, were creating a large number of newly rich, socially insecure Americans, who used the trip to Europe to claim membership in a cultured upper class.

As early as the 1830s, according to Edward Pessen, the moneyed urban elite spent "the warm weather months" enjoying "the delights of the Rockaways and other ocean resorts or . . . the waters of Saratoga and regularly traveled to Havre in ships blessed with luxurious accommodations."[9] By the end of the Civil War, this traveling class was large and familiar enough to evoke criticism and satire. "It is not easy to analyze the vague and confused motives which induce our wealthy people to travel abroad," wrote Robert Tomes in 1865. "Many of them go for no better reason than because traveling costs money, and being necessarily more or less exclusive, is approved by fashion."[10] "To go or not to go—abroad—is the question which has long agitated many of our households," an anonymous *Putnam's Magazine* article declared in 1868. Young people yearned for the glamour and culture and commodities; they pined for the chance to see certified European sights, present themselves on the fantasy stages of the European scene, and buy European goods.

> "I want to see Eugenie skate, to hear the *Miserere*, and to swim in a gondola, before I die," pleads the grown-up daughter. "And I long to ride in the Bois, to loiter in the Louvre, and see a rowing match on the Cam," adds her brother; while the smaller children dream of Swiss toys and French bonbons.[11]

Their mothers, meanwhile, sought in Europe the social successes that had eluded them at home.

> At home she never could succeed, even with the aid of Brown's list, in gathering about her the *élite* of the city where her lord had made his fortune. She was snubbed by her old school-friend, who had been polished at

a French school, and married a popular attorney. She was laughed at for murdering the King's English, and wearing *outré* apparel. In short, her social aspirations had been ruthlessly disappointed; so she coaxed her gudeman to come abroad; and, in Paris, her beautiful apartments, her showy landau, her opera-box, her elegant toilette, and, above all, her luxuriant dinners, do attract her errant countrymen and women, even those who ignored her on the Fifth Avenue. (532)

In addition to the idle or the vacationing rich, the expanding nineteenth-century American economy was able to support a considerable class of professional people who produced no material wealth and provided no materially essential service.[12] Members of these nonproductive classes—clergymen, artists, teachers, writers—frequently used their European travels to prepare for or advance their careers. When twenty-three-year-old George Ticknor set sail from Boston in 1815, accompanied by Edward Everett and two sons of John Quincy Adams and carrying a list of books that Thomas Jefferson wanted for his library, he was on his way to the university at Göttingen, where, he reported to his father, "my chief objects are still Greek and German, my subsidiary objects Italian and French, my amusement literary history, chiefly ancient, and books that will fit me for my future travels."[13] Ticknor was a serious intellectual, the first occupant of the Harvard chair in Spanish and Italian literature which was later held by Longfellow and James Russell Lowell. He was also the forerunner of a whole class of materially nonproductive Americans who helped create an artistic and intellectual culture that valued European travel as a flight from various distasteful aspects of life at home. As the century wore on, this class came to include a wide range of journalists and social activists, women, African Americans, and middle-class white males, as well as the sons of Ticknors, Everetts, and Adamses. As we will see, study tours, writing assignments, and attendance at international conferences gave a large number of Americans, undistinguished by birth or fortune, the chance to define themselves and their groups in the context of European culture and history and to report on the process and its results in print.

The historian Ann Douglas reads this whole phenomenon as part of "the feminization of American culture" in the first half of the nineteenth century. She sees travel, travel writing, and other combinations of leisurely enjoyment and intellectual cultivation as falling in this period more and more to women and a group of their social allies made up primarily of professors, clergymen, and sentimental writers, all of them, men and women alike, supported by the surpluses that a thriving capitalist economy generated. The "contiguity of travel and writing" in this period "was not accidental," she writes; "it expressed the fact that these authors built their professions on a form of evasion—of their country, of their own identity, and of their occupation itself."[14] Her judgment of these men and women is overly severe—her contention that her subjects were evading their country, for example, rather than rejecting or criticizing it seems to adopt the dominant ("masculine") point of view and thus belittles their very real accomplishments—but her theory as a whole helps to explain the popularity of European travel throughout the century and to account for the large number of women, clergymen, popular journalists, and academics who published reports of their European travels.

However the phenomenon is explained, some combination of the allure of European culture and society, the underlying strength of the American economy, and the developing class structure sent thousands of Americans to Europe throughout the nineteenth century. With the large-scale introduction of fast, comfortable, and fairly reliable North Atlantic steamships[15] and the roughly simultaneous expansion of European railway networks, the tide of the early nineteenth century became a torrent, and the American tourist in Europe became a commonplace. Recent histories of tourism have documented the rapid expansion of the industry;[16] contemporary writers noticed it as well. "If the social history of the world is ever written," *Putnam's Magazine* declared in 1868, "the era in which we live will be called the nomadic period. With the advent of ocean steam navigation and the railway system, began a travelling mania which has gradually increased until half of the earth's inhabitants, or at least half of its civilized portion, are on the move."[17]

To put it schematically, an underlying economically, socially, and culturally driven demand for European travel joined with a new technology to stimulate provision of a large supply of transatlantic transportation, which in turn helped increase the demand for improved travel services in Europe. This generated an ultimately vast supply of couriers and guides, hotels, banking services, and reading rooms, which made European travel even more attractive by linking it to luxury, convenience, and conspicuous consumption. Traveling Americans used Europe as a stage to enact their personal and social fantasies and as a treasure trove of learning, culture, and commodities. The booming travel industry used Europe as a device for marketing hotel rooms, wagons-lits, package tours, and courier services.

If this dynamic helps explain the growing popularity of European travel in the nineteenth century, however, it cannot fully account for the

American Travellers in Europe

Should not fail to remember that

THEIR CROWNING NATIONAL LUXURY,

THE

PULLMAN PALACE CARS

CAN BE FOUND ON THE

Great Midland Railway,

OF ENGLAND,

SUPPLYING PASSAGE BETWEEN

LONDON, & LIVERPOOL, LEICESTER, DERBY,
&c., &c.,

WITH AMERICAN CONDUCT AND MANAGEMENT,

AND

All the Modern Conveniences,

Which mark the " PULLMANS " as the

Travelling Wonder and Glory of the Age,

AND THE

LEADING SUBJECT OF AMERICAN PRIDE.

Due announcement will be made of the putting on of the **Pullman**
Palace Cars, already under contract and admitted to
be indispensable, on

OTHER LINES OF GREAT BRITAIN AND THE CONTINENT.

"Wonder and Glory of the Age," from *Morford's Short-Trip
Guide* (1874).

popularity of travel writing, to which a number of other factors contributed. The sentimental closeness of the bourgeois family and the development of a reliable international postal service certainly stimulated letter
writing from abroad; travelers with a literary bent naturally recorded their
impressions in order to share them with or show them off to others; stay-
at-homes interested in the subject or the author, as well as people plan-
ning or dreaming of similar tours, naturally provided a market for these
impressions. The peculiar status of writing in antebellum America also
contributed to the success of travel writing. Among the many contradictions that helped structure the American upper middle class in the early
nineteenth century was that between the neo-Puritan work ethic and the
economy's new ability to support more and more economically unproductive members. While the culture at large continued to extol the virtues of productive labor, the field of activity for well-to-do women nar-
rowed, and the number of men in economically marginal occupations
increased. The result was a redefinition of the idea of work to include
these peoples' activities, especially writing.[18] One way for economically
nonproductive men and women to justify their privilege, minimize their
guilt feelings, and make their mark in the world was to record their
thoughts and experiences in writing. In fact, writing was the ideal work
for the marginalized male and the only respectable public channel for
the voice of the supposedly private and domestic female. According to
Charles Butler, the author of popular books of etiquette and advice, the
"American gentleman" of 1836 who chose a "literary and retired life" was
not thereby excused from the cultural imperative to work. "The fire of the
mind," Butler wrote, "has burned with a clear and constant flame, when
open and ventilated by perpetual motion, as it has been smothered and
extinguished in smoke, when suffered to remain long without disturbance." Literature and retirement are all very well, but sloth and torpor
certainly are not. The literary gentleman must justify his privilege by the
products of his pen or suffer the shame of invidious comparison with his
social inferiors who must work for a living:

> A hackney writer of catch-penny compilations, the editor of a newspaper,
> the maker of a magazine, will perform, in a few months, a portion of literary
> labour, which shall infinitely exceed that of whole colleges inhabited by
> those who slumber in literary retirement.[19]

The best defense against such accusations of indolence and self-indulgence was clearly to produce a text.

For women, writing was an even more valuable, because rarer, form of productive activity. Letter writing was a valued social skill; handbook after handbook instructed young ladies on the production of elegant, grammatical, and tasteful prose in their social correspondence. For women who moved on from letters to belles-lettres and moralistic prose, writing combined a private activity, a conventionally commendable desire for "influence," and the opportunity to make a public name for themselves and take a public position without actually appearing in public. "Where a knock-down in-person plea would be out of place, a well-written 'effusion' was by definition polite."[20]

Writing, then, was a respectable activity: the lady or gentleman who wrote could be proud of filling time productively. It was a kind of work, and as such it could turn an idle holiday into a serious mission, a desultory grand tour into a purposeful investigation of foreign institutions, manners, and art. Its association with travel lent the respectability of productive labor to an activity more frequently associated with frivolity and conspicuous consumption. The happy conjunction of the two helps account for the popularity of both travel and travel writing in the United States in the nineteenth-century.

Another factor that certainly contributed to the popularity of travel writing had to do with its attractiveness as an established, respectable, and relatively undemanding literary genre. Travel writing offered aspiring authors a ready-made form, a surefire subject, and the opportunity to adopt one of several widely respected cultural roles. Like the pilgrims at the beginning of *The Innocents Abroad*, inexperienced writers thought that nothing could be easier than spending an hour or two a day recording their impressions and nothing more fascinating to a homebound audience than an account of their foreign adventures. A travel account, to their minds, was simply a collection of foreign impressions, all written down in a book.

The results of their efforts were predictably mixed. Most of Twain's pilgrims soon ran out of steam; traveling writers who managed to publish their work often evoked indifference or even hostility from the reading public. "Nothing is more slipshod," wrote a censorious Henry James, "than the style in which publications of this kind are habitually composed. Letters and diaries are simply strung into succession and transferred to print."[21] Despite their misgivings, however, both Twain and James remarked on the presumed easiness of the genre, and the fact that many hundreds of otherwise unpublished writers managed to finish books of travel suggests that its ready-made quality gave aspiring authors the confidence they might otherwise have lacked.

More important than the genre's easiness, and more appealing to all but the least ambitious of writers, was the chance it offered travelers to claim respected cultural roles for themselves. Travel writing provided a stage on which they could act out their desires for authority and importance. In preface after preface writers admitted their cultural belatedness, apologized for leading their readers over well-trodden ground, but went on nonetheless to cast themselves as teachers, guides, mentors, models, and, they hoped, successful authors.

Fanny W. Hall introduced her *Rambles in Europe . . . in 1836* by disavowing all claims to novelty: "In her rambles, she . . . looked only upon things which a thousand times before have been seen and admired."[22] In admitting her belatedness as a traveler, however, she also claimed the authority of a writer and a guide. Before she left for Europe, she wrote, "the countries which she traversed were known [to her] only from books" (vii). Now that she has returned, she will take her turn as author, and "furnish a telescope, through which [her] home-staying friend, sitting at ease in his elbow-chair, may reconnoitre, and at his leisure trace the course of the wayfarer, and enjoy with him the elegancies of foreign cities, or the exciting vicissitudes of adventurous travel" (vi).

Lydia Sigourney, in the preface to *Pleasant Memories of Pleasant Lands*, admitted that for "a traveller in climes so generally visited" it would be "difficult to say what has not been said before" and agreed to "forfeit the right of discovery" if she could only "retain the power of promoting good and pleasurable feelings."[23] She did not presume to inform her readers, but rather aspired through her travel writing to please them, and above all to influence their behavior and affections. In keeping with the genteel and pious conventions of her class, gender, and time, Sigourney renounced the title of explorer and adventurer, asserting the preeminently feminine power of "influence" and claiming a position of authority parallel to that of the minister.[24]

Bayard Taylor was less apologetic than Hall and Sigourney and even more conscious of his place and the place of his travels in literary culture. His early reading inspired two parallel ambitions: to be a traveler and to be a writer. "When a boy of ten years," he wrote, "I read Willis's 'Pencillings by the Way' as they appeared from week to week in the country newspaper, and the contemplation of those charming pictures of scenery and society filled me with a thousand dreams and aspirations."[25] When he was fifteen Putnam's *The Tourist in Europe*, "fell into [his] hands" (18). Although the budget Putnam proposed was beyond Taylor's means, the book set him to dreaming of Europe again, and when two years later he found his dream of inexpensive European travel confirmed in "Howitt's Rural Life in Germany" (18), he began to plan for his departure. The remaining problem was cash, and the solution was obvious. Taylor called upon "all the principal editors and publishers" in Philadelphia, and several more in New York, and secured commissions for travel letters. This done, he paid ten dollars for passage in the steerage to Liverpool, spent fourteen more on food and bedding for the voyage, and launched a thirty-year career as a traveler and writer. What had started as a quest for travel funds became an initiation into the world of periodical publishing. Taylor had placed himself very clearly in a thriving literary tradition and set out quite consciously to fill the culturally available role of man of letters.

If one way of accounting for the important place of European travel and travel writing in nineteenth-century U.S. culture is provided by a historically specific combination of economic, social, and cultural factors and personal desires and ambitions, another, more theoretical source of the appeal and the power of all kinds of travel and travel writing may be found in the features they share with the whole range of human activities—exploration, research, reading, and so on—included under the general heading Interpretation. Writing and travel are *creative* acts, ways of giving form and meaning to actions and perceptions, of shaping experience for comprehension, use, and pleasure. As such, they are also necessarily *interpretive* acts, based on particular understandings of their subjects, governed by the interpretive conventions of their practitioners' social and historical situations, and closely related to reading, whether it is understood literally as the perusal of a text or figuratively as the interpretation of data.[26]

The parallels among travel, reading, and writing were as real for nineteenth-century Americans as they are for poststructural literary critics. The traveling class was a reading class, and travel was seen as a preeminently literary activity. Itineraries were drawn up with the monuments of literary history in mind, and the pleasure of travel derived in part from the way it reminded the traveler of past literary pleasures. Hardly a tourist landed in Liverpool in the antebellum period without heading for "the Scott country" (by way of the equally heavily inscribed "Wordsworth country"); no one went to Venice or Rome without thinking of Byron, if only because the most popular guidebooks quote the key passages from canto 4 of *Childe Harold*. (Twain boasts that he is "the only free white man of mature age" to have "written about the Coliseum and the gladiators, the martyrs and the lions, and yet never once have used the [Byronic] phrase 'butchered to make a Roman holiday.'")[27] American travelers in Europe made their way through a landscape already heavily inscribed by poets, travel writers, and even novelists. Mme de Staël's *Corinne, ou de l'Italie* was a popular vade mecum early in the century,[28] supplemented later by Hawthorne's *Marble Faun* and James's international fiction. The connection between travel and the literary pursuits of reading and writing was an inescapable fact of nineteenth-century American culture, each contributing to and sharing in the prestige, the glamour, and the respectability of the others.

The theoretical relations among traveling, reading, and writing were also noted from the beginning. As early as 1819 the *North American Review* reminded readers of "the analogy which exists between travelling and reading." A little later in the century, Margaret Fuller and Henry Tuckerman agreed that travelers had to interpret experience if they wished to convey its true meaning to their readers. The traveler, Fuller wrote, "must have a poetic sensibility to what is special and individual both in nations and men." "This poetic sensibility ought to be common to every one," she went on,

> but now minds highly endowed in many respects, are often so deficient in this, that no observation of theirs will ever reproduce the reality. In the world of writers we find very few, among our daily companions almost none, that look through the veils which are hung over the realities of life—few or almost none that hold "the golden key, which, turned so softly, turning with so sweet a sound, unlocks the hearts of men." And you can see nothing of the institutions and manners of a nation, unless you can look into the heart from which they grew.[29]

Fuller's ideal traveler, like her ideal writer, should be a poet, and a poet for Fuller was always a kind of interpreter, a visionary with the power to see into the life of things. Tuckerman, in contrast, saw the ideal traveler as a philosophic rather than a poetic interpreter. His goal was to work "by the light of philosophy," "to think, not to create—to see, not to imagine," but at the same time "to elicit the ideal from the real, to look beyond the immediate and material, without distorting the perspective."[30] For both, intelligent travel entailed the careful, informed reading of experience and perception.

In apparent contrast to the views of Fuller and Tuckerman, Henry James seems at one point in his review of Howells's *Italian Journeys* to reject active interpretation in favor of mere stenographic reportage. One long Jamesian sentence begins, "Mr. Howells . . . takes things as he finds

them, and as history has made them; he presses them into the service of
no theory, nor scourges them into the following of his prejudices." The
stenography James advocates, however, turns out to be the most cultivated, literary kind of reading; taking things "as history has made them"
involves underscoring their historical and literary meanings. "Mr. Howells . . . takes things as he finds them" indeed, but, the sentence continues, "he leaves them as the man of real literary power and the delicate
artist alone know how to leave them, with new memories mingling, for
our common delight, with the old memories that are the accumulation of
ages, and with a fresh touch of color modestly gleaming amid the masses
of local and historical coloring."[31] Howells transforms the "things" of
travel into the experience of art by reading them for their depth and their
richness, for their associations and their inherent value, and then writing
out his reading.

At their best, Michel Butor writes, traveling, writing, and reading are
double journeys, entailing horizontal progress along a predetermined
path—the line of the text, the route of the voyage—and "perpendicular"
flights and soundings, moments of exaltation and insight, spots of time
in which linearity is suspended and understanding is heightened.[32] At
their most characteristic, he believes, travel and writing are forms of inscription by which human beings record their passage and shape their
history.[33] Travel, reading, and writing were among the most favored activities of a growing class of privileged, influential Americans in the nineteenth century. They exploited all of the features of their favorite pas-
times to claim social and professional positions for themselves, to gratify
their desires for pleasure and especially for prestige, and to justify their
privileges by demonstrating their superior taste and sensitivity.

CHAPTER TWO

Travel as Ritual

Reading and writing are convention-bound, rule-governed, culturally and historically contingent activities. *What* people write and read is influenced by the dominant values of their cultures and the historically and technologically determined ways in which writing is commissioned, paid for, reproduced, and distributed. *How* they write and read depends to a large extent on generic conventions and culturally sanctioned standards of interpretive legitimacy.

Since travel combines the structuring and the interpretive functions of writing and reading, of making plots and educing meanings, it makes sense that it, too, should be influenced by culturally determined patterns of action and interpretation. Just as narratives are necessarily produced in the context of previously existing narratives and related to a previously existing system of narrative kinds, so trips are planned in the context of other trips, their shape and content influenced by their a priori definition as grand tours, sightseeing junkets, pleasure jaunts, or adventures. Just as any individual reading of a literary work depends on—even if it violates—a set of shared assumptions, so any individual understanding of foreign lands and travel experiences relies on earlier, culturally transmitted views, if only to contradict or refute them. And like the appropriate use of a sonnet, an opera, or a triple-decker novel, the use of a European tour is defined by social practice.

Indeed, travel is if anything more convention-bound than either reading or writing, because it is a public and a physical act, governed by material possibilities and standards of outward behavior. It is possible to travel alone, or even to travel incognito, but it is not possible to move one's body through space with the freedom and impunity one enjoys as a reader or a writer in the privacy of the boudoir or the study, confined only by the bounds of the individual imagination. It is possible to use travel for unconventional, nonrespectable purposes, but such use is by definition more public than, say, the clandestine reading of trashy romances.

On a practical level, the itineraries of nineteenth-century Americans

traveling in Europe were governed by the availability of transportation, which in turn was governed by geography and technology as well as the economics of shipping lines and land routes. Guidebooks made the traveler's choices clear. According to George Palmer Putnam's *The Tourist in Europe*, the traveler arriving in Liverpool in 1838 could continue by steamboat to Dublin, by coach to the north via Carlisle, or "direct to London, in 24 hours."[1] It was also possible to take the railroad to Manchester and make a more leisurely journey to the capital by way of the Midlands, Stratford, and Oxford. Morford's *Short-Trip Guide* (1874) is even more specific. To reach the Lakes from Liverpool, Morford writes, one should travel "by the London and Northwestern railway, to Oxenholme, on the Lancaster and Carlisle branch of that road, and then by the Kendal and Windermere spur of the same road to Windermere. This route will be pursued, whether the visit is paid as merely an excursion from Liverpool, to return,—or the temporary break is made at Oxenholme from the main line from Liverpool to Carlisle and Edinburgh."[2]

If one's choice of itinerary depended on the transport services available, however, these services were presumably instituted to supply a need generated at least in part by tourists, whose agendas were set by cultural as well as practical considerations. Agendas varied with the particular situations of individual travelers, but they also varied within culturally determined parameters. Americans abroad in the early nineteenth century saw themselves primarily as learners and appreciators; their goals were knowledge and experience; if they wrote, their overt purpose was to provide their readers with information and to share privileged sensations. These earnest pilgrims investigated historical, technological, literary, artistic, and natural wonders; they went to Chester for a whiff of Rome and a good dose of the Middle Ages, to Manchester by rail to experience modernity in its glory and its horror, to "the Scott country," "the Burns country," and the Lakes for scenery imbued with literary association.

The sights that they went to see, and even the thoughts and feelings that they expected to have, were dictated by tradition and passed down in guidebooks and travel accounts. Manchester, for example, is repeatedly described as worth visiting but not lingering in. "Manchester, by railway at 6 or 7 a.m.," writes Putnam in 1836. "Time to see cotton factories & c., and proceed same day by coach to Birmingham."[3] "Enter the cab, and drive to Manchester station, if you desire to visit a town renowned for its manufactures, its bustle, and smoke," Siddons recommends twenty-two years later, hastening to add that "a few hours will exhaust Manchester."[4]

"Those who may have even a day more of time on their hands at Liver-pool than originally contemplated," says Morford, "can see both [Manchester and Sheffield], hurriedly, within that space."[5]

Chester, however, requires historical musing:

> A fine walk on the walls that surround the old town. I went to the tower on the wall, from which it is said that Charles I beheld the rout of his army on Rowton Moor. I ascended those steps, which I imagined he went up that day, with eager and anxious hope, and which he came down, doubtless disappointed, dispirited, and foreboding evil.[6]

> Passing round the cathedral, I came to an old gateway which led to the cloisters, which are a covered walk, opening into a square interior quadrangle, of soft, green sward. Here the monks had paced to and fro, five hundred years before. . . . It was strange to me, to find myself walking in these quiet passages which holy feet (or at all events monkish feet) had worn so long before.[7]

The Lakes require meditation, too, but of a more literary nature. In the 1830s Orville Dewey took the occasion of a rural walk to evoke an appropriately Wordsworthian "spot of time."

> What a power lies in association! I was already in sight of the far famed Windermere, and . . . , as I stopped to pick a few raspberries by the hedge, that simple action—the memories that it brought with it—the thoughts of those hours of my early days, passed near my own native home—passed by those hedges, thronging ever since with a thousand inexpressible recollections—passed in the fond romance of youth, amid the holy silence of the fields and all the thick coming fancies of an unworn imagination and sensibility—all this moved me as no scene of mere abstract beauty could ever do![8]

Twenty years later James Freeman Clarke made Wordsworth himself the subject of his Lake Country musings.

> But the main thought in my mind was, that Wordsworth had looked upon this scenery day by day; that here his mind had been fed and strengthened; that this hill, that lake, had been his muse; every thing around me bore the coloring of the poet's mind.[9]

European travel in the nineteenth century was a highly conventional activity, controlled at one level by the layout of transportation networks and a list of canonical sights, at another level by the socially sanctioned

purposes of travel, and at a third, most intimate level by the appropriate responses to individual sights suggested (and repeated) by cultural authorities and previous visitors. It was, in other words, a kind of secular ritual, complete with prescribed actions, promised rewards, and a set of quasi-scriptural writings.

Since the vocabulary, the intellectual categories, and the rhetoric of religion pervaded thinking and writing in the nineteenth-century United States, it is not surprising that European travel was routinely conceived in these years as a pilgrimage to sacred shrines in quest of the ineffable distinction of the initiate. This notion is among the governing conceits of two such dissimilar texts as Twain's *The Innocents Abroad; or, The New Pilgrim's Progress*, and Henry Adams's *Mont-Saint-Michel and Chartres*. It dominates Lydia Sigourney's concluding dissertation on the "benefits of travelling"[10] and motivates the Reverend C. W. Winchester's impressive step-by-step allegorization of his European tour in *The Gospel of Foreign Travel*.[11]

Dean MacCannell has written extensively about the ritualistic meaning of twentieth-century mass tourism; the subtitle of his book, *A New Theory of the Leisure Class* (emphasis mine), suggests turning to Veblen for insight into earlier tourist travel. Veblen considers travel, religious observances, and many other social customs versions of "honorific expenditure," proofs of one's own or one's society's pecuniary power, demonstrations of one's own or one's society's ability to dispose of time and energy for no immediate practical purpose. For him, the leisure and the priestly classes are parallel manifestations of a society's ability to support nonproductive activity: their occupations, the rituals of "decent" expenditure and divine service, are parallel ways of using the surplus time and money generated by a booming bourgeois economy to create a stable, "respectable" society.[12]

Veblen's reading of the meaning of leisure-class ritual, secular and sacred, makes perfect sense. That rituals function as Veblen says they do on the level of the economics of consumption and the behavior of classes cannot, however, explain their significance in the experience of individual celebrants, whether shoppers, travelers, students of Greek, or religious communicants. The sociologist Steven Lukes provides an alternative definition of ritual which helps balance Veblen's. Ritual, he writes, is "rule-governed activity of a symbolic character which draws the attention of its participants to objects of thought and feeling which they hold to be of special significance."[13] Ritual behavior, in other words, is conventionally structured; it bears cultural meaning; it generates for its participants an

experience they consider more meaningful than their daily round of activities. Just as it is impossible on one level not to see the applicability to
travel of Veblen's account of the place of conspicuous consumption in
bourgeois society, so I think it is easy on another to see the connection
between Lukes's account of ritual and the experience of earnest individual
travelers, for whom travel is a conventional activity, to be sure, but also
one that is fraught with "symbolic character," whose whole purpose is the
provision of "objects of thought and feeling" which they hope will be "of
special significance."

Veblen and Lukes come at ritual from opposite perspectives, the former examining its place in the social economy of bourgeois capitalism,
and the latter attempting to account for its significance in the private
experience of individuals. Their understandings of the subject have, however, several points in common, which help underline the parallels between ritual and travel. They agree, first, that ritual is a form of behavior
that is "sacred" in the sense of "nonordinary."[14] It need not be religious,
but it is also not routine and utilitarian; whether it involves a moment's
pause or a lifetime's service, whether it is distinguished by its participants'
socioeconomic status (Veblen) or their sense of its extraordinariness
(Lukes), it is set apart from the workaday grind. Second, ritual activity is
culturally prescribed; it is not an original, unrepeatable action, but a conventional performance, whose rules may be embodied in a prayer book,
an explicit oral tradition, or a set of unspoken community values and
expectations. Third, a ritual is a symbolic *action*, an *acting out* of some
cultural meaning, a *performance*. And finally, ritual is experienced as important; its participants are not merely passing time, they are serving God
or maintaining respectability or acquiring culture but in every case seeking some kind of grace, some version of redemption, whether from sin,
ignorance, social insignificance, or the monotony of daily life.

The anthropologist Victor Turner's more detailed accounts of ritual
corroborate all four of these points and further illuminate its social nature
by relating it to other forms of "cultural performance" ("ceremony, carni-
val, theatre, and poetry"), which he sees as "expressions" of personal and
cultural "experience," as "explanation[s] and explication[s] of life itself."[15]
For Turner, ritual at its most productive is not merely sacramental and
demonstrative, the outward and visible sign of an inward and spiritual
grace, or an instance of the conspicuous consumption of leisure; it is also
exploratory, tentative, experimental, a culturally sanctioned, culturally
structured activity that allows for, even demands, some measure of personal growth and discovery.

Turner's description of ritual is especially relevant to the study of travel because its three-stage structure, adapted from the early-twentieth-century anthropologist Arnold van Gennep, clearly parallels the structure of a journey. For Turner and van Gennep, rituals begin with a "phase of *separation* [which] clearly demarcates sacred space and time from profane or secular space and time." This separation may or may not involve a change of place, but it always involves a change in the participant's experience of time, a sense that he or she has moved from an ordinary to a sacred dimension. The phase of separation is followed by a transitional or marginal state, "a sort of social limbo which has few of the attributes of either the preceding or subsequent profane social statuses or cultural states." This stage is followed, naturally enough, by the "reaggregation" of the participant into ordinary society, as a changed (cleansed, reborn, rededicated, adult) individual in a basically unchanged world.[16]

The most important of these phases is the central one, in which the significant ritual action takes place. Van Gennep, who was primarily interested in rites of passage in tribal societies, calls this the liminal phase and sees it as a rigidly prescribed stage in a process designed to perpetuate a particular social order. The participant's actions in this stage may seem playful, anarchic, or even subversive, but the ritual as a whole is profoundly conservative. "The tribal liminal," writes Turner, "however exotic in appearance, can never be much more than a subversive flicker. It is put into the service of normativeness almost as soon as it appears."[17]

Ritual takes place in industrial societies as well as tribal ones, however, and Turner believes that it follows the same pattern, with a couple of crucial differences. First, ritual in industrial society is optional: it is seen as one possible activity among many, rather than as a necessary part of the natural cycle of life. For this reason, the liminal phase of modern, bourgeois, and industrial ritual can become what Turner calls a liminoid phase, not a conventionally (and illusorily) subversive period between two normative states, but an actually subversive period between a conventional, conservative view of the world and one's place in it as fixed, and a new perception of the world as changeable and the self as capable of effecting change.

Reading Turner's studies of pilgrimage helps clarify the applicability of this theory to travel and the advantages of thinking of travel as a kind of ritual. Travel obviously involves a separation, a move into a privileged region of time and space, then a period of privileged activity, free from the demands of work and home, a period of more-than-ordinary freedom from which one hopes to gain more-than-ordinary benefits, and finally, usually, a reintegration into the home society. Some travelers experience the ritual as a tribal rite of passage in van Gennep's sense: for them the central phase is merely liminal, and the reintegration into an unchanged society an inevitable, foregone conclusion. For others, however, the trip is a liminoid experience, an occasion for real change. Some of these travelers never return at all; others return as troubled and troubling members of the home society.

Some writers on travel emphasize the maleness of this pattern—Eric Leed, for example, calls it "the spermatic journey"[18]—and although I must admit that the characterization is technically correct (the pattern does parallel male initiation rites), it does not seem to me that this ritual pattern is either essentially or exclusively male or that its putative maleness is finally very important.[19] A brief account of two roughly contemporary, geographically parallel, self-consciously literary, and fundamentally dissimilar European journeys may help clarify this point by demonstrating anew Carroll Smith-Rosenberg's observation that nineteenth-century bourgeois men were often the champions and exemplars of conservative domesticity, whereas women were often active in the public sphere. An understanding of travel as ritual, in other words, can help distinguish not between male-coded and female-coded activities, but between conventionally conservative and potentially revolutionary ones.

On the first of July 1844, Bayard Taylor set sail from New York to fulfill his boyhood dream of European travel. His voyage was financed in part by an advance of fifty dollars from the *Saturday Evening Post*, and his resolve was strengthened by a commission from Horace Greeley for a series of "sketches of German life and society."[20] On the first of August 1846, Margaret Fuller set sail from New York to fulfill her girlhood dream of European travel. Her voyage was financed in part by an advance on a book called *Papers on Literature and Art* from the publishers Wiley and Putnam, who were just then bringing out Taylor's *Views A-foot*, and her resolve was strengthened by a commission from Horace Greeley for a series of European letters. Taylor's German sketches were not published until he returned home, but Greeley printed Fuller's letters as he received them. As a result, the *New-York Tribune* ran two sets of European letters concurrently in the fall of 1846, Taylor's "Glances at Modern Germany, by a Young American," and the first installments of Fuller's "Things and Thoughts in Europe."

After docking in Liverpool, Taylor reembarked for a short excursion to Northern Ireland. He joined the more conventional itinerary in the Scot-

tish Highlands, paid Scott the requisite passing tribute of reverent quotation, waxed lyrical on the subject of Ben Lomond,[21] commented on the
Gaelic songs of the Loch Katrine boatmen and the regrettable desecration
of the lake by a small steamboat, passed on to the Burns country, and
from there to Edinburgh, Abbotsford, Newcastle, and London. Fuller
docked in Liverpool, too, and from there went to the Lakes to call on
William Wordsworth and Harriet Martineau. She continued to Scotland,
quoting Scott and Burns along the way, took excursions to Loch Katrine,
where she, too, commented on the steamboat and the Gaelic singing, and
to Ben Lomond where she, too, waxed lyrical,[22] and proceeded to Edinburgh, Abbotsford, Newcastle, and London.

Taylor and Fuller patterned their experiences on existing cultural models. Taylor's models were primarily contemporary: he read Washington Irving on England and Spain, followed Byron's Childe Harold
through Italy, and learned the geography of Scotland from Scott's poems
and novels.[23] His immediate inspirations, however, were the fashionable
journalist N. P. Willis and the publisher and traveler George P.
Putnam.[24] Like millions of tourists and thousands of aspiring writers who
followed him, Taylor was entranced by the glamour and exoticism of
foreign travel, fascinated and challenged by the details of transport and
the exigencies of a budget, and lured by the prospect of producing a travel
book of his own. Fuller's original inspiration to travel was altogether
more high-toned: steeped in European culture from childhood on, by
the age of sixteen she was reading de Staël, Epictetus, Racine, Mil-
ton, Castilian ballads, Dante, Petrarch, Tasso, Ariosto, Alfieri, and Man-
zoni. Four years later she had learned enough German to translate
Goethe's *Tasso* and to conceive the ambition of writing his biography.[25]
Her longing for Europe was prompted by her desire to gather material for
her biography, "see the best literary society," and "love" those "scenes"
which her reading had led her to imagine.[26] But Fuller's early European
plans were frustrated by her father's death and the family's lack of funds;
when she finally did go abroad, in 1846, her motives were in part "professional," governed by the journalist's need for material and the intellectual's desire for knowledge,[27] in part political, governed by her passionate
advocacy of reform,[28] and in part conventionally touristic, governed by a
desire to see the sights and meet the people that others had seen and met
before her.

Notwithstanding its conventional elements, furthermore, the trip to
Europe represented for both Taylor and Fuller a long-dreamed-of journey
from ordinary to sacred ground, from the everyday to the magical. Tay-

lor's journal record of his approach to Great Britain reveals both his sense of the sacred quality of his journey and his penchant for conventional, cliché-ridden prose:

> Oh! if the mist could rise up like a veil from the ocean, and show us Ben Lomond, standing blue in the dim distance, the first herald of the romantic land we approach! Now that we are so near the Old World, I feel a kind of fear, that I cannot at first realize my situation. I have so long and ardently wished to visit the scenes hallowed by the spirit of many a mighty bard, or consecrated by the noble deeds of the men of former times, or marked by acts of tyranny or crime, and standing as silent but eloquent lessons, bequeathed to us by antiquity, that now, when I shall behold them, I fear I cannot reconcile the real with the ideal.[29]

Fuller's mature prose is not so breathless, nor is her sense of Europe's "sacred" difference from the American norm so romantic. Still, it is clear that life in Europe represented for her, too, a step away from the limiting "normal" toward the liberating ideal. "I find myself much in my element in European Society," Fuller wrote to Emerson shortly after arriving in Paris. "It does not indeed come up to my ideal; but so many of the encumbrances are cleared away that used to weary me in America, that I can enjoy a freer play of faculty, and feel, if not like a bird in the air, at least as easy as a fish in water."[30]

Taylor and Fuller also saw European travel as performance, as the acting out of a cultural drama. The arrival in Italy, for example, is a classic moment for the nineteenth-century traveler; Taylor and Fuller dramatized it fully for their readers and, one suspects, for themselves. Taylor approaches on foot, over the Gotthard Pass, self-consciously acting out the classic transition from north to south: "I thought, as we went down, that every step was bringing me nearer to a sunnier land—that the glories of Italy, which had so long lain in the airy background of the future, would soon spread themselves before me in their real or imagined beauty."[31] Fuller approaches from the sea, and instead of simply acting out the conventional arrival in Italy, uses its very conventionality to emphasize the unpleasantness of her first view of Genoa and the disappointment of her first week in Naples, only to declare at last that not even its indisputable banality can detract from the charm of Italy in its proper sunny condition.

> The excessive beauty of Genoa is well known, and the impression upon the eye alone was correspondent with what I expected, but, alas! the weather was still so cold I could not realize that I had actually touched those shores

to which I had looked forward all my life, where it seemed that the heart would expand, and the whole nature be turned to delight. (*Dispatches*, 129)

Here at Naples I *have* at last found *my* Italy; I have passed through the Grotto of Pausilippo, visited Cuma, Baia, and Capri—ascended Vesuvius, and found all familiar, except the sense of enchantment, of sweet exhilaration this scene conveys. . . . Nature here, most prolific and exuberant in her gifts, has touched them all with a charm unhackneyed, unhackneyable, which the boots of English dandies cannot trample out, nor the raptures of sentimental tourists daub or fade. (*Dispatches*, 129–30)

Finally, both Taylor and Fuller saw their travels as bearing more than literal meaning, as symbolizing important steps and connections in their thought, their lives, and their careers. To Taylor, the trip to Europe was an initiatory act, a necessary step in a well-planned career. The decision to go abroad represented "a crisis, which I seemed instinctively to feel was either to carry me on to that station in the hearts of men which is my highest ambition, or to condemn me to a life of obscurity and spiritlessness."[32] According to his wife and first biographer, "the two years which Bayard Taylor spent in travel and study were his university education."[33] Their conscious purpose was to qualify him for the life of a respected poet (a life that, ironically, he was able to maintain only by undertaking more and more travel books as his debts grew and his poems did not sell).

If Taylor saw his travels as qualifying him for the life he intended to lead, Fuller believed that her life abroad, and especially her experiences in Rome, had a transformative, sacramental value.

You say truly, I shall come home humbler. God grant it may be entirely humble! In future, while more than ever deeply penetrated with principles, and the need of the martyr spirit to sustain them, I will ever own that there are few worthy, and that I am one of the least.[34]

The elements that Taylor's and Fuller's travels have in common are what made them possible, both culturally and economically. Neither would have gone to Europe if the European tour had not been a culturally recognized and codified phenomenon, and if the "Letter from Europe" had not been a marketable literary product. Their differences are partly cultural, too—the differences between a Cambridge child reading Goethe and a Pennsylvania child reading Lydia Sigourney, between a serious intellectual and an ex-transcendentalist on the one hand, and a sentimental poet and genteel litterateur on the make on the other—but they are also personal and temperamental, the differences between Fuller's intense personal honesty and public conscience and Taylor's grand, self-serving literary ambitions. These differences are at least part of what distinguishes the uses of their two journeys and makes Taylor's an example of the "tribal" ritual whose middle phase is strictly liminal, and Fuller's an example of modern "industrial" ritual whose middle phase is liminoid, and so capable of producing genuine change.

Taylor's move from the ordinary world of West Chester, Pennsylvania, to the sacred realm of Europe was largely instrumental. He knew before he went what it was to mean; it was undoubtedly a thrilling adventure, but it was also a shrewdly calculated step in the career of an aspirant to literary fame. Taylor expected his travels to make his fortune, and it is fair to say that they did. *Views A-foot* was his most popular work; it set his name before the literary world and the larger public and launched his career. It changed him, however, not a whit. His own brief summary of the trip concludes with a self-congratulatory self-christening, a statement of admirable if mundane accomplishments and unswerving purpose. He had done what he intended to do, and he would move on to make use of it.

> I had been abroad for two years, and had supported myself entirely during the whole time by my literary correspondence. The remuneration which I received was in all $500, and only by continual economy and occasional self-denial was I able to carry out my plan. I saw almost nothing of intelligent European society; my wanderings led me among the common people, but literature and art were nevertheless open to me, and a new day dawned in my life.[35]

Fuller's time in Europe was by contrast fundamentally transformative. Her journey transformed itself gradually from a literarily and sociologically oriented grand tour—already a common mode in 1846—into a revolutionary odyssey. By the time she reached the sacred soil of Italy, she had seen and learned a great deal, as Taylor no doubt had before her. She had also, however, witnessed and begun to experience a kind of political passion that had a *trans*formative, not just an *in*formative power. Her Roman experience nurtured this passion, and her last letters from Italy bear witness to her transformation from a reporter and a theorist into an activist:

> I believed before I came to Europe in what is called Socialism, as the inevitable sequence to the tendencies and wants of the era, but I did not think these vast changes in modes of government, education, and daily life, would be effected as rapidly as I now think they will, because they must. The world can no longer stand without them. (*Dispatches*, 320)

It is not surprising that her friends' grief at her death in a shipwreck within view of the Long Island shore was mixed with relief, both that she would not have to face a hostile America and, I think, that they would not have to face a radicalized Margaret Fuller.[36]

Neither Taylor nor Fuller was rich; they were, however, members of what Veblen would call the leisure class because their occupations produced not material goods, but rather intellectual products in return for which their relatively prosperous society could afford to support their literary activities. From the wide perspective of social analysis, they can be seen as members of a new clerisy, acting out a ritual whose function is to demonstrate their society's ability to pay some of its members to think and to write. Taylor and Fuller would not have thought of their travels in these terms, nor did they refer to the personal meaning of their journeys in terms of ritual patterns. From our perspective, however, it seems clear that they were "rule-governed activities of a symbolic character," that they drew "the attention of their participants to objects of thought and feeling which they [held] to be of special significance," and that they marked crucial transitions in their lives. Whether they knew it or not, in other words, in their European travels Taylor and Fuller were participating in a cultural ritual that paralleled certain religious practices. They were acting out, in Judith Adler's terms, an overdetermined "trope" based on a culturally generated narrative paradigm[37] capable of being simultaneously understood as rite of passage, cultural credentialing, political awakening, "New Pilgrim's Progress," "search for the homeland of the soul," and "descent into hell."[38]

An understanding of travel as a ritual activity suggests a related understanding of travel writings as quasi-religious texts, paralleling the scriptural, liturgical, and testimonial texts of Western religious traditions. Nineteenth-century Americans in Europe were inspired by a wide range of texts. Classical writers, Petrarch, Dante, Shakespeare, Scott, Byron, Goethe, de Staël, and many others served as scripture for many travelers, but no single author or work inspired them all. Individual travelers knew *Corinne* and *The Prelude*, *Childe Harold*, the *Italienische Reise*, the *Confessions*, the *Divine Comedy* and the *Aeneid*, but none of these texts had the status of scripture for the culture as a whole. Popular guidebooks quoted Virgil, Abelard, and Byron as needed to flesh out and glamorize their descriptions of sights and cities. Because none of these texts is an example of American travel writing, however, and because no single text seems to have had the authority for European travelers that the Bible had in religious matters (or, for that matter, in travel to the Holy Land), I leave consideration of the scripture of travel for another time and place, and turn in the two chapters that follow to the liturgy of travel—the guidebook—and its testimonial literature—the travel chronicle. In the chapter on guidebooks I show how faithful adherence to the liturgy of travel could liberate and empower the celebrant as well as guarantee the orthodoxy of his/her travel plans. In the chapter on chronicles I outline the generic conventions at work in travel writing and show how they, too, could have an empowering effect for writers as different as Lydia H. Sigourney and William Wells Brown.

CHAPTER THREE

Guidebooks:
The Liturgy of Travel

G UIDEBOOKS are at once the most practical and the most magical of texts: they give the hours of trains and the prices of breakfasts; they set the planner dreaming of foreign scenes, great works of art, moving scenery, and unaccustomed luxury. They certify, furthermore, that long-imagined sights and experiences are actually available for consumption in some specific, physical location, that the would-be traveler's dreams of foreign places can actually be fulfilled. They provide an order of worship at the shrines of the beautiful, the historic, and the foreign, telling the potential tourist what kind of behavior is appropriate to each site and indicating what kind of fulfillment to expect from it. They serve as directories of services, aids to meditation, and handbooks of devotion. They are both modest and powerful, at the same time effacing themselves and asserting themselves, serving culture and shaping it by influencing the way in which it is experienced and understood.

Nineteenth-century American travelers used the standard European guidebooks—notably Baedeker and Murray—but they also had guides of their own, published in the United States, often providing overviews of the European tour and intended as general introductions to the European experience. Reading these texts in chronological order suggests an outline of the development of American tourism. Analyzing their language and their rhetoric provides additional insight into the ways nineteenth-century Americans used travel to construct and reinforce a sense of themselves as powerful and independent actors on a broad international stage.

GUIDEBOOKS AND TOURIST READERS: 1838–1900

The experience of the first wave of what can fairly be called tourists, Americans traveling in Europe for pleasure after the initiation of scheduled North Atlantic packet service, may be represented by two guidebooks, George P. Putnam's *The Tourist in Europe* and *A Hand-Book for American Travellers in Europe, Collated from the Best Authorities*, by "Roswell Park, D.D., President of Racine College, Wisconsin."

Putnam's romantic goal is to make "the long dreamed of attractions of the 'Old World'" accessible to the youth of the new.[1] His "new world" is no longer a colonial or even a postcolonial extension of Europe,[2] however, but a bumptious Jacksonian republic, proud of its independent, democratic ways. It is a nation that has turned its imagination westward and seems to be daring the effete Old World to measure up to its standards of grandeur and vitality. Putnam's tourist is therefore liable to contradictory errors: shame at his[3] nation's uncouthness may lead him to "slander" it in the hope of seeming more European than the Europeans; pride in its principles may lead him to denigrate the countries he is visiting, through "invidious comparisons, or lofty boasts" (6). Putnam deplores both responses, arguing that the "American, who conducts himself as a patriotic and gentlemanly American should do, has no reason to be ashamed of his name or nation" (6), and therefore no reason to run down his own country or anyone else's. He "belongs," Putnam goes on, "to Nature's nobility" (6).

In one sense, then, Putnam's reader is nature's nobleman, a dignity he shares with all honest, democratic sons of the New World; in another, more literal sense, however, he is a simple, middle-class tourist out to see certified sights and experience dreamed-of sensations. He is no bumpkin, but he does need help in sorting out the sights and deciding how to deport himself in foreign lands. Putnam's "Notes for the Way" and the descriptive "Memoranda" of his own tour help the reader move from sight to certified sight, take pleasure in his travels, and maintain a proper attitude toward the social and political concerns of the countries he is visiting. His suggested itinerary is chockablock with hints and orders, with what must be seen and what may be skipped, where to dine, and what hotels to patronize. The new National Gallery in London, he writes, is a "day's work," "scarcely equal to the Louvre! but yet should not be omitted." The Tower is "worth a visit, however vulgar Mr. Cooper may deem it," and the Zoological Gardens "well worth visiting. Omit not to go through the tunnel and see the Giraffes, &c." (15). The road into Italy is "very sublime" (33); the landlord at Como "intelligent" (33). The approach to Rome evokes overwrought grandiloquence ("If thou hast a grain of enthusiasm, unbar the floodgates of thy feelings and thy memory—whelming thy former littleness of conception in the grandeur that awaits thee. Rome bursts upon thy view!" [39]) followed by a brief apology ("I am but a guide and yet, forsooth, must soliloquize and lecture. Pardon, gentle reader, and on" [39]). The feeling of the whole is genuinely rough and ready: Putnam's tourist is out to get what is to be gotten and to do so efficiently and with good humor. Everything he sees, however, seems to fall into the same category: it is all curious, *sehenswert*, and somehow interchangeable. The cotton factory, the National Gallery, the "Giraffes &c." at the zoo, and the Alpine glaciers all pass in review while the eager traveler takes them in or at least looks them over. There is no engagement, no contact with anyone but mountain guides and "intelligent" or "facetious" landlords, no attempt to understand the experience as more than intellectual and imaginative window shopping or the places visited as more than spectacles to observe.

The same is true of Putnam's own European tour, described in the second half of this volume. He went where he was supposed to go, saw what others had seen, quoted the suitable passages (Scott in Scotland, Shakespeare at Windsor, Byron in Venice), visited where he had introductions, and commented on whatever presented itself to his view.

> In the afternoon I went with Mr. T—— to the beautiful chapel of Magdalen college, to hear the chanting, which is performed by a choir of boys, in the most perfect and touching manner. It was the sweetest, most expressive, and most appropriate church music I had ever heard. . . . In this chapel is a painting by Carlo Dolci, valued at eleven thousand guineas! Addison was educated at Magdalen College; and his favorite walk, on the banks of the Isis, is yet called "Addison's Walk." Gibbon, whose stately style is so strongly in contrast with the classic ease and purity of the "Spectator" took his degree here, also. (163)

The passage suggests a kind of gaping passivity, a naive American willingness to be impressed. It records experience ("In the afternoon I went"), registers taste ("perfect," "touching," "most appropriate"), betrays a naive and appealing philistinism ("eleven thousand guineas!"), and asserts literary authority ("stately style" as opposed to "classic ease"). It is curiously random, however—the response to transient stimuli rather than the result of a considered purpose.

Putnam's comments on contemporary life also represent ad hoc responses rather than considered opinions. He praises the efficiency of the London police force ("Disorder is consequently rare, and is always checked in the bud; and drunken vagrants, if ever seen, are soon disposed of" [166]) and its public visibility ("to be seen at every corner, day and night, always on the watch for the least show of disturbance" [166]) as

opposed to the oppressive secrecy of the French police, without consider-
ing the similar effects of the two systems of surveillance. He values American equality of opportunity ("But with us, all classes have books; and the
mechanic's apprentice, with the penny paper in his hand, may discuss the
politics of the day as wisely, perhaps, as his master, or the president himself" [172]) but is quick to adopt the class prejudices of the countries he
visits ("Verily, the lower classes of the French are a filthy people" [205]).
His valedictory catalog of experiences ("I have promenaded the Regent-
street of London"; "My hand has been in Rob Roy's purse, and on the
skull of Charlemagne"; "I have seen Daniel O'Connell!" [281]) is impressive in its randomness, and his conclusions are predictable in their
complacency.

> I have seen much, very much, to admire; much that we of the "New World"
> might imitate with advantage, and more still to make me better satisfied
> than ever that we are, on the whole, or ought to be, the happiest people in
> the world. Let us but pay a little more attention to our manners (for they
> certainly may be improved,) and let us check the spirit of lawlessness and
> fanatical agrarianism, which has shown itself to be already dangerous to our
> liberties and prosperity, and we may with conscious pride take our station
> first among the nations of the earth. (281–82)

There is no indication here that Europe has changed Putnam's way of
thinking, though it has certainly given him a good deal of information to
digest and ammunition in the fight for his favorite causes. He returns to
America with all the smug authority of the traveler and the very same
mental and political horizon with which he set out. The tourist who followed his advice would probably enjoy himself immensely, assimilate a
great deal of information and experience, and remain quite secure in his
American beliefs and prejudices.

Park is no more open than Putnam to fundamental challenge and
change, but he does expect his readers to use their European experiences
for earnest self-improvement. The pleasure he advocates is not that of
dreams fulfilled, but of long-studied subjects made concrete, of worthwhile learning consolidated.

> None but those whose principles are firmly established, whose educa-
> tion, both literary and scientific, is far advanced, and who have a strong
> curiosity to learn what is best worth learning; none else can reap the full
> benefit of such a tour as it is the object of this work to delineate. And those
> who have already studied most carefully the Geography, and History, and

Literature of Europe, will derive the greatest pleasure and profit from visiting in reality those scenes through which they must already have wandered
in imagination.[4]

Europe for Park is a reward for the tired scholar, a worthwhile experience
for the American who has not just read books and dreamed over maps,
but studied literature and geography. This "philosophic traveller, who is
a scholar, a patriot, and a Christian," is not out for idle pleasure. His goal
is rather to "see both nature and art, both men and things, in their true
aspects, however various; and to see the best specimens of each class of
objects in their appropriate localities" (10–11).

Park's step-by-step guide is even more prescriptive than Putnam's: he
postulates an actual day of departure and conducts the tourist practically
hour by hour along a route that he himself has followed and can therefore
guarantee. One imagines a small gaggle of earnest Americans, all of whom
have booked passage "from New York, by a Collins steamer, on Saturday,
the 19th of March, 1853" (73), moving from sight to sight, hotel to hotel,
consulate to consulate, shop to shop, in lockstep, with their noses in
Park's *Hand-Book*, oblivious of each other and of anything Park does not
mention. Not that Park misses many tricks. On arrival in London he
suggests not only what map to buy, but where to buy it ("Lee's, 440
Strand" [75]). In the House of Lords he recommends that the tourist
"observe the Lords sitting with their hats on" (77). In his Sunday entries
he reviews the claims of various churches and preachers and suggests attending morning and afternoon services in different churches to sample
their wares. In Paris, Park suggests a morning at the banker's ("Messrs.
Greene & Co." [91], by choice), the American embassy, and their fashionable environs and advises that "it is desirable to reach the Exchange
before 3 o'clock, and witness the scene of confusion and excitement," and
proceed from there to "the office of Messrs. Livingston, where a register
is kept of Americans visiting Paris" (96). The tour continues in this
mode, and a tedious brief journey it proves to be. Park is continually
urging his reader on to the next important site. "You may now rest," he
writes, uncharacteristically, in his entry for May 22, a Sunday, but in the
very next sentence reminds his reader that "those whose time is limited
should now hasten northward to the valley of the Arno, by the short-
est way, which will be by sea. The inland route is interesting; but will
require time, which in the writer's opinion may be more profitably spent"
(162–63).

Park is also concerned for his travelers' physical and spiritual well-being in foreign lands. "Ripe and sound fruits are doubtless wholesome," he opines, "but as their tendency is aperient, and may be cathartic, they should not be used in excess; and should be laid aside entirely when there is any laxative tendency" (61–62). His anxious Protestantism reminds modern readers of just how cast away (and how relieved, in many cases) the descendants of American Puritans could feel in the less pious, even the popish lands of Europe. "The usual tendency of travel," Park writes, "is to secularize the mind," so "the traveller who would not miss the way to heaven, while wandering over the earth, must endeavor to collect his thoughts in some exercise of daily devotion, which ought to be at some stated hours, or hour, as in the morning and evening" (70–71). "Even in Italy," to his apparent surprise, "the Bible will be allowed him" (71), and Protestant chapels may be found in all the major cities, with the exception of Milan and Venice.

Unlike Putnam, Park thinks of himself primarily as a Protestant and only secondarily as an American, but their books are more alike than different when compared with later guidebooks. Putnam's combination of naive self-assurance, reasonable patriotism, and a susceptibility to awe and enjoyment may be more appealing than Park's stern prescriptions, but they were both writing at a time when traveling Americans were the slightly hesitant, self-conscious representatives of a new democracy, out for self-improvement. The European tour was—in theory, at least—an occasion for education, a chance to submit oneself to the influence of older civilizations, to round off one's sharp American edges, to polish up one's dull American surface, but not to relinquish one's proud American values.

By the time of Twain's innocents, James's Americans, and the readers of postwar guidebooks, the chief purpose of many travelers was not to submit to Old World influences but to acquire choice bits of culture and experience at a good price. Education was all very well, and a little polish never hurt anyone, but the new American travelers of the sixties, seventies, and eighties were not about to purchase these European commodities on any terms but their own. These successful capitalists and their wives, children, and servants were no longer diffidently, painfully aware of their shortcomings, but proud of their own and their country's new-found economic power and eager to experience the very best that their hard-earned money could buy. They required a lighter and at the same time more assertive tone in their travel guides and found it in such books as *Morford's Short-trip Guide to Europe*.

The 1874 edition of this work combines the good humor of the after-dinner speaker with the self-confidence of the successful businessman. Its presumptive reader is motivated by no earnest cultural, ethical, or educational imperative; he simply wants to travel comfortably and economically, take in or at least pass by a reasonable number of certified attractions, and get home to business before too many weeks have elapsed. "The most important question" before him, Morford declares, is, "what need be the expenses, for a certain round, of a traveler going first-class and demanding all the comforts, and yet indisposed to waste money on costly luxuries?"[5] The answer, for a six- to seven-week tour of the British Isles and northern France, is "$460 gold or $550 currency." For "$200 gold additional" the traveler may "secure" "the Cumberland Lakes and Shakspeare Neighborhood of England" and "a rapid run through the more frequented parts of Switzerland" (12). Morford's traveler is a canny consumer who wants value for his time and money, a successful, self-confident American with a "well-founded pride" in his country (33) and no sense that Europe is anything more than a vast gallery of curiosities. He has paid his money and is more than ready to take his choice of sights and souvenirs.

Unlike Putnam's and Park's guidebooks, which encourage their readers to think of themselves as students or pilgrims, Morford's resembles contemporary periodicals in frequently reminding its readers of their status as consumers. Advertisements appear at the end of the volume ("'Heat is Life.' Nicholls' Patent Volta Medicated Cloth cures Neuralgia in five minutes" [n.p.]), and Morford unblushingly puffs the advertised products in a section called "Reminders for Ramblers." Nothing is "referred to here or elsewhere in the book, not *bona fide* within the knowledge of the author-proprietor" (418), he avers, and then gives us the following, in the same tone and typeface as his sightseeing recommendations:

> Medical authorities inform us that "heat is life"; and it is upon a knowledge of that fact that the inventor of Nicholls' Patent Volta Medicated Cloth has proceeded, in providing his invaluable remedy against neuralgia, rheumatism, gout, etc., of which the principal depot is to be found at No. 292, High Holborn, London—not far from Chancery Lane. (428)

Morford's recommendations for sightseeing are calculated to serve the traveler without overtaxing his attention. Invoking the "seen one, seen 'em all" principle, he remarks:

> English rural scenery, among the most beautiful on the globe, is also the least varied, so that one excursion through it affords, with rare exceptions,

a type of all, and neither time or [*sic*] money need be expended in dull repetitions. To some extent, the same remarks will apply to old churches and old buildings. (18)

His tours of the principal cities prefigure the three-hour Cityramas of today. On the second day in Paris, for example, he recommends hiring a cab by the hour and catching glimpses of some nineteen attractions, including not only Notre Dame ("perhaps the most impressive ecclesiastical object in Paris" [258]) and the Conciergerie, but also the "Church of St. Eustache, where a common courtesan was once enthroned in the place of God" (257), the Morgue, and, after dinner, the Jardin Mabille, "where the *cancan* may be enjoyed in what the Parisians (and some of the Americans) consider its 'purity'" (261). His suggestions for Rome, under the heading "Rome in a Hurry," are even more perfunctory, though he does provide the fascinating information that twelve full-scale replicas of New York's Trinity Church could be assembled under the dome of St. Peter's, with room to spare.

Given his minimal interest in making contact with European people and cultures, Morford's attitude toward foreign languages is predictably cavalier. His tourist's purpose in conversation is purely instrumental, his goal, like James's Christopher Newman's, to emerge "from dialogues in foreign tongues, of which he had, formally, not understood a word, in full possession of the particular fact he had desired to ascertain."[6] James, however, spares us the sounds that Newman must have uttered to initiate these dialogues; Morford lays them out in appalling detail in one of his appendixes, where the French is often incorrect and the suggested pronunciation painfully familiar to the ears of generations of European travelers. "*Cocher*," he is heard to demand, "*ète* [*sic*] *vous libre?* (*Pro.* Coshay, ettay voo leebr?)", or even better, "*Mille remercièments* [*sic*], *Mademoiselle.* (*Pro.* Meel raymayr shemons, Madmwasel)" (344).

The changing tone of travel after the Civil War was also evident in guidebooks intended for less prosperous travelers. Europe had long appealed to the adventurous, impecunious young. Bayard Taylor's *Views A-foot* described a young man's extensive European travels at an average cost of fifty cents a day and concluded with a budget demonstrating the feasibility of making "a two years' pilgrimage" at a cost of precisely $472.10, which figure Taylor generously rounded upward to $500 to account for the two years' worth of "amusements, guides' fees, and other small expenses" (505–6). Whereas Taylor, however, maintained a modest tone and a Whitmanesque openness to experience in his travels, William Hemstreet's *The Economical European Tourist: A Journalist Three Months*

Abroad for $430 adopts Morford's bluster and seems to betray an underlying social and cultural insecurity. "Europe is the biggest show I ever went to," Hemstreet trumpets,[7] and goes on to list four pages of attractions, from the Killarney Lakes and a "water-cure establishment" in Ireland to "Gondola rides, Doge's palace, Bridge of Sighs . . . , etc." in Venice, which "were visited in person by the writer" (13–17). He is an enthusiast for Europe but also a quick and oversensitive defender of the United States. He is harsh on the ignorance and prejudice of those inferior ranks, "the middle class of English" and "more particularly" the "intolerant, absurd, and bigoted who have raised themselves just above want" (213). His point is clearly that America, the American system, Americans, and he himself are all superior to anything Europe can offer. Our "average dignity, tone, and honesty of private character is above other peoples'" (217), our public priorities sensible when compared with the "barbarism" of English monarchism, hero worship, and grinding poverty (218). Hemstreet's true colors and the fears of the bourgeois Americans whom he and Morford represent, come out in his conclusion, where he makes it clear that not even America is nowadays immune from the influence of "the lower half of foreign peoples" who make "our seaports the dumping-grounds of the Old World's social slough, . . . where, widely, American society itself is degenerated by the infection of foreign fraud, vice, cowardice, disloyalty" (227). Despite his enthusiasm for Europe, Hemstreet is a xenophobe, insecure in his class position and always in need of asserting his superiority to those beneath and different from himself. Hemstreet and Morford announce the arrival on the European scene of the still-familiar figure of the American tourist as well-meaning boor, a proud, jingoistic bourgeois democrat—equally disdainful of the social and political remnants of feudalism and of the malodorous and socially disruptive lower classes—who uses travel and Europe to affirm the superiority of his class and nation to all challengers at home and abroad.

A welcome contrast to this figure is suggested in three guidebooks specifically intended for women travelers—the only three I have discovered among the scores of general-purpose (that is, male-oriented) guides. Two of these, *Studying Art Abroad: How to Do It Cheaply* (1879), by May Alcott Nieriker (the Amy of her sister's *Little Women*), and *European Travel for Women* (1900), by Mary Cadwalader Jones (the sister of Edith Wharton), are remarkable chiefly for their assumption of female independence and their matter-of-fact acceptance of European customs and conditions.

Nieriker assumes that her reader is a serious art student, "no gay tourist . . . but a thoroughly earnest worker, a lady, and poor, like so many of the profession."[8] She is out not to judge foreign customs and societies, but to get an education. When she comes across some disagreeable aspect of the foreign scene, she neither scolds nor gloats, but takes note of it, and passes on:

> To some people, the first sight of a poverty, vice, and misery of which one before could form no adequate conception, proves most startlingly interesting; but of course, a young American lady in London would oftener give the preference to other streets. (22)

When her educational program is threatened by a ban on sexually mixed life-drawing classes in, of all places, Paris, the young lady from, of all places, Massachusetts bands together with other female artists to hire a studio and a teacher to get on with the business of learning to draw the male and female figure (48–49).

Jones's implied reader is wealthier, less earnest, but equally self-assured. She needs to know who bows to whom, when, and in what order, and how much to give the butler at the end of a weekend stay in a country house.[9] She is also, however, scrupulously modest and determined to enjoy what is distinctive about Europe, rather than carp at what she misses or show off her purchasing power.

> It is scarcely worth while to go to Europe for the purpose of proclaiming all the time that America is in every way better; if that is your opinion you may show it by going home and never leaving it again, but while you are abroad try to get all the pleasure and profit possible out of the visit. (2)

The pleasure and profit that Jones's tourist seeks are conventional enough: she will visit, dine, drive in the park, and attend the theater; she will accumulate cultural capital, "widen" her "mental horizon" (4), stimulate her "intelligent curiosity" (5), and open herself to moral improvement through aesthetic contemplation.

> If we . . . feel a thrill . . . in the little church at Stratford-on-Avon, or in Canterbury Cathedral, where the Black Prince lies . . . , it means that we have the capacity to be stirred by the memory of words and deeds which were higher and nobler than anything which we shall say or do in all our lives; and although we are told that no man by taking thought can add to his bodily stature, it is certain that the best aid to mental growth is a healthy sense of our own littleness. (18)

Her air of well-mannered self-confidence, however, is a welcome relief after the assertive bluster of Morford and Hemstreet.

A third guidebook for women, *A Summer in England, with a continen-*

tal supplement: A Hand-Book for the Use of Women (1894), published by the Women's Rest Tour Association (WRTA) of Boston, makes an even more striking contrast. Its presumed authors are neither New York society women, like Jones, nor the daughters of eminent if ineffectual transcendentalists, like Nieriker, but benevolent Boston club women, the sisters and wives, in some cases, of the Morfords and Hemstreets, who made up the vanguard of the bourgeois New Woman movement.[10] Its presumed readers are also independent, middle-class women, schoolteachers, settlement-house workers, or even, perhaps, office workers, with no particular claims to social, intellectual, or artistic distinction.

Like Nieriker's book, and Jones's, the WRTA handbook is notable for its calm self-assurance, its assumption that women can travel, alone or in groups, as easily and with as little fuss as men, that they are perfectly capable of walking twenty-five miles over an Alpine pass, and as entitled as men to a restful, regenerative vacation in foreign parts. Nieriker and Jones, however, like Morford and Hemstreet, have points to make and missions to fulfill. Their books betray a certain amount of performance anxiety. If Morford is worried about demonstrating that he is as good as anyone else, or better, and Hemstreet needs to prove that he has gotten the most for his money, Nieriker must convince herself that she has done her duty to future waves of female art students, and Jones must uphold the honor of the upper-class American woman on her visits and in her public demeanor. Each of these texts is certainly intended to aid travelers, but each also serves as a vehicle for self-presentation. Each of these authors uses European travel as a source of pleasure and improvement, variously defined, and as an occasion for producing him- or herself as a strong, authoritative figure on a broad, conspicuous, and prestigious stage.

The WRTA handbook is different. Its title page lists no author; its voice is kindly, helpful, but impersonal. It uses no first-person pronouns, either singular or plural, which gives it the air of a collective product, a compendium of sisterly advice. The preface informs the reader that the WRTA was established to serve "women who might enjoy a vacation abroad if they but knew how cheaply it can be accomplished, and how easy the paths of travel may be made by confidence and commonsense."[11] Its founders' purpose was to provide an information bureau and introduction service to which "the timorous and inexperienced may apply for aid" (5). The handbook assumes that the "gracious motherland" of Europe offers women a unique combination of relaxation and cultural enrichment; its authors assume that European travel is neither a duty nor a quasi-public performance, but a source of physical and intellectual pleasure.

> Every foot of ground has, indeed, its uncounted memories; almost every name is instinct with historic interest. Add to such intellectual charms the fact that, in summer, the climate is full of a sweet serenity, the days long, melting into a soft twilight, the scenery rich in beauty, and that the daily life flows like a quiet stream, and one who has never set foot in this gracious motherland may guess what its soothing influence must be. Even in busy London . . . it is possible to find a lotus-eater's paradise, where she may truly rest, feeding the eye on pictures, the mind with memories. (6)

If the preface suggests a certain languid passivity, the book is quick to dispel any notion that the traveling woman is a helpless invalid. The authors balance the language of sentiment and sisterly cooperation with a bold and hearty individualism, urging women to cultivate vigorous independence by undertaking challenging walking tours (13–14), "'knocking about'" on the tops of buses (33), exploring regions of the city "that respectability wots not of" (37), or even enrolling at Oxford or Cambridge ("if she has sufficient leisure, e.g., two or three years" [54]). Further, they see no reason that an American woman, having taken sensible precautions, should not travel by herself on Continental trains (73) or brave the Italian summer, provided she "close her windows at night, . . . rest after the mid-day meal, carry a wrap when visiting subterranean grottos or mouldy churches and, if possible, wear silk or flannel undergarments" (71).

All three of these guidebooks demonstrate the New Woman's newfound independence; all three, but especially the WRTA handbook, suggest that whatever historical factors made this independence possible also helped make the New Woman more self-assured and less aggressively self-promoting than many of her male contemporaries. All three, finally, suggest that women had particular uses for Europe, but none of them gives any hint that women questioned the general belief in the personal and cultural value of the European tour that had dominated tourist travel throughout the century. Women travelers had special requirements, and they were distinguished one from another by their means, their goals, and their backgrounds, but they shared their culture's faith in the benefits of combining pleasure and improvement in a grand European adventure.

The most important advocate of this combination at the turn of the century was the prolific, popular, genial, and cultivated guidebook writer Grant Allen, whose estimation of the uses of European travel rests on his belief that the best education is based on personal observation. The "notion that Latin and Greek constitute 'a liberal education,'" he writes in *The European Tour*, "was natural enough in the sixteenth century, when most knowledge had still to be dug out of books, and when books were mainly written in the dead languages. It is absurd at the present day, when knowledge is chiefly to be gained by contact with things."[12] Using the analogy with the physical sciences, Allen argues for a cultural education based not on classic texts and established authorities, but on personal experience. "Travel holds the same position with regard to mankind, its history, its industry, its arts, its organisation, as laboratory work holds to chemistry, field work to geology, and dissection to biology" (11). Further, "the direct method of observation and experiment" is as valid in "the sciences which deal with man" as it is in the natural sciences (14). This sounds like a familiar late-nineteenth-century argument for an empirically based social science, but Allen has something quite different in mind. He is interested not in contemporary social and economic conditions in the countries he visits, but in the history and the "culture" embodied in their tourist attractions. His goal is not to redefine culture, but to suggest a new way of approaching it. He still believes that an understanding of "American institutions" must be based on their historical precedents rather than on the social and economic conditions in which they were adopted and are maintained, but he thinks these precedents are best understood through personal experience of their material remains.

> If you want to know the origin of American institutions, American law, American thought, and American language, you must go to England; you must go farther still to France, Italy, Hellas, and the Orient. Our whole life is bound up with Greece and Rome, with Egypt and Assyria. (11–12)

The best introduction to "France, Italy, Hellas," is not study, not even studious travel, but aesthetic pleasure.

> Once you have learned to love and sympathise with Hellenic art . . . , the language, the poetry, the history of Hellas will become easy and simple to you, because you want to know them: you will study them now out of enthusiasm and pleasure, out of pure desire to understand and appreciate the beautiful things that have begun by interesting you. (7)

The point is to move not from texts to artifacts, but the other way around. The goal (like the goal of progressive educators of later years) is to combine education with pleasure, to motivate learning by promoting spontaneous interest.

This is, the tricky point for progressive education, as it is for educational travel. One does not "learn by doing" just anything or the same thing over and over. Experiential education is structured by the teacher who provides ordered occasions for curiosity and the facilities for following it out. The learner's activity must be pleasurable but not random or aimless. This must also be the case with travel, if it is to have the desired educational effect. Like the kindergartner absorbed in a puzzle, the enthusiastic traveler is engaged in the most attractive and therefore most effective kind of learning, learning that seems to be absorbed through the pores but that is the result of intense, and intensely pleasurable, concentration on the subject or the task at hand. Like the kindergartner, too, the traveler needs a teacher to help structure his experience, to help him use his time efficiently, and to provide the resources he needs to satisfy his awakened curiosity.

This is where Allen comes in. *The European Tour* suggests a careful, rational itinerary, moving from modern London to "more ancient" Paris to the "pure medievalism" of Belgium, tracing the old Frankish empire up the Rhine, and connecting at last with Rome, "Hellas," and the East. Entrust the structure of your tour to me, he seems to promise, and the education will come of itself. "I am telling you how to make the best use of your time . . . in the deeper sense of taking you round on a *definite plan*, so that at the end of your trip you may have *enjoyed* yourself thoroughly, and yet *learned and digested* as much as was possible" (26, emphasis Allen's).

A tour in Europe is for Allen a source of pleasure and a goad to curiosity: the combination of aesthetic sophistication and historical knowledge that it produces is what he calls culture, at once a faculty and a possession, a pleasurable and a useful attainment. "The use of Europe," he writes, "is that Americans should employ it as a means of culture. Other incidental uses it may possess, of course—for Europeans; as a place to make a living in, to love, to die for. But these are unessential. Its true purpose in the scheme of nature is clearly for you and me to enjoy ourselves in, without prejudice to a little concomitant instruction. At least, I shall say so to my American readers" (19). This is ironic but also serious. Allen knows that Europe has "other incidental uses" "for Europeans," and that these "uses," and even modern Europeans themselves, hold little interest for the average American tourist, whose command of languages is rudimentary (8–9) and whose serious purpose in going to Europe, if he has one at all, is to visit, reimagine, and consume the past.

The progress from Putnam and Park to Morford, Nieriker, the

WRTA, Jones, and Allen quite properly suggests a developing sophistication among American travelers. There were Putnam tourists, Park tourists, and Morford tourists in Jones's and Allen's day, just as there are all
of these kinds and more today, but the sequence of these guidebooks
suggests a trend parallel to what would be suggested by the sequence of
Irving's *Sketch Book*, Longfellow's *Hyperion*, Twain's *Innocents Abroad*,
and Adams's *Mont-Saint-Michel and Chartres*, from awestruck wonder to
confident, even smug self-assurance by way of earnestness and bumptious
self-assertion.

The Rewards of Travel

Celebrants of the rites of travel were clearly aided in their offices by
guidebooks, which in turn offer evidence about the evolution of travel
practices and attitudes. Many guidebooks also provide explicit commentary on the ultimate purpose of the ritual, the boon to be gained by its
practice. In addition, a close analysis of these texts suggests that nineteenth-century Americans used Europe and European travel in less overt
and explicit ways, to assert and defend social and cultural positions of
privilege and domination.

Most nineteenth-century American guidebooks claim that their version of the European tour provides a combination of pleasure and improvement far superior to anything available at home. Putnam defines the
exalted pleasures of travel in explicit contrast to ordinary amusements.
"For scarcely a greater sum than is often wasted in unsatisfactory pleasures," he writes, travelers "may glide in a gondola on the moonlit waves
of the Adriatic . . . or tread the classic soils of the lava-crushed cities of
Vesuvius" (5). John Henry Sherburne makes a similar contrast between
the idle life of the American watering places and the "information and
improvement" to be derived from a summer's tour in Europe, visiting
"three or four kingdoms, their capitals, institutions, and people" and enjoying "a pleasant sail of seven thousand miles on the Atlantic."[13] Later
writers are less prim, but they still have the tourist's intellectual and spiritual improvement in view. William Hemstreet follows up his opinion
that "Europe is the biggest show I ever went to" by advising "all Americans who . . . are willing to pay money for substantial education, [to] go
to it" (2). Grant Allen, as we have seen, gives the formula a prescient
pragmatic twist by suggesting that "going about the world to amuse ourselves . . . is the way to preserve and enlarge . . . our interest in knowl-

edge" (2). From Putnam to Hemstreet to Allen, guidebooks sold themselves as manuals for pleasant and productive worship at the shrines of
Europe. From one end of the century to the other, travelers expected to
enjoy and improve themselves by following the orders of service proposed
by these trusted authorities.

Guidebooks also promulgate more specific, historically determined relations between travel, knowledge, and satisfaction. Some of the earlier
ones maintain the eighteenth-century tradition of the traveler as amateur
natural and social scientist by defining travel as a kind of improving research.[14] Roswell Park advises his readers that "to *see* the curiosities of
nature and of art, to *observe* the manners and customs, and to *examine* the
laws and institutions of the old world, should certainly *expand the mind*
and *improve the understanding* of a citizen of the new" (9, 10–11; emphasis
mine). Murray assumes that the European tourist will be interested in a
detailed account of the hydrology of Amsterdam's canals and a description of a high-speed diamond polisher powered by four horses.[15] Other,
more properly romantic authorities neglect description to exalt the benefits to be gained from coming to know Europe in a more spiritual way.
Some years before Park and Murray, Putnam was already touting the romantic frissons available to the tourist "beneath Buonarotti's dome" (5).
And at the end of the century Grant Allen combines the two approaches
by claiming that the only real, the only lasting knowledge is that which
is obtained by the enthusiastic spirit.

> Few men remember in middle life any of the beggarly stock of Greek and
> Latin they acquired for the moment at school or college. Why? Because
> they never cared for it; therefore they never learned it. . . . How different is
> the knowledge one has drunk in with pleasure in examining some stately
> cathedral, some exquisite temple, some fresco of Fra Angelico's, some relief
> from the perfect chisel of Pheidias! Those things, and the knowledge of
> them live with one forever. You don't try to remember them. You couldn't
> forget them. (5)

The ideal tourist experience combines pleasure and instruction, exaltation
and study to produce improvement. Like a ritual celebrant, the traveler
returns with a boon: with knowledge, memories of exalting, enno-
bling experience, and a magically transformed sensitivity to history and to
art.

Immediate pleasure, knowledge, and the salutary effects of exalted experience may be the most obvious benefits of travel, but they are not
necessarily the most important. The rite of travel also provides its votaries

with an exhilarating sense of freedom and power. Traveling is as close as most people come to truly independent action: the security of organized group travel has always commanded less prestige than the independent traveler's putative freedom;[16] Hans Magnus Enzensberger has suggested that the *Wandervogel*'s footloose irresponsibility is so appealing because it is all that remains of the romantic revolutionary's heroic "*liberté*."[17]

Of course, few nineteenth-century travelers used their freedom to do anything except follow the standard tourist itineraries, but within these fairly narrow limits guidebooks encouraged them to think of themselves as the knowledgeable creators of their own European experiences. Indeed, it seems to me that one of the guidebooks' most important functions was to endow the traveler with all the freedom and power of the bourgeois consumer by serving as a catalog of tempting products among which he or she was free to choose and by constructing an implied reader who felt well informed, authoritative, and ultimately superior to other tourists, indigenous peoples, and previous generations.

Most guidebooks emphasize their readers' freedom of choice, even when the number of options is limited by convention or by such practical matters as the availability of transport. George Putnam makes the tourist's freedom clear from the very beginning of his "Notes for the Way." After a few words on Liverpool, he lays out a number of options for the independent traveler:

> *If* you intend to visit Ireland, a steamboat goes daily from Liverpool to Dublin. A short tour *may* be made thence to Belfast, *or* to the Giant's Causeway, and *if* Scotland is an object, before proceeding to London, cross from Belfast to Glasgow: (See Tour in Scotland,)
>
> —*or*—
>
> you *may* go to Scotland via the northern counties, the lakes of Cumberland &c. (11, emphasis mine)

More prescriptive guidebooks can also be used by independent travelers as catalogs of choices rather than strict instructions. The hortatory Roswell Park is less permissive than Putnam: his "mays," interspersed with imperative "wills" and simple commands, are those of a schoolmaster and really mean "should," or "must." "Here you *will* save time by taking a cabriolet to visit the tomb of la Fayette, the patriot of two worlds," he remarks at one point, apparently leaving the presumably patriotic tourist little room to object that she might prefer a second visit to the Louvre. "You *may* next . . . visit the famous cemetery of Père la Chaise," he goes on, and then, even more peremptorily, "*Observe* the monuments of Abelard and Eloise . . . *visit* . . . the largest of the five slaughterhouses constructed by Napoleon" (94, emphasis mine). In his introduction, however, Park admits that the individual tourist will ultimately decide whether to follow his very good advice and suggests that it be used as what he calls a general itinerary, "by means of which [the tourist] will be able to estimate his own progress, and proportion his own time; so as not to linger too long amid scenes of minor interest, nor pass too rapidly by those of greater importance, unless for special reasons" (73).

Murray's *Handbook for Travellers in Central Italy and Rome* sums up this aspect of the guidebook's appeal very clearly:

> We believe that most travellers form some plan for themselves . . . and that no general rule can be laid down to which exceptions may not be taken. . . . With this view, therefore, we have arranged the different objects of attraction in Rome under separate classes, observing, as far as possible, a systematic arrangement of the details. For facility of reference, there is, we are convinced, no plan which presents so many advantages; and it has this additional recommendation, that it brings within one view a complete catalogue of objects which would be scattered over various and detached parts of any work in the topographical or chronological arrangement.[18]

Murray uses the word *catalogue* here to mean exhaustive list, as in the catalog of a museum's collections or of a library's holdings, but the commercial sense of the word is at least as appropriate in this context. The guidebook shares features of the catalogs of the Library of Congress and Sears & Roebuck. The traveler is a reader and a researcher but also, and perhaps primarily, a consumer. Successful travel, in other words, combines the satisfactions of the free, imaginative construction of experience with the joys of shopping. Guidebooks facilitate both activities by describing the available attractions, experiences, and commodities and by providing practical advice on how to enjoy or acquire them most conveniently and economically.

Pleasurable though it may be, however, shopping is not a particularly prestigious activity in official nineteenth-century culture, and to become an accomplished shopper is not a widely honored ambition. It is not surprising, therefore, that the authors of even the most utilitarian catalogs of European goods, services, and sights should choose more honorific (and more masculine) metaphors to describe their texts' missions and to provide their readers with more heroic, masterful figures for the tourist *him*self. "A man without [a guidebook]," writes W. Pembroke Fetridge in the self-serving preface to the fifth edition of *Harper's Hand-book*, is "like

a ship at sea without a compass, dragged round the country by a courier."[19] The purchaser of *Harper's Hand-book*, by contrast, will be not a
passive drifter but the purposeful captain of an obedient crew, the master
of a well-run ship.

Fetridge's authoritative traveler may resemble a shopper in his daily
activities, but he is encouraged to think of himself as a captain of men in
a more general sense. The implication that the tourist shares the masculine force and independence of the sea captain flatters the male traveler,
helping the writer, the clergyman, the artist, or the student to feel that as
a traveler he is filling a powerful, independent male role, and it also em-
powers in a backhanded way the large number of travelers who were
women, by encouraging them to appropriate this same independence for
themselves. By inviting all travelers, men and women, rich, like John
Quincy Adams, and poor, like Bayard Taylor, white and, as we shall see
in the next chapter, black, to identify with the upper-class sons of Anglo-
American colonists, by encouraging the tourist to think of him- or herself
as a deservedly masterful member of a deservedly dominant gender, class,
and ethnic group, and by referring explicitly and disdainfully to other
groups, guidebooks helped make tourist travel a profoundly empowering
activity for individual Americans.

One important element in this empowerment was the tourist's notorious ethnocentricity. John Pemble provides an extensive analysis of the
British traveler's sense of superiority to the "sensual" and "childlike" peoples of the South;[20] William Vance, in *America's Rome*, does the same for
the American.[21] Fetridge's description of the "Sicilian character" can
stand for the superior attitude toward foreign "races" most frequently
adopted in American guidebooks. "'They are cheerful, inquisitive, and
fanciful,'" he writes, "with a redundance of unmeaning compli-
ments, showing they are not so deficient in natural talents as in their due
cultivation. . . . The upper classes are incorrigibly indolent, and fond to
excess of titles and such like marks of distinction" (379–80). The "natives"
of Europe, and particularly southern Europe, are altogether different
kinds of beings from the Anglo-American tourist: they are exotic, quaint,
childlike, and even primitive in their old-fashioned delight in titles and
display.[22]

The guidebook's class assumptions can be equally overt. Dean Mac-
Cannell describes the treatment of workers as tourist attractions in nineteenth-century Paris and remarks on Baedeker's disdainful attitude toward wretches condemned, unlike his readers, to work for a living.[23]
Mary Cadwalader Jones advises her readers that "many of the nicest English people always travel third class," "but if you are going through the

'black country,' or into the mining district, where there is a rough population, it will be, perhaps, wiser to choose first class" (89). The most common treatment of the lower classes in guidebooks, however, is simply to
write them out of existence. Putnam, Park, Fetridge, and Morford all
mention the palaces, parks, and noble houses of London, but none so
much as suggests the existence of the urban poor.

Guidebook writers encourage tourists to claim positions of dominance
by exercising the economic power of the consumer, then, and by assuming the "natural" superiority provided by some combination of actual or
honorary gender, class, race, or nationality. They also empower tourists
by treating their activities as ways of coming to know and hence to dominate the world. As we have seen, tourism is often understood as a form
of study. Dean MacCannell relates the tourist and the ethnographer;[24]
Georges Van Den Abbeele suggests that the tourist's ambitions parallel
those of the theorist, since "both theory and tourism imply a desire to see
and to totalize what is seen into an all-encompassing vision."[25] Judith
Adler reminds us of the scientific pretensions of early travelers, which
persist well into the nineteenth century, to "'envision' whole countries
through a detailed inventory of their flora, fauna, antiquities, and monuments."[26] Totalizing and envisioning imply domination. Tourists are
sightseers: their subjugating gaze reduces individuals, institutions, art-
works, and landscapes to bits of knowledge and elevates the tourists and
their class, race, gender, and nation to the position of the authoritative
knower. The method of the traveling gentleman-scholar, as Adler points
out, was closely related to "techniques developed to rationalize the infor-
mation-gathering practices of absolutist states" and instrumental in the
mercantile project of the "European cultural and intellectual elites" as
they "sought to take title to 'the whole world' then coming into view."[27]
Tourists in this sense are the not-so-secret agents of social, political, and
economic domination.

One way of knowing and controlling the world is to reduce complex
objects, phenomena, and experiences to sets of easily graspable facts. The
most obvious manifestation of this practice is the guidebook's notorious
addiction to numbers. Vasi's *New Picture of Rome*, first translated into
English in 1818 and recommended to American tourists by Putnam and
Park, among others, sets the tone. Its description of St. Peter's moves
immediately from vague appreciation to measurement and enumeration.
"The front of the cathedral" is "magnificent." "To give an idea of its size,
it is sufficient to say that it is 370 feet wide, and 149 high." "The effect
produced by this front . . . is truly astonishing," "particularly when the
whole is illuminated by 4,400 lamps, and afterwards by 784 flambeaus."[28]

Murray reinforces the tourist's sense of control by presuming to criticize as well as describe: "The façade is 368 feet long and 145 feet high; but it is more adapted to a palace than to a church, and is ill calculated to harmonise with such a structure as the dome."[29] *Osgood's Complete Pocket-Guide to Europe* retreats from judgment but provides even more figures, presumably to help the reader grasp the church's immensity and gauge its importance: "It cost over $50,000,000; took 176 years (the reigns of 28 popes) to build; and covers 212,231 sq. ft., being the largest ch. in the world."[30]

Just as numbers are presumably easier to master than the complex aesthetic and spatial experience of architecture, so are simple facts, objects, and anecdotes easier to register than complex systems of economic and cultural life. Vasi again sets the tone by reducing bustling public spaces to collections of objects, some with "interesting" stories attached. His description of the Piazza del Popolo takes no notice of the "popolo" that presumably animates it, but rather points out the gate, the obelisk, the garden, and the two matching churches, integrates the whole as a single, satisfying "coup d'oeil," and then adds a two-sentence history of the obelisk, from its erection "at Hieropolis, by Sesostris king of Egypt," to its ultimate relocation here in 1589 (3–4). Osgood similarly reduces the bustling Piazza di Spagna to a group of commercial establishments, buildings, and monuments: "The Piazza di Spagna is surrounded by the hotels and shops of the foreign quarter, and contains Bernini's Barcaccia fountain; Pius IX.'s Column of the Immaculate Conception (with 5 statues); the Palace of Spain (Spanish Embassy); and the College of Propaganda Fide (1662)" (343).

Tourists, however, do more than visit squares and monuments, and some are even interested in the economic activities of the places they visit and the lives of the inhabitants. Guidebooks cater to their interests by reducing even these objects of interest to figures, facts, and images. Murray describes Italian economic and social life with cool detachment, treating their details as independent bits of information. "The vitriol works of Viterbo," he informs us, "produce upwards of 100,000 lbs., of which about one-half is exported. The salt works of Cervia, the Comacchio, and Corneto, give an annual production of 76,000,000 lbs." (xiii). His paragraph on farming contains parallel figures ("the number of sheep collected on the Campagna at the season is said to amount to 600,000" [xv]) along with matter-of-fact accounts of the lives—and deaths—of migrant workers: "They work in the harvest-field all day under a scorching sun, and at night sleep on the damp earth, from which the low heavy vapour of the pestilent malaria begins to rise at sunset. Even the strongest and healthiest are often struck down in a single week" (xv).

Reducing public places, work, lives, and national customs and institutions to figures and "objective" descriptions is one way of turning them into information, of coming to "know" and, presumably, to "master" them. The combination of what the tourist actually sees and the information that the guidebooks provide produces something that the tourist is eager to call knowledge and to use as a basis for establishing himself as an authority. Having seen a building or a group of peasants and read an explanation of their composition, history, and function, the tourist credits himself with having "experienced" and so, by unjustified extension, understood them.[31] Having negotiated the omnibus system, found a hotel, changed money, and bought some gloves, the tourist claims to know Paris.

Another, related way of establishing one's authority is by assuming a central and usually superior position in relation to one's surroundings, of placing oneself, like Stevens's jar, upon an eminence and forcing the slovenly wilderness of the "foreign" world to surround it. The most obvious way to do this is to climb a hill or a tower. Guidebooks invariably recommend the ascent of the Campanile or the towers of Notre Dame or the heights of Fiesole to the connoisseur of "views."[32] Georges Van Den Abbeele traces this practice back at least as far as Montesquieu, who always began his visit to a city by climbing the highest tower "pour voir le tout ensemble,"[33] and relates it to the tourist's inveterate "desire to see and to totalize what is seen into an all-encompassing vision."[34] The *Satchel Guide* proposes a more pleasant means to a similar end, suggesting that a ride on the top of a London omnibus—making the self the moving center of the passing panorama—is "the quickest way of obtaining a general view of its most remarkable features."[35] Jones (109) gives the very same advice and provides another image of the tourist as a centered, ordering perceiver and knower (as well as underlining her ethnic and class assumptions) when she suggests that "if the next Sunday after church, during the season, you will take a chair at Hyde Park corner while some of the handsomest men and women in the world, belonging to the English upper classes, walk up and down, you can form a good idea of the mighty strength of our common race" (109). Sherburne suggests studying maps as a more private way of centering oneself, obtaining a grand, synthesizing vision of the "tout ensemble," and "mastering" the lay of the land or the layout of the city and makes it very clear how such study can liberate and empower. "The tourist, immediately upon his arrival, should step into one of the numerous bookstores, and for a shilling purchase a neat pocket map." He should then study the map until he has a clear picture of the layout of London in his head. This "will enable him to move about the city and see all that is to be seen without asking many questions" (78).

These examples suggest that at least one image of the ideal tourist is the unseen seer who dominates the world around her by observing it, processing it, and ultimately comprehending it. The purpose of the map and the guidebook is precisely to make this process possible. With a guidebook in hand and a map in mind, one is an independent viewer of the passing scene, possessing the necessary information to understand what one sees and to move through it without impinging upon it or being impinged upon by it.

If the substance of the guidebooks' advice helps the tourist dominate the passing scene, their rhetoric also reinforces her sense of authority. Guidebooks make tacit assumptions about their ideal readers and in the process help construct their actual readers' views of themselves and their positions as tourists. They assume, as I have suggested, that the tourist is free to organize her time and choose the sights she wants to visit. They also encourage their readers to adopt the role of social, moral, and aesthetic critic and pass supercilious judgment on the people and places they visit. Mariana Starke sets the tone here, Fetridge chimes in in midcentury, and Allen carries the practice on into the twentieth century. "The German villages at the foot of the [Carinthian Alps]," Starke opines in 1823, "in some measure spoil the beauty of the scene, as nothing can be more uncouth than the wooden buildings which compose them, except the fences, which are possibly worse."[36] It is difficult to wash here, she goes on, since the bedrooms lack washstands; the table linen is so dirty that the tourist is advised to purchase her own; "the peasantry have fine complexions," but "the women are said to be depraved in their morals" (306). Nothing eludes the censorious eyes, nose, hands, and imagination of Starke's tourist, who clearly knows what is right, judges what is wrong, and distances herself from all deficiencies, whether of taste, cleanliness, or behavior. Fetridge in Paris forty years later is equally critical—on what grounds he does not say—of the people's superficial pleasantness and deep moral corruption.

> Beneath this pleasant surface, however, a strong and polluted current is perpetually running, and there is no part of the world where the more substantial virtues are more rare, and where so much dissoluteness exists within such narrow limits. (96)

And finally, at the turn of the century, Allen reasserts the serious tourist's authority and his aesthetic priorities, dismissing vast reaches of London, the homes of millions and the shrines of the unenlightened, as without interest for the really cultivated traveler. "The northern area," he writes, "you may entirely neglect. It contains nothing of interest, . . . is entirely modern, stucco-built, and repellent." St. Paul's Cathedral is "vast, bare, pretentious, unimpressive. The monuments are nightmares." In sum, London is an aesthetic disappointment. "Architecturally and artistically, London has done nothing in any way worthy of its commercial supremacy. It ought to be as fine as fifty Venices: it has not one St. Mark's, one Doge's Palace" (71–72).

Allen's strictures suggest yet another aspect of the guidebook reader's implied superiority: her claim to cultural authority, artistic connoisseurship, and refined sensibility. Some guidebooks, to be sure, treat all European "attractions" as interchangeable commodities, to be "secured" by a canny purchaser, but even the crassest of these catalogs assume that their readers are interested in and at least minimally knowledgeable about history and art. Morford's *Short-Trip Guide*, to take the most egregious example, is peppered with allusions to artists and writers, emperors and kings, and even occasional quotations from Scott, Burns, and Byron. Other guidebooks typically encourage their readers to think of themselves as the kind of people who can catch allusions to Virgil and Byron, know the difference between Louis Quatorze and Pio Nono (Pope Pius IX), and appreciate the works of Salvator Rosa, Guido Reni, and "Michael Angelo." Mariana Starke's early description of the *Dying Gladiator*, for example, expresses the aesthetic tourist's enthusiasm in its adjectives and exclamation points and assumes the connoisseur's erudition in its allusions to writers and artists.

> This super-excellent statue, found in the gardens of Sallust, has been so well restored, by Buonaroti [*sic*], that the arm he made is deemed nearly equal in merit with the other parts of the figure!!!!! Winckelmann supposes the statue called The Dying Gladiator to represent a herald; other antiquaries think it more like a shield-bearer: it seems, however, to be generally considered as a copy of that masterpiece in bronze, by Ctesilaus, which represented a wounded man in the agonies of death. (151)

Forty years later, Fetridge also recommends the *Gladiator* as "this brightest gem of art," adds a sentence of appreciation ("the wonderful, simple, and natural position of the limbs," "the lineaments of the face, expressive of the utmost anguish, yet endowed with manly fortitude"), quotes Pliny, and includes Byron's famous stanza from *Childe Harold* without attribution, assuming it is part of the reader's cultural baggage.[37]

The most revealing treatment of the famous statue for our purposes, however, is provided by George Stillman Hillard, whose *Six Months in Italy* (1853) was an essential part of the midcentury tourist's library.

> But the charm and power of the statue consist in the amazing truth with which the two great elements of humanity and mortality are delineated. A vigorous animal life is suddenly stopped by the touch of death, and the "sensible warm motion" becomes a "kneaded clod" before our eyes. The artist gives us all the pathos and the tragedy of death without its ghastliness and horror. The dying man is no longer a trivial person, stained with coarse employments and vulgar associations, but an immortal spirit breaking through its walls of clay. The rags of life fall away from him, and he puts on the dignity and grandeur of death. We feel ourselves in the presence of that awful power, before whose icy sceptre all mortal distinctions are levelled. Life and death are all that for a time we can admit into the mind.[38]

In the time-honored manner of critics of and lecturers on art, Hillard tells his readers how *they* ought to react by pretending to describe how "we" actually react. Hillard's "we" do not suffer from museum fatigue or worry about the differences between Roman life and our own. "We" are serious aesthetes and deep thinkers, transported by the masterpiece and reminded of Shakespeare (the quoted phrases are from *Measure for Measure*) and mortality. We are superior beings for whom the experience of art is an exalting, spiritual escape from the trivial concerns of daily life. We are also connoisseurs, who can be expected to follow and agree with Hillard's next paragraph demonstrating the artist's skill and appreciating more particularly his taste, and the wonderful way it affirms our own superior judgment. Given such a subject, Hillard writes, too many artists would fall "into the weakness of overdoing the tragic element, and of laying such a weight upon our sympathies that they would have given way under the pressure." Too many artists, in other words, would fall victim to sensationalism and court the common emotional reactions of the mob. "Here," however, "nothing has been done for effect. No vulgar applause is courted, and the decency and dignity of truth are scrupulously observed" (182). The sculptor of the *Gladiator* lives up to the high standards of George Stillman Hillard and his readers, who use their cultivated, noble reaction to the work of art to affirm their superior appreciation of true artistic merit and their immunity to vulgar effects.

Guidebooks underline the important connection between point of view and sense of self, between the position of the eye and the power of the "I," between seeing and being. They help demonstrate the function of travel in the constitution of group and individual identity. Travelers are performers, actors of well-known scenes, players of well-known roles, and adopters of approved attitudes, all of which are laid out for them in the guidebooks' liturgy. At its best, the traveler's performance is no mere literal reading of a part, but an individual, "artistic" enactment of a conventional action, an imaginative attempt, as Judith Adler puts it, to discover, create, and communicate meaning as one "move[s] through geographical space in [a] stylistically specified way."[39] Guidebooks provide an outline of the action and suggest the central features of the main character. The individual tourist may choose to use the guidebook slavishly, like a paint-by-numbers canvas (Adler's image, 1385), or she may draw on it for the advice and the information she needs to create her own original version of a conventional cultural experience.

If guidebooks can be prescriptive and liberating, limiting and empowering, according to how they are used, the same is true for the generic conventions of the travel chronicle. In the next chapter I show how the easy expectations of what I have described as the testimonial dimension of travel ritual made writers out of many travelers and provided an occasion for significant personal, literary, and cultural work to some of their number.

CHAPTER FOUR

Travel Chronicles: Testimony
and Empowerment

THE TRAVEL CHRONICLE offered its practitioners the opportunity to testify to what were often transformative, always extraordinary, passages in their lives and to court the prestige of authorship by contributing to an established literary genre. The allure and the cultural cachet of testimony can be traced to evangelical religious practices and the confessional writings of romantics like Rousseau and Wordsworth. The appeal of writing in an established genre goes back at least as far as the Renaissance sonnet sequence and manifests itself in such disparate nineteenth-century forms as the sentimental novel and the African-American slave narrative.[1]

As we have seen, travel is often understood as a kind of ritual whose participants bestow "meaning on the self and the social, natural, or metaphysical realities through which it moves"[2] by enacting variations on traditional patterns of action and modes of being. Like the celebrants of a religious ritual, travelers enact a kind of drama, following a scenario that they have adapted from available models or copied from a guidebook or bought from a "travel packager." Travel writing can be seen as a similarly conventional, similarly empowering mode of literary behavior, whose practitioners exploit and expand a set of conventions, partly to record their experiences and partly to create for themselves appealing, powerful, and prestigious cultural personas.

Travel chroniclers put Europe to at least double use, acting out the ritual of travel in their experience and reenacting it in words. Such reenactments could be explicit fictionalizations of experience, like Irving's *Sketch Book*, purportedly faithful accounts, like Silliman's *Journal*, or complex hybrids, like Dorr's *Colored Man Round the World*. In every case, however, the chroniclers had the opportunity to rewrite and in a sense to relive their travel experiences, and to recast themselves as the kind of narrators, protagonists, and travelers they most wanted to be. Like spiritual autobiographies and saints' lives, travel chronicles attest to certain nonordinary events, reformulate them to match approved cultural patterns, and depict their protagonists as ideal incarnations of respectable models, from

the objective, superior scientific observer to the sensitive, sympathetic reformer, the social critic, the intrepid explorer, the professional writer, and
the responsible, respectable American.

In this chapter I survey the range of models available to the potential
travel chronicler and then show how two African-American writers, born
in slavery, used the conventions of the travel chronicle as part of a strategy
for producing themselves as free, independent men, worthy of their readers' admiration. My purpose here is not to generalize on African-American history and literature, but more simply to show how two African-
American writers adapted the conventions of a common literary genre to
their own purposes. My point is not that travel writing provided an ideal
vehicle for African-American cultural empowerment, but rather that the
travel chronicle genre offered William Wells Brown, the writer and political activist, and David F. Dorr, the author of *A Colored Man Round the
World*, a chance to testify to their unusual European experiences, generate
powerful social identities for themselves, and create in the process an extremely useful model for understanding how travel writing functioned in
the lives and works of nineteenth-century American travelers in Europe.

MODELS

The simplest form of the travel chronicle in the first part of the nineteenth century was the "Letter from Europe," which typically appeared in
a newspaper's "Miscellany" column alongside such respectable, informa-
tive, and improving items as a local poet's lines on the death of Napoleon,
a précis of Sir Humphry Davy's theory on the formation of mists, and the
unrelated stories of an "Extraordinary Resuscitation" and an "Extraordinary Cucumber."[3] Such letters gave their authors the opportunity to produce themselves as authorities on a subject of general interest and to
display to their homebound neighbors some combination of the poet's
artistry, the scientist's attention to the details of the natural world, the
moralist's profundity, and the ordinary person's affection for curious and
amusing facts. These letters vary enormously, but they are most frequently personal accounts, combining description and testimony. The report on St. Peter's Basilica in the September 29, 1821, *Providence Gazette*
includes a description of the piazza, the colonnade, the obelisk, and the
vast interior and an account of a mystical, musical experience, a spiritual
boon, the product of the travel ritual which testifies to the writer's aesthetic sensitivity.

[The singing] thrilled my whole frame, and brought tears into my eyes, and kept them there for many minutes. Such tenderness, such melody, such unison, such power and compass of voice, I did not suppose possible in human beings.

A description of Aix-la-Chapelle in the same paper on July 30, 1825, is more objective in tone. Its author claims the role of knowledgeable informant in his detached description of such social types as farmers known as "Kappesbauern, a name derived from a kind of cabbage," "manufacturers and merchants, whose establishments derived great benefit from the French government," and "tradesmen of every description, who profit considerably from the influx of strangers." The *New York American* correspondent's account of his first romantic view of Scotland focuses in contrast on personal experience and invites the reader to share a thrill rather than acquire some information.

Land of Song and Story; home of Philosophy and Chivalry; synonym of Virtue and Valor; Scotia, hail! How my heart bounded with wild emotion when from the moor hills of England's Northumberland, my eyes caught in the blue tops of thy Cheviots, standing like faithful sentinels to guard the entrance into thy sacred dominions![4]

Newspaper travel accounts instructed and amused their readers and enticed the potential travel writer with the prospect of authorship. Whether he or she aspired to be a poet or a scientist, an enthusiast or a genial man or woman of letters, the easy conventions of the travel column promised a well-prepared stage to accommodate the role and a ready-made audience to applaud the performance.

   The book-length travel chronicle is a slightly more ambitious form, often compiled from newspaper dispatches and private letters, with a clear reportorial purpose and an overall shape dictated by the outline of the author's actual travels. Its author typically claimed the authority of experience and often used that authority to adopt a didactic and in some cases moralizing or pedantic tone. When Benjamin Silliman set out from New Haven in 1805 to buy books and scientific equipment for Yale College, for example, he began a series of letters to his brother, which he subsequently edited for publication in book form. His avowed purpose was to provide pleasant instruction for his readers by permitting them to relive his experiences and perceptions as they happened, rather than presenting them with a series of essays on his observations and conclusions: "I trust that a faithful picture of some portion of real life, actually led in a foreign country, interspersed with a reasonable number of remarks, will be more interesting and useful than a collection of mere dissertations or general accounts."[5] Silliman invites the reader to join his tour, describing the inns, the scenes, the people he meets, and the sensation of riding fifteen feet above the ground on the top of an English coach. In addition to being a tourist, however, he is also a scientist and an educator, eager to relay technical knowledge, and a moralist, eager to explore the ethical problems that his experience poses. So he describes an electrical demonstration, explains Dalton's theory on "aeriform bodies," compares his results with those of Gay-Lussac, and outlines manufacturing processes in great detail (see, for example, 102–7). Not content with mere description, he goes on to comment on the moral effects of the factory system and the problems posed to society by what he sees as a concentration of highly paid and underpoliced operatives (108). Whatever we think of Silliman's politics, we cannot deny that he considered travel writing a serious undertaking, an occasion to inform his readers and to air his social and moral concerns as a prominent scientist, educator, and contributor to the nascent U.S. industrial revolution.

In his popular *Sketch Book of Geoffrey Crayon, Gent.*, Washington Irving adopts a more casual, less earnest voice and combines familiar varieties of magazine writing to develop a third, extremely productive model for the travel book. Crayon was widely perceived as "a 'genial' though diffident tourist indulging his fancy for aristocratic culture amidst the finery of the Old World."[6] Irving's narrator assumes the attractive persona of the tourist as an inveterate explorer ("Even when a mere child I began my travels and made many tours of discovery into foreign parts and unknown regions of my native city" [743]), independent literary dreamer, and flaneur. "I cannot say that I have studied [the shifting scenes of life] with the eye of a philosopher," he tells his reader, "but rather with the sauntering gaze with which humble lovers of the picturesque stroll from the window of one print shop to another; caught sometimes by the delineations of beauty, sometimes by the distortions of caricature and sometimes by the loveliness of landscape" (745). His title describes his project clearly: this is no journal, no conscientious record of experiences undergone and knowledge acquired, no collection of dilemmas for moralists and problems for social critics, but an album of sketches.[7] Irving's avowed desire to "prompt a benevolent view of human nature, and make my reader more in good humour with his fellow beings" (961–62), belies his insouciant pose, however, and shows how even the self-styled American dilettante feels compelled to testify to the improving qualities of his travel and his writing.

Crayon achieves this purpose by combining conventional—and, as it turned out, convention-setting—travelogues, such as his famous trip to Stratford-upon-Avon, with descriptive essays ("Rural Life in England"), literary journalism ("English Writers on America"), moral exempla ("Roscoe," "The Wife," "The Broken Heart"), and interpolated, unrelated fiction ("Rip Van Winkle," "The Legend of Sleepy Hollow"), all conceived as promoting benevolent good humor. Like the newspaper travel column, the form appears undemanding, a perfect showcase for the wares of a budding writer, or a catchall for the productions of a literary amateur. Not surprisingly, it founded a long line of similar collections, including not only such obvious imitations as Longfellow's *Outre-Mer* (1846), Donald Grant Mitchell's *Fresh Gleanings* (1847), and Joel Tyler Headley's *Rambles and Sketches* (1850), but also, I would argue, such important hybrids as Fuller's *Summer on the Lakes* (1844) and Thoreau's *Week on the Concord and Merrimac Rivers* (1849).

A fourth form of travel chronicle could certainly be seen as a variation on the Geoffrey Crayon model, but its tone seems to me sufficiently different and its progeny sufficiently numerous to merit separate consideration. It is embodied in Lydia H. Sigourney's *Pleasant Memories of Pleasant Lands* (1842), a pleasantly sentimental album of sketches, poems, engravings, and meditations, dominated by its author's pleasant but imposing presence. "Mrs. L. H. Sigourney," as the title page styles her, presents herself as a serious literary artist and a witness for Christian piety and human love. She offers her book as partial payment of the "debt" incurred "to his Preserver" by anyone "who leaves his native land to take note of foreign realms, and is brought again in safety to his own home and people." She ends her preface with the pious tone and archaic grammar of prayer, combining conventional modesty ("dear reader, if any such there be") with high-style diction ("perchance") and a devout belief in the resurrection of the body, to project a narrative persona that is the very model of the high-toned Christian woman.[8]

> And now, dear reader, if any such there be, who shall have patiently finished these my pages, thou art for this very kindness, as a brother or sister unto me. And as we have thus communed together of pleasant things, without, perchance, having seen each other's faces in the flesh, may we be so blessed as to dwell together in that country where no stranger sorroweth, where no wanderer goeth forth from his home with tears, and "where there is no more sea." (v)

Sigourney's text combines conventional description, sentimental reverie, and explicitly religious testimony. It takes the form of a chronological narrative, frequently interrupted by non-narrative passages. Sigourney

tells where she went and what she saw and rarely misses an occasion for
religious or moral improvement. Her chapter on Calais includes the
obligatory descriptions of the French *diligence* ("cumbrous"), the land
("flat"), and the "hovels . . . miserably planted in the midst of an expanse
of mud" (229). It is largely taken up, however, with a poem on the legend
of the siege of Calais and the role of Queen Philippa in securing the
release of those noble burghers who had offered themselves as sacrifices to
prevent the sacking of their city. Sigourney tells the story, and then comments on woman's proper power by exhorting her readers to exercise
their influence through love and prayer.

> Oh woman! ever seek
> A victory like this; with heavenly warmth
> Still melt the icy purpose, still preserve
> From error's path the heart that thou dost fold
> Close in thine own pure love. Yes, ever be
> The advocate of mercy, and the friend
> Of those whom all forsake; so may *thy* prayer
> In thine adversity be heard of Him,
> Who multiplies to pardon.   (226–27)

   "Among the advantages of travelling," Sigourney writes in her final
chapter, "it is common to allow" such things as an increase of knowledge,
self-knowledge, charity, sympathy, patriotism, and the love of home
(368–71). The ultimate value of travel, however, is its effect on individual
piety. The enforced separation from loved ones together with the knowledge that they may be sick and dying at home while the traveler is enjoying the wonders of the foreign scene evokes "an intensity of prayer, before
unknown," "a stronger faith, a deeper humility, a more self-abandoning
dependence on the Rock of Ages." "Thus," she concludes, "amid the
gains of the reflecting traveller, may be numbered that which is above all
price, a more adhesive and tranquil trust in the 'God of our salvation,
who is the confidence of all the ends of the earth, and of those who are
afar off upon the sea'" (372–73). Beginning and ending with prayer, Sigourney's album of verses, stories, and reflections, linked by the narrative
thread of her European travels, provides a model, actual or potential, for
a range of works from Harriet Beecher Stowe's similarly titled and equally
pious *Sunny Memories of Foreign Lands* to the European letters of Margaret Fuller, whose purposes are surely moral but whose piety is directed
toward political freedom and social justice rather than conventional
Christian obedience.

Writing and publishing a travel chronicle was a way of both inventing and laying public claim to a social role and a literary persona. From the simplest newspaper column to the most elaborate multivolume memoir, the travel chronicle testifies to a privileged experience and constructs an authoritative voice. Even the least ambitious newspaper chronicler longed to claim a certain personal distinction by testifying to his or her extraordinary experiences in public print. More ambitious "scientific" reporters like Silliman claimed an even broader authority for themselves by testifying not only to experience but to "truth." Artful chroniclers like Irving and Sigourney used the conventions of travel writing to create and then claim identity with narrative selves they considered worthy of public regard. For all of them, and many others as well, testifying to a European experience by writing and publishing a travel chronicle was a personally satisfying, culturally legitimating activity. Howells, Twain, James, and Adams all used travel writing to help build and consolidate their literary reputations; hundreds of others burst into print for the first and often the only time with accounts of their European travels.

EMPOWERMENT: DAVID F. DORR AND WILLIAM WELLS BROWN

Among those who availed themselves of the travel chronicle form in the antebellum period were two African Americans, the otherwise obscure and unpublished David F. Dorr and the celebrated William Wells Brown, already a frequent orator for the causes of abolition, temperance, and peace and the author of the *Narrative of William W. Brown, a Fugitive Slave*. Both men wrote book-length accounts of their European sojourns; both combined the conventions of the straightforward travel narrative with the looser ones of the travel sketchbook and the edifying album of impressions and comments; both developed distinctive narrative personas. Whereas Dorr, in *A Colored Man Round the World*, casts himself as a knowledgeable bon vivant, Brown uses *The American Fugitive in Europe* to help solidify his already considerable reputation as a speaker, a writer, and an intellectual.

In his study of early African-American autobiography, *To Tell a Free Story*, William L. Andrews emphasizes the ways in which African-American authors use autobiography "to open an intercourse with the white world."[9] Their narratives, he argues, were intended not only to tell a story but also to assert by their very existence their authors' standing in the public world of letters. They were meant to be "declarative" as well as "constative," to claim authority for a previously silenced black voice, and to create between a black author and a white reader the unusual relationship of speaker and listener. Dorr's book and Brown's are both declarative texts in this sense, claiming rhetorical, social, and political power for their narrators. Their very titles stake their authors' unusual claims to cultural authority by juxtaposing noun phrases identifying their authors' marginal social status (*A Colored Man, The American Fugitive*) with adverbial phrases denoting a socially privileged experience (*Round the World, in Europe*). The fact that Brown's narrative persona turns out to be easier to admire than Dorr's should not blind us to the fact that both men used their travel writings to assert strong African-American identities in the face of nearly overpowering racial prejudice.

A Colored Man Round the World is a problematic text; the narrative persona Dorr creates for himself is as often repugnant as appealing. Dorr's book provides us, however, with an unusual and illuminating glimpse of an African-American slave's struggle to re-create himself as a free man. Deprived of legal selfhood, Dorr uses the conventions of a common literary genre and the clearly inadequate model provided by his master's circle of New Orleans men-about-town to construct an imaginary literary self. His efforts can help us understand both the usefulness of travel writing for aspiring authors and the kinds of limitations that slavery could impose on a young person's understanding of responsible, free man- or womanhood.

The most remarkable feature of Dorr's text is its counterfactual narrative persona. Dorr acknowledges in his preface that he was still a slave when he returned from Europe,[10] but in the narrative he speaks and acts as if he were a free man, the master of his time and of his destiny. He uses travel writing as a dry run for freedom, a vehicle for fantasy, a way to dream of what it might be like to be free, to imagine himself into an equal relationship with everyone he meets.

Dorr's double sense of self is replicated by a double sense of purpose in the text. In his preface he claims high moral authority and serious purpose. The authority is that of the fugitive slave who was betrayed by his master, took his fate into his own hands, and fled. The purpose is to foster racial and national pride by displaying "the ruins of the ancestors of which he is the posterity" (11) and claiming "from what he has seen in the four quarters of the globe" that "the American people are to be the Medes and Persians of the 19th century" (12). In his preface, Dorr sets himself up as the servant of all the people, sharing with them the fruits of his travels in the hope of freeing them from the limitations of their ignorance.

And as he believes that the rights of ignorant people, whether white or black, ought to be respected by those who have seen more, he offers this book of travels to that class who craves to know what those know who have respect for them. (12)

In his text as a whole, however, Dorr follows a more personal agenda, using his tour and his book as occasions to assume the coveted role of independent, well-heeled young bachelor, emphasizing his assumed status and his power of choice by his constant use of the first person singular pronoun,[11] referring to his master as if he were an old and valued acquaintance,[12] and imagining himself as a knowledgeable traveler and bon vivant, making (awkward) pronouncements on the standard sights,[13] nudging the reader with insinuating sexual remarks, and participating in race- and class-based jokes and pranks.

The contradictions between the author's actual enslavement and the narrator's apparent freedom, between Dorr's noble purposes and his occasionally ignoble narrative help energize his text and begin to suggest the bewilderingly complex task confronting a young African-American slave in his attempt to become his own free self. A passage from Dorr's opening pages gives us a sense of this struggle; I quote it at length because the original text is hard to find.

This day, June 15th, 1851, I commence my writings of a promiscuous voyage. This day is Sunday. I am going from the Custom house, where I have deposited my baggage to be searched for contraband goods, and making my way along a street. . . . It was raining; consequently there was not a person to be seen. All of a sudden the coachman drew up to the side walk, and, opening the coach, said, "Adelphi, sir." I was looking with considerable interest to see the hotel of so much celebrity on board the ship. Captain Riley had informed me that it was a house not to be surpassed in the "hotel line" . . . I, under this dispensation of knowledge, looked around to see the towering of a "St. Charles or Verandah," but when I saw a house looking like all the rest, I came to the conclusion that the English were trying to get along without making any improvement. . . . Just then a well-dressed gentleman opened the door and descended the steps with an umbrella to escort me in. "Come right in here, sir," he said, leading me into a large room, with an organ and hat-stands as its furniture. The organ was as large as an ordinary sized church organ. The gentleman took my overcoat and hung it up. He then asked me some questions concerning the voyage, after which he asked me to walk to the Bureau and register my name. This done we ascend one flight of stairs and enter my room. He asked me if I wished fire. I answered in the affirmative. He left me.

Having seated myself *a la American* [*sic*], I listened very attentively to "those chiming [church] bells." Tap, tap on my door called forth another American expression, "come in." The door opened and a beautiful girl of fifteen summers came in with a coal scuttle and kindling. She wore on her head a small frilled cap, and it was very small. A snow white apron adorned her short, neat dress. A man is a good deal like a dog in some particulars. He may be uncommonly savage in his nature, and as soon as he sees his sexual mate, his attention is manifested in the twinkling of an eye. She looked so neat, I thought it good policy to be polite, and become acquainted. Having finished making a lively little fire, she rose up from her half-bending posture to follow up her duty through the hotel. "What is your name, Miss," said I; "Mary," said she, at the same time moving away. "I shall be here a week and want you to take care of me." Mary's pretty little feet could stay no longer with propriety the first time. (13–15)

I descended and found a good dinner, after which I walked into the newsroom, where I found several of the merchants of Liverpool assembled to read and discuss the prevailing topics of interest. . . . [Two] noblemen . . . were quietly discussing the weak points in American policy. One held that if the negroes of the Southern States were fit for freedom, it would be an easy matter for four millions of slaves to raise the standard of liberty, and maintain it against 250,000 slaveholders. The other gentleman held that it was very true, but they needed some white man, well posted in the South, with courage enough to plot the *entree.* . . . I came to the conclusion that they were not so careful in the expression of their views as I thought they ought to be. I was quite sure that they would not be allowed to use such treasonable language at Orleans or Charleston as that they had just indulged in.

Sitting in my room about an hour after hearing this nauseous language, Mary came for the clothes, for that is what she asked for. (16–17)

The contents of the first part of this passage are completely conventional: parallel descriptions of hotels and maidservants can be found in many contemporary chronicles. In the opening pages of *Haps and Mishaps of a Tour in Europe*, for example, Grace Greenwood reported that "the Adelphi, the best house in Liverpool, does not compare with our first-class hotels, either for comfort or elegance."[14] James Freeman Clarke described the "smiling young lady, with curls on her cheeks and a smart cap on her head," who met him at the door of the Waterloo Hotel in Liverpool,[15] and S. W. Fiske's Mr. Dunn Browne commented appreciatively on "our bright, tidy, black-eyed, rosy-cheeked Susan, with her coquettish muslin cap and her merry laugh."[16]

Dorr's tone, however, is unusual for a midcentury American traveler.[17] His attitude toward the chambermaid combines the Boswellian with the sophomoric, an uneasy match that produces a disturbing canine simile: "A man is a good deal like a dog in some particulars. . . . [A]s soon as he sees his sexual mate, his attention is manifested in the twinkling of an eye." His suggestions of sexual intimacy—"I shall . . . want you to take care of me"—and his hint that the servant later obliged his desires— "Mary's pretty little feet could stay no longer with propriety *the first time*" (emphasis mine)—cast him in the role of an upper-class lecher rather than the elegant man-about-town he desires to impersonate.

Dorr's observation of the after-dinner conversation at his hotel reveals another surprising effect of his adopted persona. A discussion of the likelihood of slave rebellion in the South would have given Fuller or Brown a welcome opportunity to elaborate on English and American attitudes about race and slavery. Dorr, however, uses the occasion to identify himself as a "Southerner" (14) and a "gentleman" rather than a "colored man" and a slave. What shocks him is not the fact of a quarter-million whites holding four million blacks in bondage, or even the assumption that the four million would require white leadership to revolt against the quarter-million, but the audacity of these foreigners' even suggesting such a threat to *American* law and order. He is for the moment a Southern gentleman traveling with other Southern gentlemen, and if their relationship is anything less than comradely—if he is, in fact, a slave—he gives no sign of it.

In some senses and at some moments Dorr is an individualist rather than an abolitionist, and his purpose is to demonstrate his superiority, not to advance the cause of African Americans in slavery. The very fact of his travels serves as prima facie evidence of his personal equality with other travelers; his descriptions of foreign scenes and customs lay implicit claim to the traveler's superior knowledge; the conventional persona of the man of the world gives him the opportunity to develop his own more daring persona as a sexual as well as a cultural connoisseur. At the same time, Dorr does not ever completely forget his avowed desire to teach "ignorant people, whether black or white," about their European and African heritage. He wants to play the teacher as well as the dandy, but his problematic narrative persona repeatedly undermines this ambition.

In the course of his visit to Athens, Dorr makes much of the contributions of Egypt to Western culture and of Homer's description of the Egyptians as black Africans (134). In Turkey, however, Dorr seems to condone the grossest racism as he observes the cruel baiting of a black sailor and describes its target in grotesque, subhuman terms. "At the hind part of one of these yawls," he writes, "was a large, fat, and shiney [*sic*] black African" reclining half naked at the tiller of a small boat. "He attracted the attention and caused amusement for the passengers; and some one threw some orange peelings on his naked rotundity as he was half lying on his back with no clothes on above his loins. . . . After his patience gave out, he turned lazily around and looked up, like a duck at thunder, and shook his head; they followed up this amusement until he got agoing on the gibberish dialect, and that was more amusement yet" (118–19). Dorr may not have thrown orange peels himself, but his language is no kinder to the African than his fellow passengers' missiles: "naked rotundity," "lazily," "like a duck at thunder," and "gibberish" do not betoken respect.

Dorr's position on racial matters is inconsistent. He sometimes speaks as the "colored man" of the first part of his title, but more often as the white Southern "gentleman" he is trying to imitate. Dorr clearly felt empowered by his travels, and he seems to have written his book as a testimony to that empowerment. Like many other Americans, mostly white and male, it is true, but also black, like Brown, and female, like Fuller, Dorr treated his European journey as a rite of passage. He used travel, in other words, to test his knowledge and his skill, and he used travel writing to show how well he did on the test. That his experiences in Europe and the text that represents them have disturbing elements of both sexism and racism tells us more about the models for strong, independent manhood that were available to him than it does about his own character.

The confusion that available models could produce is further evident in the book's concluding paragraphs, which read like a pastiche of slogans from *Poor Richard's Almanac* and an uplifting sermon on the brotherhood of "man."

> Henry kindled his own fire, Washington paddled his own canoe, and for a bright manhood, youth must find his own crag on the mountain, rivet his eye of determined prosperity up the cliffy wiles of life, kick asunder impediments and obstacles, and climb on! When you hear *can't*, laugh at it; when they tell you *not in your time*, pity them; and when they tell you *surrounding circumstances alter cases* in manliness scorn them as sleeping sluggards, unworthy of a social brotherhood.
>
> All are obliged to unite when a question of *might* against *right* comes up, as it is now before the world. Dickens says, "no doubt that all the ingenuity of men gifted with genius for finding differences, has never been able to

impugn the doctrine of the unity of man." He further says, "The European, Ethiopian, Mongolian, and American, are but different varieties of one species." He then quotes Buffon, "Man, white in Europe, black in Africa, yellow in Asia, and red in America, is nothing but the same man differently dyed by climate." Then away with your *can't*; when backed to the wall by the debator, you had better say *nothing* than *can't*. You had better say, as I say while taking leave of you, *au revoir*. (191–92, emphasis Dorr's)

The first of these paragraphs asserts the effectiveness of plucky American individualism in the fight against the "impediments and obstacles" of "*surrounding circumstances*," without taking any note of the differences between the obstacles confronting a white apprentice in Boston and a black slave in Louisiana. The second paragraph begins like an appeal for interracial solidarity, but turns into an affirmation of the power of the individual and concludes with a final, anomalous demonstration of the widely traveled narrator's bilingual sophistication, "*au revoir*."

Dorr uses the readily available form of the travel chronicle to create and attempt to play the barely compatible roles of the "colored" dandy as European traveler and the African-American fugitive as exemplar of Franklinesque grit and determination. However we judge his success, it is clear that travel writing provided him with a stage for the enactment of his fabricated public self and an occasion for asserting his self-worth.

Travel and travel writing played a part in William Wells Brown's self-construction, too, strengthening his claim to the cultural and political power of the cultivated gentleman of letters. Brown left the United States in 1849 as a fugitive slave, a well-known orator, an elected delegate of the American Peace Society to the Peace Congress in Paris, and the author of an autobiographical narrative that sold ten thousand copies in the two years after its publication.[18] Stranded in Europe by the passage of the Fugitive Slave Law, he remained there, earning his living and supporting his daughters by his pen, until his freedom was purchased in 1854. He returned to the United States as a well-connected gentleman of letters who had savored the pleasures of high European culture and literary society and experienced for himself the tragic contrast between "monarchical Europe," where he felt free and equal to all, and the "democratic" United States, where "since [his] face was not white, [his] hair was not straight, [he] must be excluded from a third-rate omnibus."[19]

As its subtitle suggests, Brown's travel book, *The American Fugitive in Europe: Sketches of Places and People Abroad*, shares many of the conventional features of Irving's, Sigourney's, and Dorr's work, providing its

readers with the usual descriptions of tourist attractions, sketches of ce-
lebrities, and personal anecdotes. Sales of the book were brisk,[20] and the
reviews underlined Brown's distinctive contribution to the literature of
travel. "When before," asked the *Liberator*'s reviewer, "has the world had
submitted to its perusal a volume of travels from the pen of a fugitive
slave?"[21] "It is something new," says the *British Friend*, "for a *self-liberated
slave* to publish such a work."[22] The book's success was doubtless due in
part to the novelty of its authorship and the passion of its rhetorical passages, but it certainly also had something to do with Brown's use of the
familiar conventions of the travel narrative. *The American Fugitive in Europe* would have struck a mid-nineteenth-century reader as a welcome
variation on a familiar genre. Like many other European travelers, Brown
writes much of the time as a sightseer, relying on the intrinsic interest of
the foreign to provide him with marketable copy (and occasionally approaching Murray's and Baedeker's dullness in doing so).

> The obelisk [in the Place de la Concorde] was brought from Egypt at an
> enormous expense, for which purpose a ship was built, and several hundred
> men employed above three years in its removal. It is formed of the finest red
> syenite, and covered on each side with three lines of hieroglyphic inscrip-
> tion commemorative of Sesostris,—the middle lines being the most deeply
> cut and most carefully finished; and the characters altogether number more
> than sixteen hundred. The obelisk is of a single stone, is seventy-two feet in
> height, weighs five hundred thousand pounds, and stands on a block of
> granite that weighs two hundred and fifty thousand pounds. (81)

Like other travelers, he views the landscape as if it were a painting and the
aesthetically pleasing qualities of the "straggling cottages" as signs of their
"comfort," and takes vociferous pride in "the progress of civilization and
the refinement of the nineteenth century" (56). Like other travelers, too,
Brown realizes that he must provide his readers with testimony as well as
description, that his experiences as a cultured African-American gentleman are what will distinguish his travel book from all the others.

He comments frequently, therefore, on his treatment by Europeans.
His description of the obelisk in the Place de la Concorde concludes with
the remark that it arrived in Paris "on the 23d of December, 1833,—just
one year before I escaped from slavery," and is followed by a comment on
dining in Paris as a person of color.

> Having missed my dinner, I crossed over to the Palais Royal, to a dining
> saloon, and can assure you that a better dinner may be had there for three

francs than can be got in New York for twice the sum,—especially if the person who wants the dinner is a colored man. I found no prejudice against my complexion in the Palais Royal. (82)

The courtesy and respect with which Europeans treat Brown naturally lead him to bitterly ironic comparisons with his treatment in the U.S. "In America," he writes, "I had been bought and sold as a slave in the Southern States" and "treated as one born to occupy an inferior position" "in the so-called Free States" (40). In Britain, by contrast, "I was recognized as a man, and an equal." "The very dogs in the streets," he continues in a bitter contrast with the "republican . . . bloodhounds" (18) of his native land, "appeared conscious of my manhood" (40). His description of his treatment in France is more succinct, and more poignant. "I was not laughed at once while in France" (97).

The prevailing atmosphere of tolerance at the Paris Peace Conference even gives Brown the rare opportunity to turn the tables on a white bigot. While conversing with Victor Hugo, Brown notices standing near him, hat in hand, the white man who had "appeared the most horrified at having a negro for a fellow-passenger" on the trip from Boston to Liverpool.

> This gentleman, as I left M. Hugo, stepped up to me and said, "How do you do, Mr. Brown?" "You have the advantage of me," said I. "O, don't you know me? I was a fellow-passenger with you from America; I wish you would give me an introduction to Victor Hugo and Mr. Cobden." I need not inform you that I declined introducing this pro-slavery American to these distinguished men. (60–61)

In a less personal vein, Brown uses the authority of firsthand experience to expose "the utter fallacy" of a slaveholder's commonplace, the notion that British workers are worse off than American slaves.

> Whatever may be the disadvantages that the British peasant labors under, he is free; and if he is not satisfied with his employer, he can make choice of another. He also has the right to educate his children; and he is the equal of the most wealthy person before an English court of justice. But how is it with the American slave? He has no right to himself; no right to protect his wife, his child, or his own person. He is nothing more than a living tool. (140)

Brown writes as a conventional traveler, then, and as an African-American opponent of slavery and racial discrimination. He is interested in other social questions, too, and quick to turn his experiences into texts for other kinds of social commentary. His visit to Wordsworth's grave reminds him of the sad life of Hartley Coleridge, buried nearby, and he takes the occasion to produce a two-page discourse on the evils of drink, using the conventional language and rhetoric of the temperance lecture to conjure up "the enslaving appetite," "the wild vortex of London life," "the treacherous wine-cup," and the inevitable outcome of overindulgence, in which "the wine destroys the intellect, and the man of wit degenerates into a buffoon, and dies a drunkard" (189–91). Other encounters call forth homilies on "determination" (213–14) and the importance of "education, determination, and self-culture" (229).

Brown's testimony, furthermore, is not exclusively social and economic. He claims the cultural authority of one who has been inspired by high art and historic sites. In the British Museum, he turns from the aesthetic appreciation of a statue of Venus, "one of the most precious productions of the art that I have ever seen" (113), to a conventional meditation on "the uncertainty of the human character" prompted by a portrait of Cromwell ("Yesterday, a common soldier; to-day, the ruler of an empire; to-morrow, suspended upon the gallows" [114]). At the grave of Wordsworth he permits himself a few pious generalizations on the subject of poetry. "England has the greatest dead poets," he writes, "and America the greatest living ones. The poet and the true Christian have alike a hidden life. Worship is the vital element of each. Poetry has in it that kind of utility which good men find in their Bible, rather than such convenience as bad men often profess to draw from it" (187). In Paris, he treats himself to some historical frissons at Robespierre's house, "the residence . . . of that blood-thirsty demon in human form, Marat" (83), and "the place where the guillotine stood when its fatal blade was sending so many unprepared spirits into eternity" (85). His narrative, in other words, reports on a heritage and a set of experiences that he shared with his white countrymen and fellow tourists and testifies to the particular experiences and reflections of "the American fugitive in Europe."

Even more important, his adoption of the highly conventional form of the travel narrative can be seen as part of a conscious strategy for presenting himself as the (self-)educated equal of the writers, diplomats, delegates, and humanitarians with whom he associates. Writing and publishing *The American Fugitive in Europe* was a political as well as a commercial act for Brown: its very conventionality supports its author's implicit claim that African Americans are the spiritual and intellectual equals of their white compatriots. The long and frequent passages in which Brown demonstrates his social successes, his aesthetic sensibility, his powers of reflection, and his ability to write midcentury magazine prose after the manner of Lydia Sigourney and N. P. Willis must be read with this political project in mind (see pp. 74, 138, 156, 195). I have been to soirees and concerts, Brown declares; I have visited great monuments, old and new, and been moved by them. I have enjoyed the glamour of ambassadorial receptions, the sublimity of grand organ music, the slightly melancholy medieval splendor and the poetic associations of Tintern Abbey, and the up-to-the-minute modernity of the Crystal Palace. His conventional appreciations of the conventional high points of European travel constitute a strong claim to membership in an influential group of writers and cultural authorities and an assertion of not just equality with but similarity to his (mainly white) readers. His visit to the Poet's Corner in Westminster Abbey, an indispensable stop on any literate American's tour of London,[23] reinforces this claim and this assertion by demonstrating his appreciation for the English literary past. For Brown, as for his contemporaries, great writers appeal to the noblest qualities of "mankind," and individuals can demonstrate the nobility of their thoughts and feelings by responding to their works and venerating their memories. "The genius of these men," Brown writes, "spreads itself over the whole panorama of nature, giving us one vast and varied picture, the color of which will endure to the end of time" (132). As if to demonstrate his own appreciation of this genius, Brown stops at the Royal Academy on his way home from the abbey and takes the occasion to show off the breadth and intensity of his reading and his critical acumen.

> Our first interest for [Dante] was created by reading Lord Byron's poem, "The Lament of Dante." From that hour we felt like examining everything connected with the poet. The history of poets, as well as painters, is written in their works. The best written life of Goldsmith is to be found in his poem of "The Traveller" and his novel "The Vicar of Wakefield." Boswell could not have written a better life of himself than he has done in giving the Biography of Dr. Johnson. It seems clear that no one can be a great poet without having been sometime during life a lover, and having lost the object of his affection in some mysterious way. Burns had his Highland Mary, Byron his Mary, and Dante was not without his Beatrice. (133–34)

In the course of his five years abroad and in the pages of his travel narrative William Wells Brown claimed a stake in the Anglo-European tradition and exploited the authority he gained by this claim to expound his ideas on social justice and Christian morality. He was not ready to reject European-American culture or to criticize the class structure of British and American society. His strategy was to appropriate the prevailing class structure and cultural norms in order to gain respect for himself as a writer and an intellectual and promote the cause of racial justice. The travel book provided a convenient vehicle for this strategy. It also documents an important aspect of Brown's strategy as a respectable public opponent of slavery in the United States. In his impassioned conclusion to the book, Brown writes that neither his race nor his "legal" status as a fugitive had barred him from respectable literary and intellectual society in England. In London, for example, he had "eaten at the same table with Sir Edward Bulwer-Lytton, Charles Dickens, Eliza Cook, Alfred Tennyson, and the son-in-law of Sir Walter Scott" (313). Brown clearly sees his social successes as an important victory in the fight against slavery and an inspiration to further struggle. I "returned to the [United States]," he goes on, "for the express purpose of joining in the glorious battle against slavery" (314).

> I came back to the land of my nativity, not to be a spectator, but a soldier—
> a soldier in this moral warfare against the most cruel system of oppression
> that ever blackened the character or hardened the heart of man. (314–15)

Brown embraced European culture, took inspiration from European models, and cultivated a conventionally elevated aesthetic sensibility; he dedicated the skills and the prestige these acts betokened to the fight against slavery and "Negrophobia" (314). In *The Narrative of William Wells Brown* (1847) he had testified to his experiences as a slave, a fugitive, and an abolitionist. In *The American Fugitive in Europe* (1855) he presents his credentials as an intellectual, a reformer, a cultivated gentleman, and a fighter for freedom.

Dorr and Brown believed in the American promise of liberty and justice for all. They also recognized two important obstacles to its fulfillment: slavery and the widespread ignorance of the history and the capabilities of African and African-American peoples. Both men escaped from slavery; Brown fought it in his speeches and writings; and both used the conventional travel chronicle—the testimony of privileged experience—to dispel ignorance in their readers and to claim places for themselves in what they wanted to see as one unified American meritocracy. Both, however, underestimated the virulence and the persistence of American racism. If the demonstration that black people were as resourceful, as intelligent, as receptive to high culture, as capable of literary self-construction, of bonhomie in Dorr's case and of gentility in Brown's, had ever been enough to secure liberty and justice for them, then travel writing might have done more to achieve this goal. Neither *The American Fugitive in Europe* nor *A Colored Man Round the World* struck a decisive blow in the struggle for African-American liberation. Both, however, gave their authors the opportunity to assume what they understood to be culturally accredited voices, and both demonstrated in the process how adaptable conventional travel narrative could be to a wide range of personal and collective agendas.

Travel and travel writing provided nineteenth-century Americans with broad but not unbounded fields for the creation and the performance of personal and social meaning. Time abroad was sacred to them, in an anthropological if not a strictly religious sense; the texts that inspired, structured, and reported on that time served as secular versions of conventional religious texts. The sense of travel time as a time apart and of Europe as a distant, quasi-sacred ground enabled nineteenth-century American travelers to experiment with alternate identities and construct tentative though often very serious systems of belief and structures of commitment. The sense of travel writing as an available, respectable, and unintimidating genre enabled many of them to share their experiments with a well-prepared audience back home.

In the rest of this book I will show how five writers used the opportunities travel afforded for their own widely disparate aesthetic, political, commercial, philosophical, and personal purposes. Emerson, Fuller, Twain, James, and Adams are not the only writers who used travel and travel writing in this way. A short list of others includes Longfellow, Stowe, Hawthorne, Cooper, Howells, and Wharton. Any of these writers and many others besides would have lent themselves to treatment here, but I think the ones I have chosen provide a good sense of the ways in which many of the most distinguished nineteenth-century American writers and thinkers exploited the challenges and the opportunities of European travel and travel writing.

CHAPTER FIVE

Ralph Waldo Emerson:
The Reluctant Traveler

GIVE ME HEALTH and a day," Emerson wrote in *Nature* (1836), "and I will make the pomp of emperors ridiculous. The dawn is my Assyria; the sun-set and moon-rise my Paphos, and unimaginable realms of faerie; broad noon shall be my England of the senses and the understanding; the night shall be my Germany of mystic philosophy and dreams."[1] This is Emerson at his most exalted, seductive, and troubling, a self-sufficient idealist who seems to think he can generate all the places and experiences he needs by hard, bold thinking. Travel for him is both frivolous and superfluous, producing at great expense of time and energy nothing more than could be created, given "health and a day," in a New England study.

This Emerson exemplifies one aspect of what Robert Weisbuch calls "American actualism," a kind of "reverse verisimilitude" by which history, life, and experience can "be imagined as creative invention, and then implemented." To dwell in such a stimulating possibility is not necessarily to live at ease. A thoroughgoing actualism denies its practitioners the comfort of the given and demands that they be constantly creating new versions of history, culture, and experience. The resulting "ontological insecurity" leads in the case of such writers as Emerson, Dickinson, Whitman, and Melville to that "epistemological daring," that breathtaking freshness of thought that distinguishes the best nineteenth-century American writers from their English contemporaries.[2] It can also lead to an ambivalent relationship with cultural authority, often embodied in the general idea of Europe. "We have listened too long to the courtly muses of Europe" (*E* 70), Emerson wrote, but there were not many other muses available, and he continued all his life to put their songs to his own peculiar uses.

Emerson's "American actualism," his romantic intellectual idealism, and his contradictory feelings about Europe naturally informed his attitude toward travel. Even at its best, he wrote, "travelling," like "conversation, music, pictures, sculpture, theaters . . . , war, mobs, fires, gaming, politics, or love, or science, or animal intoxication," is a mere substitute for "the true nectar" of successful, exhilarating thought (E 460). His comments on his own travels acknowledged the benefits he derived from them while claiming distaste for the actual activity. "It is more than meat & drink to see so many princely old Greek heads[,] Apollos, Dianas, Aristides, Demosthenes, Seneca and emperors & heroes without end," he wrote from Naples in 1833. He enjoyed the paintings, too, and the "sublime old temples, so lofty & many-chapelled, covered with marble & gold of ages & every wall & nook alive with picture, statue, or inscription." Still, he went on, "I hate travelling. Happy they that sit still! How glad I shall be to get home again."[3]

Despite his doubts about the practice, however, Emerson traveled widely, not just in Concord, like Thoreau, but up and down the United States, all through Europe, and as far away as Egypt. A therapeutic trip to Florida in 1827 not only arrested his incipient tuberculosis but taught him something about the differences between places and their effect on theoretically unchanged selves.[4] The European tour that followed the death of his first wife and the end of his brief career as a parish minister helped mend his health and set him on a new intellectual course, "directing him away from theology, preaching, and scholarship," as Robert D. Richardson, Jr., writes, "and providing a new imperative to become a naturalist and a teacher."[5] These trips were followed by a lecture junket to Great Britain in 1847–48, which included a visit to revolutionary Paris and led to the composition of *English Traits*, an extended tour to England, France, Italy, and Egypt, with his daughter, Ellen, between October 1872 and April 1873, and numerous forays on the American lecture circuit, one of which took him as far as California, showed him the Yosemite Valley, and introduced him to John Muir. All this peregrination on the part of a man who declared that "the soul is no traveller" and "the wise man stays at home" (E 277) invites comment. In his actions as well as in his thought and the style of his writing, the man who early disdained "a foolish consistency" (E 265) embodied contradictions, implicitly challenging his readers and critics to make them fruitful.[6] My intention here is to explore the contradictions embodied in Emerson's European travels, his opinions of travel and of Europe, and his book on England and to show how some conventional features of European travel and travel writing combined or clashed with Emerson's temperament and purpose to produce a tension that challenged both Emerson's presuppositions and the genre's limits.

Emerson Traveling, 1833

The story of Emerson's first European tour is well known. He told it clearly and vividly in his notebooks; his biographers recount its outlines and anecdotes; and it has even inspired a photographic essay.[7] In her critical work on Emerson's early years, however, Mary Kupiec Cayton devotes only one sentence to the six months between his arrival in Malta and his visit to the Jardin des Plantes in Paris,[8] and among recent scholars only Robert D. Richardson, Jr., and Evelyn Barish treat the journey with any depth or seriousness. They consider it, respectively, as a part of his intellectual and his psychic biography; I will discuss it here in cultural terms and read the journals and the letters from the period as indications of the way in which an extraordinary individual used an established cultural ritual.

As I have suggested, Americans in the antebellum period rarely admitted to traveling for mere pleasure. Their avowed purposes were less frivolous and usually included a quest for health or cultural "improvement" or both. These motivations were neither trumped up nor misguided. Tuberculosis was one of the great killers of the age, and travel was properly considered one of the best ways of returning an active case to a state of latency.[9] European guidebooks often included sections on travel for health, and a number of travel narratives reported on the beneficial aspects of European resorts and climates.[10] In addition, many Americans who enjoyed perfect health deplored the lack of culture in their homeland and crossed the Atlantic to improve their minds and cultivate their aesthetic sensibilities.

The primary motivation for Emerson's 1833 tour was therapeutic. Like several members of his family, he was early afflicted with a form of tuberculosis and suffered from tubercular "rheumatism" all his life. An alarming flare-up of tubercular pleurisy when he was twenty-five prompted a trip to Florida, which not only produced the desired physical effect, but taught him the value of distance and detachment for personal growth and change. By the time this trip was over, Evelyn Barish writes, "he had left home psychically as well as physically, and he was aware of the importance of his sea change."[11]

Perhaps the success of this trip convinced Emerson of the effectiveness of travel, distance, and change as physical and spiritual therapy. Something must have, because on December 25, 1832, less than two months after the proprietors of the Second Church voted to accept his resignation, still suffering from the crisis of conscience that had provoked him to resign and from his wife's death some twenty-two months before, in a state of health so poor that the captain was convinced he would never survive a winter crossing, he sailed for Europe. Two weeks earlier he had written to his brother William, in New York, announcing his intentions and partly explaining his motivation:

> My malady has proved so obstinate & comes back as often as it goes away, that I am now bent on taking Dr Ware's advice & seeing if I cannot prevent these ruinous relapses by a sea voyage. I proposed to make a modest trip to the West Indies & spend the winter with Edward but in a few hours the dream changed into a purpureal vision of Naples & Italy & that is the rage of yesterday & today in Chardon St. A vessel sails this week for Sicily & at this moment it seems quite probable I shall embark in it. (*L* 1:359)

Emerson never explained any further why he changed his mind and went to Europe instead of the West Indies. His early writing betrays none of that longing for Europe evinced by Washington Irving, Margaret Fuller, and Bayard Taylor and very little interest in any of the visual arts on which Europe still held a virtual monopoly. What turned the balance may have been simply the serendipitous fact that the very brig *Jasper* in which Edward had traveled south was now bound for the Mediterranean. Emerson had read *Childe Harold*, however, and the phrase "purpureal vision" does suggest that he was not entirely immune to romantic dreams of the Coliseum by moonlight. No such certified inspirational possibilities existed in Puerto Rico, where Edward Emerson had been exiled by his soon-to-be-fatal disease, but if Emerson was attracted despite himself by the classical glamour of the Continent, I suspect that he was also drawn to Europe by its sheer distance from Boston, by the bold break and the personal isolation that such a journey, in contrast to a "modest trip" to join his brother, would imply.[12] Whatever his reasons, he sailed for Malta on Christmas Day and was soon "thank[ing] the sea & rough weather for a truckman's health and stomach" (*J* 4:106–7). He landed in New York early the following October, having traveled in the interval from Malta to Scotland.

Emerson returned from Europe in excellent health, already contemplating a "book about nature" and poised on the verge of a long, successful career as a lecturer. He had enjoyed his travels, especially the first months in Italy, in spite of himself; he had accumulated a store of images, memories, and perceptions about art and history and literature that would enrich his writing and his thinking for the rest of his life; he had also freed himself from the doctrinal, the social, and the psychological bonds that had constricted him as pastor of the Second Church of Boston, without adopting any Old World standards or codes to replace them. "I wish I knew where and how I ought to live," he wrote on the return voyage. "I am glad to be on my way home yet not so glad as others and my way to the bottom I could find perchance with less regret."[13] Rather than allowing the "ontological insecurity" that this statement evinces to lead him to despair, however, Emerson took it as a challenge. He would spend much of the rest of his life seeking to know the ground of his own being, "finding his way to the bottom" as an act of "epistemological daring" rather than mere resignation to his necessary end.

Emerson's first European tour helped prepare him for this lifelong project. His travel journals not only provide a running account of his European experiences, but bear consistent witness to the tension he felt between the claims of authority—God, Europe, the past, established figures, culture—and those of independence—his own thought, the idea if not necessarily the reality of America, nature.

He began his travel journal in a specially purchased leather-bound notebook on January 2, 1833, eight days after leaving Boston. On the following morning he rose early to contemplate the sea and participate in a solitary ritual frequently recorded by travelers and often useful in establishing their narrative personas. Geoffrey Crayon revels in such moments on his summertime crossing, welcoming the physical sensations they produce and the occasions they present for fantastic woolgathering. His musings are a celebration of leisure, pleasure, and unfettered imagination.

> I delighted to loll over the quarter railing or climb to the main top of a calm day, and muse for hours together, on the tranquil bosom of a summer's sea. To gaze upon the piles of golden clouds just peering over the horizon; fancy them some fairy realms and people them with a creation of my own. To watch the gently undulating billows, rolling their silver volumes as if to die away on those happy shores.[14]

Jane Eames, the author of *A Budget of Letters; or, Things Which I Saw Abroad*, contemplates the sea at night, adopts a far more solemn tone, and conjures up fantasies of a benevolent nature, a protective, paternal divinity, and domestic peace.

> 'Tis night upon the sea, a glorious night. The moon and the stars look lovingly down; the world of waters around me seems sleeping beneath their pure light. I have gazed upon the calm and spiritual beauty of this scene, till

I have felt almost raised above the earth. I think of my distant home across the Atlantic, and I adore the power of Him who can watch over us in all our roamings by sea and by land, and over you who are now in the still calmness of a Sabbath evening at home.[15]

Both Crayon and Eames accept, even celebrate, their conventional travelers' roles. Emerson, in contrast, seems ill at ease, eager to assert the primacy of his own thought, but not quite ready to reject the claims of divine or human authority. He begins with a simple statement: "I rose at sunrise & under the lee of the spencer sheet had a solitary thoughtful hour" (*J* 4:104). He goes on, however, not to describe the scene before him or his own reactions to it, but to state a maxim—"All right thought is devout" (*J* 4:104)—which could be read as an excuse for the fact that he is using this solitary hour not to pray but to think. To complicate matters further, he first appropriates the voice of a celebrated poet and then gives voice to nature to help him express his "devout" but not conventionally religious thought. He quotes Wordsworth's description of the sunlit dawn clouds—"'The clouds were touched & in their silent faces might be read unutterable love'" (*J* 4:104)—and then imagines how those clouds might comment on his voyage.

> They shone with light that shines on Europe, Afric, & the Nile, & I opened my spirit's ear to their most ancient hymn. What, they said to me, goest thou so far to seek—painted canvas, carved marble, renowned towns? But fresh from us, new evermore, is the creative efflux from whence these works spring. You now feel in gazing at our fleecy arch of light the motions that express themselves in Arts. You get no nearer to the principle in Europe. It animates man. It is the America of America. (*J* 4:104)

The voice and the light of the clouds are both ancient and modern; they know that the ancient sights and famous masterpieces of the Old World sprang from the same divine inspiration at work in the artists and heroes of the new. They deny, in other words, Europe's special status as the home of some animating "principle" of human greatness and affirm Emerson's place in the wide, divine universe. They welcome him wryly to Europe ("We greet you well to the place of History as you please to style it; to the mighty Lilliput or ant hill of your genealogy" [*J* 4:104]), only to deprecate his interest in mere human art ("The strong-winged sea gull & striped sheer-water . . . are works of art better worth your enthusiasm . . . and ye need not go so far to seek what ye would not seek at all if it were not within you" [*J* 4:104]). Emerson chimes in toward the end of the passage to remind his reader of the source of these comments ("So sang

in my ear the silver grey mists" [*J* 4:104]), but he gives the last pious word
to the elements themselves ("& the winds and the sea said Amen" [*J*
4:104]). The solitary American traveler who would spend much of his life
pondering the relation between the self and the nonself, between what is
within and what is outside, sees the world here through the borrowed
eyes of his favorite (English) poet and imagines that it speaks to him only
to say that he will find nothing outside himself that he did not already
possess within.

Emerson on his travels is neither casually debonair, like Crayon, nor
automatically pious, like Eames. Rather, he is genuinely troubled by the
conflicting demands of self and other, experience and authority. He de-
picts himself as an earnest listener to conflicting voices that represent the
pressing demands of freedom and authority, the self and the universe,
God and history, nature, art, and conventional culture. His solitary, contemplative hour is a small version of his European tour; both give these
voices a chance to speak to him without the interruptions and distrac-
tions of friends and family, social obligations and professional duties.

The contradictory voices are clearly to be heard in another early journal passage, which records Emerson's struggle to maintain the integrity of
his own judgment in the presence of the imposing monuments of the
past and the conventional, superficial values of the present.

> And what if it is Naples, it is only the same world of cake & ale—of man
> & truth & folly. I won't be imposed upon by a name. It is so easy, almost
> so inevitable to be overawed by names that on entering this bay it is hard
> to keep one's judgment upright, & be pleased only after your own way.
> Baiae & Misenum & Vesuvius, Procida & Pausilippo & Villa Reale sound
> so big that we are ready to surrender at discretion & not stickle for our
> private opinion against what seems the human race. Who cares? Here's for
> the plain old Adam, the simple genuine Self against the whole world. Need
> is, that you assert yourself or you will find yourself overborne by the most
> paltry things. A young man is dazzled by the stately arrangements of the
> hotel & jostled out of his course of thought & study of men by such trum-
> pery considerations. The immense regard paid to clean shoes & a smooth
> hat impedes him, & the staring of a few dozens of idlers in the street hin-
> ders him from looking about him with his own eyes; & the attention which
> he came so far to give to foreign wonders, is concentrated instead, on these
> contemptible particulars. Therefore it behooves the traveller to insist first of
> all upon his simple human rights of seeing & of judging here in Italy as he
> would at his own farm or sitting room at home. (*J* 4:141)

The tone of this passage is consistently breezy and familiar, whereas the subject—the struggle to maintain independent judgment in the face of cultural authority—could not be more serious or more central to Emerson's thought. The passage combines common, colloquial phrases ("cake & ale," "Who cares?" "the plain old Adam"), evocations of touristic romance and fantasy ("Baiae & Misenum & Vesuvius," "the stately arrangements of the hotel"), and allusions to the daily cares of the tourist's quasi-public life ("The immense regard paid to clean shoes & a smooth hat") with straightforward statements of Emersonian principle ("our private opinion against what seems the human race," "Need is, that you assert yourself"). It ends with a sentence that is characteristic of Emerson both in its sentiment and in its reliance on rural New England life for the imagery that anchors it. If the sentence concluded "judging here in Italy as he would at home," it would be a perfectly clear statement of a familiar Emersonian stricture. The addition of "at his own farm or sitting room" adds the dimension of personal particularity to what would otherwise be a remote and oracular pronouncement. It reminds us that the young man in question comes from a real place, a rural or at best provincial ("sitting room," not "drawing room") land across the sea, and that he is therefore especially susceptible to the blandishments of European culture and convention and especially responsible for maintaining his personal and national independence of judgment.

This paragraph emphasizes Emerson's principled resistance to conventional, received values and shows him strengthening his determination to rely on his own judgment even against "what seems the human race." This determination is not new, but it is perhaps more difficult to maintain when "the human race" is represented not by the Second Church of Boston and the figures, monuments, and artifacts of Puritan, Unitarian, and mercantile New England, but by relics of long-loved antiquity and astonishingly beautiful works of art.

Emerson's intention was not simply to resist Europe, but to use it for his own purposes as a testing ground for independent character, a source of insight into human nature and human history, and a quarry of beautiful scenes and images. It was not to judge negatively but to judge for himself that he came to Europe; it was not to condemn art or even pleasure but to enjoy everything he could convince himself was worthy of enjoyment. This is especially clear in his account of his visit to Florence, where the burdens of history and Catholicism lie a bit more lightly than they do in Rome, and the feast of art is if anything richer.

The conventional tourist's first objective in Florence was the *Venus de'*

Medici in the Tribune of the Uffizi. Byron spent five of the first six Florentine stanzas of *Childe Harold's Pilgrimage* describing it (canto 4, stanzas 48–53); George Stillman Hillard declared that "at first every one hurries to the Tribune, and probably no one ever opened the door of that world-renowned apartment for the first time, without a quickened movement of the heart."[16] On his own first day in Florence Emerson "hasted to the Tribune" and indulged in a fit of aesthetic enthusiasm no less genuine for its uncharacteristic conventionality. "I saw the statue that enchants the world," he writes, alluding to Thomson's frequently quoted judgment of the *Venus* in *The Seasons*,[17] and goes on to quote Byron and assert his own opinion of the gallery's artistic preeminence.

> Then I went round this cabinet & gallery & galleries till I was well nigh "dazzled & drunk with beauty." I think no man has an idea of the powers of painting until he has come hither. Why should painters study at Rome? Here, here. (*J* 4:168)

On his next visit, Emerson has recovered his sangfroid and is determined to be rational and detached, to pass his own judgment on the *Venus* rather than merely parroting the judgment of "the whole world." "I reserve my admiration as much as I can," he writes; "I make a continual effort not to be pleased except by that which ought to please me." But the statue does please him, and he declares himself happy to add his approbation to the world's judgment.

> I walked coolly round & round the marble lady but when I planted myself at the iron gate which leads into the chamber of Dutch paintings & looked at the statue, I saw & felt that mankind have had good reason for their preference of this excellent work, & I gladly gave one testimony more to the surpassing genius of the artist. (*J* 4:169)

If one of the boons Emerson was to bring back from Europe was a strengthened sense of his own authority, of his own personal judgment, another was certainly a deepened knowledge and appreciation of European art. That such knowledge and appreciation were what "the whole world" expected the traveler to acquire made Emerson initially skeptical of their value, but when he tested received valuations against his own sensibility and found them justified, he was quick to accept them.

Another boon the young traveler hoped to acquire was personal acquaintance with some of the great minds of the age. The pursuit of the intellectual celebrity as tourist attraction was a common feature of many prewar American journeys: Irving visited Scott; Fuller went to see

Martineau; everyone called on Wordsworth.[18] Emerson, too, had his letters of introduction, and he certainly hoped to profit from the conversation of the great and the gifted. Years later, when he compiled the summary of his early European literary encounters which serves as the opening chapter of *English Traits*, he suggested that "it was mainly the attraction of . . . three or four writers . . . that led me to Europe, when I was ill and advised to travel" (*E* 767). Although this statement and the chapter that it introduces are probably best understood as the well-known moralist's respectable hindsight rather than a full and faithful report of the ailing, grieving young ex-minister's motives and experience, they certainly suggest one of the major uses of the European tour in mid-nineteenth-century culture.

Like many educated travelers, Emerson wanted to believe that "writers [were] superior to their books," and that meeting them would "give one the satisfaction of reality, the sense of having been met, and a larger horizon" (*E* 768). He wanted, in other words, both to experience the authoritative presence of his literary heroes and to match his mettle against theirs, to partake of their personal aura without abdicating his own right to think and to judge. His encounters with famous authors, as recorded in his contemporary journal and letters, did not always provide the supreme intellectual stimulation that he hoped for, but if he was sometimes disappointed not to be inspired by his idols' genius, he did take a certain amount of pleasure in his own independent judgment of their characters and intellects.

The works of Coleridge had been important to Emerson as a student and continued to influence his thinking. Coleridge in person, however, was more tourist attraction than fount of comprehensible wisdom. "The visit was rather a spectacle than a conversation," Emerson wrote in *English Traits*. "He was old and preoccupied, and could not bend to a new companion and think with him" (*E* 773). In his contemporary journal Emerson was less self-important (why, after all, should the eminent poet and philosopher "bend" and "think with" an unknown Bostonian ex-minister of thirty?) but equally critical. Rather than conversing, the Coleridge of the journal "launches into discourse" and "bursts into declamation" (*J* 4:408), pays little attention to his interlocutor's comments (*J* 4:409), and dirties his clothes with snuff-taking (*J* 4:408). His talk is "like so many printed paragraphs in his book, perhaps the same; not to be easily followed" (*J* 4:411). Emerson's visit to Coleridge satisfied his curiosity rather than stimulated his thought, and it certainly contradicted his idea that writers are superior to their books. Having seen him was a bit like owning his autograph. Both the autograph and the visitor's memories testify to the great man's erstwhile presence without embodying his thought.

His visit to Wordsworth was more satisfying. The "plain looking elderly man with goggles" holds forth on the folly of universal "tuition," and "abuses" *Wilhelm Meister* as containing "all manner of fornication, . . . like flies crossing each other in the air" (*J* 4:222–23), even though he has not read beyond the first book. He also recites poetry, however, including one sonnet "more beautiful than any of his printed poems" (*J* 4:223), and Emerson's final vision of him is respectful, even affectionate.

> He then walked near a mile with me talking and ever & anon stopping short to impress the word or the verse & finally parted from me with great kindness & returned across the fields.
>
> His hair is white, but there is nothing very striking about his appearance.
>
> The poet is always young and this old man took the same attitude that he probably had at 17—whilst he recollected the sonnet he would recite. (*J* 4:225)

The greatest personal boon Emerson brought home from Europe, however, was surely his friendship with Carlyle. His visit to the farm at Craigenputtock was motivated by no pious wish to view an aging monument, but rather by an earnest desire to exchange ideas with a slightly older contemporary. Such an affinity did the thirty-year-old American feel for the thirty-eight-year-old Scot that he was already referring to him as "my Carlyle" some three months before they met (*J* 4:173). His expectations for the meeting must have been very high, and they seem to have been thoroughly satisfied. "I found the youth I sought in Scotland," he writes, "& good & wise & pleasant he seems to me" (*J* 4:219).

By this late stage of his travels, Emerson's journal had suffered the fate of most such undertakings and become a series of fragmentary jottings, but even these sketchy notes suggest the range of the two men's conversation: they seem to have discussed writers and books (Wordsworth, Coleridge, Hazlitt, *Tristram Shandy, Robinson Crusoe,* Rousseau's *Confessions*), politics (taxation, Ireland), the philosophy of history ("Christ died on the tree, that built Dunscore Church yonder & always affects us two" [*J* 4:220–21]), the practice of "puffing" new books, and muffins. Rather than posing as an authority, Carlyle joined Emerson in criticizing established authorities and in thinking originally about the legacy of the past and the problems of the present. Emerson's admiration for Carlyle was to be one of the defining features of his mature life. Some months after his return from Europe, he initiated the correspondence that was to last nearly forty years and serve as a vehicle for early statements of many of his opinions and ideas.

Emerson's pious visits to the great men of the age paradoxically strengthened his sense of independence, his confidence in his own judgment, and his high valuation of vigorous thought. Coleridge in person he found no better than his writing; Wordsworth in person was a moving monument to his own mind and poetry; Carlyle alone provided the intellectual resistance Emerson required.

Emerson's final evaluation of his first European tour embodied the contradictory nature of the experience, giving old Europe its scrupulous due but reserving the highest praise for the original thinkers of the present. "Go & see [Rome], whoever you are," he urged the putative reader of his journal. "He who has not seen it does not know what beautiful stones there are in the planet, & much less what exquisite art has accomplished on their hard sides for Greek & Roman luxury" (*J* 4:150). "Very good & pleasant & instructive it is to be here," he wrote to his brother Charles. "We grow wiser by the day, & by the hour. . . . And yet I would give all Rome for one man such as were fit to walk here, & could feel & impart the sentiment of the place" (*L* 1:372, 374). European travel edifies and instructs; it evokes meditations on history and appreciation of "beautiful stones" highly wrought for the pleasure of discerning ancients. It cannot by itself guarantee the essential thing, however: "the wise man—the true friend—the finished character—[whom] we seek everywhere & only find in fragments" (*L* 1:375).

Waiting for his ship to sail from Liverpool in September, taking stock of his eight months abroad, Emerson reveals why European travel, like every other lived experience, must disappoint him. He appreciates what he has learned, and he is grateful to have met "the men I wished to see," but neither things nor men are ultimately satisfying, because they cannot live up to his idea of them:

Liverpool, 1 September, 1833. I thank the great God who has led me through this European scene[,] this last schoolroom in which he has pleased to instruct me from Malta's isle, thro' Sicily, thro' Italy, thro' Switzerland, thro' France, thro' England, thro' Scotland, in safety & pleasure & has now brought me to the shore & the ship that steers westward. He has shown me the men I wished to see—Landor, Coleridge, Carlyle, Wordsworth—he has thereby comforted & confirmed me in my convictions. Many things I owe to the sight of these men. I shall judge more justly, less timidly, of wise men forevermore. To be sure not one of these is a mind of the very first class, but what the intercourse with each of these suggests is true of intercourse with better men, that they never *fill the ear*—fill the mind—no, it is an *idealized* portrait which always we draw of them. (*J* 4:78–79)

The contradictions here are astonishing. Emerson has traveled from Malta to Liverpool, been "instructed" in the great schoolroom of Europe, spoken with some of the age's most celebrated poets and thinkers, only to learn that his "idealized portrait" of these men and, presumably, of these experiences is more satisfying than the men and the experiences themselves. He has participated in one of the great ritual activities of his class and his culture; he has learned from it, taken pleasure in it, and is now ready to testify to its essential emptiness and vanity. He is happy to have had his idealist suspicions confirmed, happy, therefore, to have seen Europe, and righteously happy, at thirty, that his "travelling is done" (*J* 4:79).

Travel in Emerson, 1833–1847

Emerson's first European tour satisfied a certain curiosity and confirmed a certain prejudice. In the productive years that followed, Emerson frequently used travel in general and European travel in particular to exemplify the vanity of seeking in the nonself for the strength, the vision, and the authority that properly come from within. Just as Emerson's philosophical idealism never entirely canceled his awareness of the importance of the phenomenal world ("the meal in the firkin; the milk in the pan" [*E* 69]), however, so his strictest dicta on the vanity of travel and the emptiness of Europe were tempered by an appreciation for experiences that were available to Americans only through European travel.

The speaker in the passage from *Nature* quoted at the beginning of this chapter firmly believes that he can independently generate all the world he needs. His imagination is so strong, his thought is so all-encompassing that he needs no foreign places, no unfamiliar people, to complete his vision. His is the supremely transcendental ego, encompassing all and embracing the universe without doubting his place at their center. The speaker in "Self-Reliance," published four years later, similarly scolds his foolish compatriots for their weak dependence on celebrated places for pleasure and inspiration. "It is for want of self-culture," he famously declares, "that the superstition of Travelling, whose idols are Italy, England,

Egypt, retains its fascination for all educated Americans" (*E* 277). The American should keep to his own shores; if he has to travel, he should do so not in the expectation of growing and changing, but in the hope of converting others to his own values.

> The soul is no traveller; the wise man stays at home, and when his necessities, his duties, on any occasion call him from his house, or into foreign lands, he is at home still, and shall make men sensible by the expression of his countenance, that he goes the missionary of wisdom and virtue, and visits cities and men like a sovereign, and not like an interloper or a valet. (*E* 277)

The ideal American needs nothing that he does not have but takes his whole unitary, impermeable self about with him in the world, for the benefit of others. Even his less-than-ideal compatriot, whose sense of self is pitiably incomplete, can gain nothing essential from travel, since his task is to construct his self from his own resources rather than cobbling it together out of extraneous materials. His inadequacies, in other words, travel with him and cannot be remedied by anything he finds away from home.

> At home I dream that at Naples, at Rome, I can be intoxicated with beauty, and lose my sadness. I pack my trunk, embrace my friends, embark on the sea, and at last wake up in Naples, and there beside me is the stern fact, the sad self, unrelenting, identical, that I fled from. I seek the Vatican, and the palaces. I affect to be intoxicated with sights and suggestions, but I am not intoxicated. My giant goes with me wherever I go. (*E* 278)

The familiar feeling Emerson plays on here is guilt: travelers ought to be ashamed of themselves; they are motivated by a sense of incompleteness, but they are fooling themselves if they think that travel can make them whole. Ordinary, shallow, everyday people *should* not travel: travel distracts them from the cultivation of true self-reliance. Integral, mature, self-reliant Emersonians *need* not travel: travel provides them with nothing they do not already possess. "Though we travel the world over to find the beautiful, we must carry it with us, or we find it not" (*E* 435).

These arguments seem to rule out travel for everyone, always, but Emerson provides a characteristic loophole. A more positive version of the sentence just quoted might suggest that if we do carry the beautiful with us, then we can find it on our travels. In most cases this possibility makes travel redundant: why travel to find what you already possess? If what painting expresses is nothing but "the old, eternal fact I had met already in so many forms, . . . the plain *you and me* I knew so well," then "that which I fancied I had left in Boston was here in the Vatican, and again at Milan, and at Paris, and made all travelling as ridiculous as a treadmill" (*E* 436, emphasis Emerson's). In some cases, however, art overpowers even Emerson, and he admits to the charm if not the necessity of seeing a perfect expression of a well-known beauty.

> The Transfiguration, by Raphael, is an eminent example of this peculiar merit. A calm, benignant beauty shines over all this picture, and goes directly to the heart. It seems almost to call you by name. The sweet and sublime face of Jesus is beyond praise, yet how it disappoints all florid expectations! This familiar, simple, home-speaking countenance is as if one should meet a friend. The knowledge of picture-dealers has its value, but listen not to their criticism when your heart is touched by genius. It was not painted for them, it was painted for you; for such as had eyes capable of being touched by simplicity and lofty emotions. (*E* 436–37)

Raphael's *Transfiguration* moved Emerson. If what it showed him was something he had already seen, it was also something he was very willing to see again. Coming to the Vatican with a firm idea of beauty in his mind, he could recognize its manifestation in a painting and be touched by its maker's genius.

Travel is permissible, even desirable, he seems to be saying, if the traveler has a clear, achievable purpose and a firmly established sense of self. It is only a fool's paradise for the traveler who hopes to discover something really new on his journey. "Plato and Pythagoras may travel," he wrote in his journal in 1840, "for they carry the world with them and are always at home but our travellers are moths and danglers" (*J* 7:493). Even for philosophers, however, the best kind of travel is the fulfilling pursuit of the daily round:

> Travel, I think, consists really & spiritually in sounding all the stops of our instrument. If I have had a good indignation and a good complacency with my brother, if I have had reverence & compassion, had fine weather & good luck in my fishing excursion & profound thought in my studies at home, seen a disaster well through; and wrought well in my garden, nor failed in my part at a banquet, then I have travelled though all was within the limits of my own fenced yard. (*J* 8:18)

What seems to be missing from this conception of travel is the possibility of a truly productive encounter with the nonself. The "other" is apparently not a significant category for Emerson: differences between people seem to him delusive and superficial, masking the essential unity of "the human mind"; distances between times and places seem mere obstacles to an understanding of the oneness of human experience. The given, constant factor for Emerson is always the self. The historical other, the geographical other, the cultural other, whatever one encounters in studying history or traveling the world, is valuable only insofar as it provides a "commentary" on the already written text of the self.

This line of reasoning, part of a long tradition of devaluing the experience of the other by making it into a (usually inferior) version of one's own, places Emerson's ongoing critique of travel in the discredited company of ethnocentric idealists. We should not be surprised to find, however, that despite his theoretical self-reliance Emerson respected many of the "others" he encountered and that three related elements of his thinking admit the possibility of genuine difference and the value of experience (and, by extension, travel).

The first is a version of negative capability, a paradoxical recognition of the value of abdicating the self in order better to understand it. Emerson's example of this process comes straight out of his travel experience (and foreshadows, as we will see, the experience of Henry Adams). It is suggested by the problem of the Gothic cathedral, which is both familiar and unfamiliar, a manifestation of European selfhood that remains unyieldingly different from Emerson's American self. "A Gothic cathedral," Emerson writes, "affirms that it was done by us, and not done by us. Surely it was by man, but we find it not in our man" (E 241). The solution to the problem is to think oneself into the mind of the builder, to become a specific other in order to understand how that other is a version of one's self. Emerson "put[s] [him]self into the place and state of the builder" (E 241) by conjuring up the experience of the forest dweller, the development of craft and decoration, the accumulation of wealth, and the ritual of the church. "When we have gone through this process," he concludes, "we have, as it were, been the man that made the minster; we have seen how it could and must be" (E 241). The goal is still a fuller understanding of self and of the essential identity of all individuals, but the means Emerson adopts suggest a surprising respect for experience not one's own.

Second, this negative capability is reinforced by Emerson's insistence on the dialectical relations between "man" and the world. "A Man," he writes, " is a bundle of relations" (E 254). The shape of his nature implies the shape of nature itself, and vice versa. "His faculties . . . predict the world he is to inhabit, as the fins of the fish foreshadow that water exists. . . . One may say a gravitating solar system is already prophesied in the nature of Newton's mind. Not less does the brain of Davy or of Gay-Lussac, from childhood exploring the affinities and repulsions of parti-

cles, anticipate the laws of organization" (*E* 254). This suggests that studying the "other" that is nature can be a way of learning more about the self.
Similarly, Emerson goes on, we come to know ourselves by interacting
with other people.

> A mind might ponder its thought for ages, and not gain so much self-
> knowledge as the passion of love shall teach it in a day. Who knows himself
> before he has been thrilled with indignation at an outrage, or has heard an
> eloquent tongue, or has shared the throb of thousands in a national exulta-
> tion or alarm? No man can antedate his experience, or guess what faculty or
> feeling a new object shall unlock, any more than he can draw to-day the face
> of a person whom he shall see to-morrow for the first time. (*E* 255)

The relation between "man" and the world of experience is in these passages truly productive: the encounter with the other produces an otherwise unattainable understanding of the self.

A third factor that mitigates the apparently self-centered elitism of Emerson's position is the care he takes to characterize it as Protestant, democratic, and therefore in its aspirations anti-elitist. The devaluing of history
and of travel, of "Rome, and Paris, and Constantinople" (*E* 256), entails
a simultaneous revaluing of the experience of ordinary, contemporary individuals. "What food or experience or succour," he asks, "have [Olympi-
ads and Consulates] for the Esquimaux seal-hunter, for the Kanàka in his
canoe, for the fisherman, the stevedore, the porter? . . . The idiot, the
Indian, the child, and unschooled farmer's boy, stand nearer to the light
by which nature is to be read, than the dissector or the antiquary" (*E* 256).
This Whitmanesque catalog suggests that Emerson sees his theory of history and his criticism of travel as encouraging all sorts of people to seek
to understand themselves and nature, not to be cowed or dissuaded by
the claims of historians and travelers who have no better access to "the
light" than they do.

Emerson's opinions on travel and Europe, like his opinions on many
other elements of material human experience, remain dynamically contradictory. No single statement does them justice, for no single statement
can encompass the inconsistencies in Emerson's thought. The nub of this
particular contradiction, however, remains remarkably constant. Of what
value, Emerson consistently wonders, is an understanding of the other,
whether person, place, or even thing, for the creation of a true, independent self? Travel would seem to provide the ideal opportunity for exploring this question. Emerson uses it to fullest advantage in his only approach to the genre of travel writing, the collection of essays, narratives,
descriptions, and analyses, published as *English Traits*.

ENGLISH TRAITS, 1856

When Emerson returned to Concord after his 1847–48 lecture tour in Britain, the literary establishment assumed that a book of some kind would soon be forthcoming. A week after he landed in Boston, the correspondent of the *Literary World* was already reporting that "the recent struggles in Europe, of which he has been a spectator, will form a fine subject for a new series of Essays or Lectures." A year later another writer in the same journal hoped for a book from Emerson that "would be the perfection of Travels, cool, neat, omnisided, manly, and gentlemanly." Four years further on, the English magazine *The Critic* was predicting that "his new work, *Notes on Europe,* is to be of a descriptive rather than of a reflective character," and a year after that "Mr. Emerson's work on England" was reported to be "still in promise."[19]

When Emerson finally published *English Traits,* in 1856, it was immediately evident that it was neither a conventional travel narrative, like Bayard Taylor's popular works, nor a collection of philosophical meditations, like his own *Essays.* "The practical, concrete life of England is described," *Putnam's Monthly* rather cautiously reported, "but it is described from the high region of philosophy."[20] Emerson had evidently written a hybrid work, part narrative, part analysis, part meditation, a product of the interaction between abstract thought and concrete experience and of the confrontation between a self-reliant American self and an independent, simultaneously foreign and familiar other. He had used his second journey to Europe as an occasion for testing his sense of personal and national selfhood by exposing it to contact with a nation and a people with whom he shared a language, a literature, and a history of social and political differences.

Emerson's 1833 travel journal showed how little he could do with *absolute* otherness. The totally foreign was to him merely curious; the mob of promiscuous "others" he observed in the quarantine house at Malta seemed "grotesque"; they confirmed his conventional Anglo-Saxon traveler's superiority without challenging him to define or justify it.

> This p.m. I visited the Parlatorio where those in quarantine converse with those out across barriers. It looked to me like the wildest masquerade. There jabbered Turks, Moors, Sicilians, Germans, Greeks, English, Maltese, with friars & guards & maimed & beggars. And such grotesque faces! . . . I noticed however that all the curiosity manifested was on our part. Our cousins of Asia & Europe did not pay us the compliment of a second glance.

In Quarantine, our acquaintance has been confined chiefly to the Maltese boatmen, a great multitude of poor, swarthy, goodnatured people, who
speak their own tongue, not much differing from the Arabic, & most of
them know very few words of Italian & less of English. (*J* 4:116)

Emerson wrote of the "jabbering" crowds in the Parlatorio as if they were
an animal act, fit objects of the casual visitor's curiosity but without the
spark of intellect that would make them curious in return. The Maltese
boatmen, with whom he had a little more contact, were "goodnatured,"
as he condescendingly admits, but too foreign to impinge on his consciousness in any serious way. He could observe them with impunity:
they would not understand his observations, nor would he understand
their objections, if they had any. Between him and them there was contrast but no significant contradiction, because there was no common language or concern.

In England, however, the observant American was more accountable
for his remarks and had a clear personal and cultural stake in the objects
of his observation. Reporting in *English Traits* on his first arrival in England in 1833, Emerson noted:

For the first time for many months we were forced to check the saucy habit
of travellers' criticism, as we could no longer speak aloud in the streets without being understood. The shop-signs spoke our language; our country
names were on the door-plates; and the public and private buildings wore
a more native and wonted front. (*E* 767)

The first sentence in this passage describes a common source of embar-
rassment to travelers crossing national and linguistic boundaries and reminds us both of the comforts and privileges of radical otherness and of
the tact and delicacy required for successful travel in more familiar cultures. The second reflects the feeling of homecoming common to Americans crossing to England from the Continent, but it also uses the referen-
tial shifter, *native*, to suggest the doubleness of their relation to English
culture, which is obviously "native" in the literal sense of "indigenous"
but also feels "native" to American travelers in the special sense of "familiar" or "homey" ("native," that is, to North America as well as to Britain).
The central purpose of *English Traits* is to use England's familiar, native
otherness as a foil against which to construct a reasonable independence
and define a reasonable, even an "ideal" American identity by demonstrating the important ways in which English and American life and
thought both complement and contradict each other.

Emerson's abiding belief in the productive potential of conflict between identity and otherness is evident in the lectures on "representative
men," which he developed in Boston in the mid-forties, delivered in Britain during his tour, and revised for publication in 1850. In the introduc-
tory essay, "The Uses of Great Men," he declares that the desire to see
great men and experience their minds and works is the proper motivation
for travel. "The search after the great is the dream of youth. . . . We travel
into foreign parts to find his works . . . if there were any magnet that
would point to the countries and houses where are the persons who are
intrinsically rich and powerful, I would sell all, and buy it, and put myself
on the road today" (E 615). Productive contradiction, interaction with
strong others, "intrinsically rich and powerful," is oddly necessary for the
development and understanding of the self. Despite the fact that for Emerson "man" is "endogamous," growing "like the palm, from within, outward," "he seeks other men, and the otherest" as a way of becoming and
knowing himself. "I can do that by another which I cannot do alone. I
can say to you what I cannot first say to myself. Other men are lenses
through which we read our own minds" (E 616). What we gain from our
contact with great men and their works is not some mystic boon, whether
"wisdom," "health, eternal youth, fine senses, arts of healing, magical
power [, or] prophecy" (E 617), but a stimulus to new, radical, and original thought that we might never have realized without their example or
their opposition (E 622). These great "others" "clear our eyes from ego-
tism" and "defend us from our contemporaries. They are the exceptions
which we want, where all grows alike" (E 626–27). What Emerson learns
on his trip to England and demonstrates in *English Traits* is that not only
great "men," but facts and phenomena, customs, laws, and institutions
can provide helpful resistance for the thinker bent on self-definition.

England was the ideal national other for the United States in the first
half of the nineteenth century. The two nations shared a language, a culture, and a history that included close ties and violent contrasts. By Emerson's reckoning, they counted together "a population of English descent
and language, of 60,000,000, and governing a population of 245,000,000
souls" (E 790). England represented the Anglo-American's past and stood
as well for the energetic, successful present.

> If there be one test of national genius universally accepted, it is success; and
> if there be one successful country in the universe for the last millennium,
> that country is England. . . . The culture of the day, the thoughts and aims
> of men, are English thoughts and aims. (E 784–85)

The United States, in contrast, represented possibility rather than positive achievement. "The American is . . . the continuation of the English genius into new conditions, more or less propitious" (*E* 785).

One of the paramount strengths of the English "race," to make the parallel even more complete, is its inclusiveness. "We are piqued with pure descent," he writes, "but nature loves inoculation" (*E* 793). "The best nations are those most widely related" (*E* 793); the English nation, like the American, is happily composite. One of the results, in England, has been the profound contradictoriness of its customs and its culture, the sense of riches and poverty, justice and injustice, existing side by side in time-honored quiet dissonance;[21] one of the advantages of America's historical position ought to be the chance to observe the harmful contradictions in English society and avoid repeating them, to set itself up in outside opposition to the internal contradictions of its parent culture.

Emerson uses the contradictions of English society to create a dynamic rhetorical strategy for his text. "There can never have been such a virulent concentration of good & ill in such strict proximity [as there is in England]," Emerson wrote to his aunt Mary from London in 1848 (*L* 4:90); he exploits this feature of English life in *English Traits* by moving rapidly back and forth between widely admired features of English life and character and their often negative social and moral implications, making his critical point again and again through argument, example, and metaphor.

In the chapter titled "Ability," he begins by praising the "sense and economy," the hard-nosed practicality of a people who were "so vivacious as to extort charters from the kings" and so shrewd as to "drive the earl out of his castle" using the resources of modern finance ("his seven *per cent*") and industry. English capitalism, he seems to be arguing, is naturally anti-aristocratic and anti-authoritarian:

> A nobility of soldiers cannot keep down a commonalty of shrewd scientific persons. What signifies a pedigree of a hundred links, against a cotton-spinner with steam in his mill; or, against a company of broad-shouldered Liverpool merchants, for whom Stephenson and Brunel are contriving locomotives and a tubular bridge? (*E* 807)

In England, furthermore, both lords and commoners "hate craft and subtlety" and respect the power of fact and of logic.

> A man of that brain thinks and acts thus; and his neighbor, being afflicted with the same kind of brain, though he is rich, and called a baron, or a duke, thinks the same thing, and is ready to allow the justice of the

thought and act in his retainer or tenant, though sorely against his baronial or ducal will. (*E* 808)

One of the effects of this native clear-sightedness is a "spacious" "practical vision" (*E* 809), which has made the English master merchants, financiers, and manufacturers. The inbred English respect for facts and logic has produced an admirable system of justice and a sense of "fair play" that defeats prejudice and "preconceived theories" (*E* 810). "Their self-respect, their faith in causation, and their realistic logic or coupling of means to ends, have given them the leadership of the modern world" (*E* 810).

This litany of admiration, interrupted only by a brief comment on the practical Englishman's inveterate suspicion of "genius, or of minds addicted to contemplation" and a "contempt for sallies of thought, however lawful, whose steps they cannot count by their wonted rule" (*E* 809), swells to a paean of praise. Philip de Commines is quoted on the English devotion to the common good; Montesquieu is brought in to testify to English freedom and common sense. Emerson takes a sentence to criticize the limitation of this common sense ("They are impious in their scepticism of theory, and in high departments they are cramped and sterile") and then turns to what looks like a laudatory peroration, only to undercut his whole apparent line of argument with his last three words: "But the unconditional surrender to facts, and the choice of means to reach their ends, are as admirable as with ants and bees" (*E* 811). The ants and the bees force the reader to reevaluate everything that precedes them: if all this energy, logic, boldness, and even fairness culminate in a gigantic insect colony, perhaps something is amiss.

Emerson follows this line very briefly in the next paragraph, admitting that their "passion for utility" makes the English perhaps less delicate than other peoples, "heavy at the fine arts, but adroit at the coarse," but then redeems them with a wonderful epigram calculated to put the fine and the coarse in their proper places: "The Frenchman invented the ruffle, the Englishman added the shirt" (*E* 811). He goes on to praise the English proficiency at trade and at war and to admire the Englishman's freedom from superstition. "They have no Indian taste for a tomahawk-dance, no French taste for a badge or a proclamation," but they will "fight to the Judgment" to defend "a yeoman's right to his dinner." They are, in other words, practiced skeptics and perfect materialists, a combination that makes them eminently practical and consummately un-Emersonian. Their materialism has led them to sensuality, and their skepticism made them scornful of all principles not immediately related to self-interest.

Heavy fellows, steeped in beer and fleshpots, they are hard of hearing and
dim of sight. Their drowsy minds need to be flagellated by war and trade
and politics and persecution. They cannot read a principle, except by the
light of fagots and of burning towns. (*E* 813)

But self-interest, as it turns out, has not been an entirely evil master. It
has fostered the world's fairest legal system, made London "a sanctuary to
refugees of every political and religious opinion" (*E* 816), and supported
every "department of literature, of science, or of useful art" (*E* 816). It has
encouraged, too—and here Emerson steps definitively beyond the common perceptions of English genius—the creation of *practical* fictions, of
"artificial," which is to say, "created" reality. English life is a product as
much of invention as of diligence. "The native cattle are extinct, but the
island is full of artificial breeds" (*E* 817). Fished-out watercourses are
stocked with "eggs of salmon, turbot, and herring" (*E* 817). Marshes are
drained, houses are heated, "gas-burners are cheaper than daylight," and
parliamentary trains make it more expensive to walk than to ride (*E* 817).
Cold, dull, rainy England has contrived to enjoy tropical fruits and Italian
paintings and to supply the far-flung countries with products they used
to make for themselves ("ponchos for the Mexicans, bandannas for the
Hindoos, ginseng for the Chinese" [*E* 818]).

The term *artificial* seems in these paragraphs to draw its meaning primarily from the positive connotations of *art*. What they describe is a kind
of practical, concrete "English actualism," a contrast and a balance to Emerson's own brand of "American actualism," discussed at the beginning of
this chapter. There comes an Emersonian turn, however, and the term
takes on its modern, negative connotations, which then contaminate the
very notion of *art* itself. "The nearer we look, the more artificial is their
social system," Emerson writes.

Foreign power is kept by armed colonies; power at home, by a standing
army of police. The pauper lives better than the free laborer; the thief better
than the pauper; and the transported felon better than the one under im-
prisonment. . . . The sovereignty of the seas is maintained by the impress-
ment of seamen. . . . The Universities galvanize dead languages into a sem-
blance of life. . . . [A]nd we have a nation whose whole existence is a work
of art. (*E* 818–19)

Even "man" is reduced in England to a work of "art" created by a vast
industrial complex: he "is made as a Birmingham button." "The rapid
doubling of the population dates from Watt's steam-engine" (*E* 819).

There is one more turn before a final image affirms the unsettled nature of Emerson's judgment of his English cousins. The last section of the chapter begins full of admiration for the unity of the English, and their "solidarity," their "responsibleness," and their "trust in each other" (*E* 819). Unlike other nations, they have one language for rich and poor alike. Their "great ability" is "poured into the general mind," so that "each of them could at a pinch stand in the shoes of the other." "The laborer is a possible lord. The lord is a possible basket-maker." "In politics and in war they hold together as by hooks of steel" (*E* 820). They are proud, civil, prosperous, and powerful, but Emerson's final image suggests a hellish side to all their virtues and a threatening aspect to their patriotism.

> Whilst they are some ages ahead of the rest of the world in the art of living; whilst in some directions they do not represent the modern spirit, but constitute it,—this vanguard of civility and power they coldly hold, marching in phalanx, lockstep, foot after foot, file after file of heroes, ten thousand deep. (*E* 820–21)

Emerson admires the English as any observer of their phenomenal successes must; he mistrusts them, however, as each of their successes proves to derive from or encourage the growth of some regrettable practice or characteristic. His book as a whole proceeds much as "Ability" does, moving from praise to blame to devastating Emersonian metaphor, and back and around again to repeat and vary the pattern. The positive balance of the chapters on general features ("Land," "Ability," "Character," and so on) turns generally negative in the chapter on wealth, which is shown to rule the English rather than the other way around, and stays that way through discussions of specific institutions ("Aristocracy," "Universities," "Religion," "Literature," "The 'Times'").

Emerson's purpose is not mere condemnation, however, and he is careful to maintain the dialectical tension of his argument even in the context of his passionate criticisms. He enjoyed his trip to England; he admired a great many English institutions and even more English men and women. He uses the conventions of travel writing to ensure that his book will be an appreciation as well as a critique of his gracious host country. We have seen how he began his account of the 1847–48 trip with a description of his voyage. He ends it with the story of his excursion to Stonehenge, Wilton House, Salisbury, and Winchester in company with "my friend Mr. C[arlyle]," full of random details ("We took the South Western Railway through Hampshire to Salisbury" [*E* 915]), guidebook information ("The sacrificial stone . . . as I read in the books, must have been brought one hundred and fifty miles" [*E* 917]), and amiable commentary ("We crossed a bridge built by Inigo Jones over a stream, of which the gardener did not know the name [*Qu.* Alph?]" [*E* 921]).

The most serious moment in this pleasure trip comes during a discussion of the whole book's implicit subject, the contrast between England and the United States, and the serious question of whether there is such a thing as "any Americans . . . with an American idea" (*E* 922). Emerson's answer elevates his argument once more to the plane of the ideal and reminds us that the contrasts that interest him most are not between wage scales, higher-education schemes, and newspapers of record, but between radically opposed ways of thinking. "Thus challenged," he begins, "I bethought myself neither of caucuses nor congress, neither of presidents nor of cabinet-ministers, nor of such as would make of America another Europe. I thought only of the simplest and purest minds" (*E* 922). These minds, it turns out, have a "dream," which may sound "ridiculous" to English ears but is in fact the "only true" one, a dream of passive Emersonian anarchism. "So I opened the dogma of no-government and non-resistance, and anticipated the objections and the fun, and procured a kind of hearing for it" (*E* 922).

This is the greatest contrast of all, at once the most frivolous and the most intensely earnest. To the vast complexity of English government, society, and character Emerson opposes a profound unattainable simplicity. If England is strongly aggressive, let us be as strongly passive; if English government is the best organized on earth, let us have no organization at all. Let England, in other words, be full and America empty, England all past and present accomplishment and America all future potential. The contrast is impossibly "artificial," but not for that reason without meaning. Emerson anticipates "the objections and the fun" and yet "procure[s] a kind of hearing for" a set of ideas he holds dear. He certainly believes in his own criticisms of English customs and institutions, and the salutary contrast to them that he hopes American ones will present, but he is much more deeply committed to this last, extravagant, and impossible contrast, whose effect must be wholly intellectual.

If Emerson's stay in England concluded with his excursion to Stonehenge, however, his "work on England" adds two more conclusions to the narrative one. In his penultimate chapter Emerson sums up his contradictory feelings about England by developing his view that "England is the best of actual nations." English life, values, and institutions, he argues, derive from no ideal scheme, but from an accretion of precedents ultimately based on personal, national, and class self-interest. The practical results of this "makeshift" (*E* 929) jumble, however, surpass those of systems more ideally conceived.

> The American system is more democratic, more humane; yet the American people do not yield better or more able men, or more inventions or books or benefits, than the English. . . . France has abolished its suffocating old *régime*, but it is not recently marked by any more wisdom or virtue. (*E* 933)

It is grudging praise, if I read it aright. England is better than it has any right to be. Its practical strengths outweigh its theoretical weaknesses, producing a balance of freedom and creativity in defiance of oppressive custom and narrow practicality. If no honest reporter can deny its successes, however, no truly perceptive one should overlook the weaknesses that underlie them. England may be the best of *actual* nations, but is far from the best *imaginable* nation. Its present character has been to a large extent determined by an accretion of historical events and accidents spanning nearly two thousand years. The United States, in contrast, has the great advantage of starting afresh and so the possibility of building a national character and identity based on principle and choice, the possibility, at least, of becoming the best of *ideal* nations.

England's strength springs from productive tension and contradiction rather than the systematic fulfillment of an ideal. The strength of *English Traits* springs from a similar tension between genres, purposes, and intentions. It is at the same time a travel book and a set of essays, an honest encomium and a principled critique; it never settles down to one genre or one opinion. The final chapter maintains this productive doubleness. After the balanced summary of his experiences in chapter 18, Emerson turns for his peroration to a speech he delivered to the Manchester Athenaeum shortly after arriving in England, moving from 1856 back to 1847, from judgment back to experience, and apparently from judicious criticism to the unalloyed praise appropriate for such a ceremonial occasion. His speech is indeed effusive: he declares at one point that the English people's "love and devotion" to their "commanding sense of right and wrong" "is the imperial trait, which arms them with the sceptre of the globe" (*E* 935). In the context of the whole book, however, it is hard to read its last sentence as its original audience must have heard it. England was in economic crisis when Emerson arrived, and his speech was in part an exhortation to strength and confidence in dark times. It concludes with a sentence that reads very differently according to one's understanding of its conditional premise.

> If the courage of England goes with the chances of a commercial crisis, I
> will go back to the capes of Massachusetts, and my own Indian stream, and
> say to my countrymen, the old race are all gone, and the elasticity and hope
> of mankind must henceforth remain on the Alleghany ranges, or nowhere.
> (*E* 936)

England's courage must and will never falter, Emerson assures his English
audience in 1847, because if it did I would be put in the absurd position
of placing the "hope of mankind" in the Allegheny Mountains. England's
courage may well falter, he prophetically suggests to his American readers
in 1856, and when it does the hope of mankind will lie with you. The
same words have different meanings for the gentlemen of Manchester
after a celebratory English dinner and the readers of America after an
Emersonian analysis of England's contradictory strengths and weaknesses.
The last words of Emerson's book were some of the first public words he
spoke in England: they provided a rousing, upbeat conclusion for his
speech to the Manchester Athenaeum; they sound like a call for a new
beginning to the American inheritors of English traits.

Epilogue: Emerson Traveling, 1872–1873

"The soul is no traveller; the wise man stays at home" (*E* 277). And yet
Emerson traveled and profited from his journeys. England and Italy are
mere "idols" (*E* 277), false gods for misguided pilgrims, and yet Emerson
valued the treasures of Italy and made productive intellectual use of the
contradictions both within English society and between England and the
United States. Europe was an ideal other for Emerson, offering itself up
for criticism as the empty product of what Henry James would call a
"superstitious valuation," for appreciation as the home of genuine beauty,
and for use as a resistant foil to his arguments and positions, the locus of
real difference from American ways of thinking and being. He used Europe in all these ways, but it is also important to remember that even the
sage of Concord also used it for rare, irresponsible pleasure. "The enjoyment of travel," he wrote in 1872,

> is in the arrival at a new city, as Paris, or Florence, or Rome,—the feeling
> of free adventure, you have no duties,—nobody knows you, nobody has
> claims, you are like a boy on his first visit to the Common on Election Day.
> Old Civilization offers to you alone this huge city, all its wonders, architec-
> ture, gardens, ornaments, Galleries, which had never cost you so much as a

thought. For the first time for many years you wake master of the bright day, in a bright world without a claim on you;—only leave to enjoy. This dropping for the first time the doleful bundle of Duty creates, day after day, a health as of a new youth. (*J* 6:292)

Emerson valued vitality of mind, inconsistency, and productive contradiction. He found them all in travel, which, despite himself, he enjoyed.

CHAPTER SIX

Margaret Fuller and the
Discourses of Travel

L IKE MOST creators of narrative, biographers and commentators on the lifework of individual authors tend to mold their material into standard plots. The writer's career takes the shape of a quest for maturity, for example, or an early triumph followed by a period of mannerist decline, or an apparently random series of brilliant successes and ill-conceived failures. The biographer/critic's implicit claim is that his/her interpretive schema matches the facts in question, but the choice of an interpretive schema—the imposition of a genre—is as much a rhetorical as a mimetic device. It is influenced by the critic's own agenda and justified by its persuasive and explanatory power as well as its simple mimetic truth.

Over the last 140 years, the life and works of Margaret Fuller have provided the raw material for a variety of compelling narratives. Each of these represents a variation on a standard generic formula, and each necessarily serves the ideological purposes of its author as well as conveying some version of the substance and meaning of its subject's life and work. In his excellent brief history of Fuller's reputation, David Watson goes so far as to accuse Fuller's critics and biographers of "distort[ing] her aims and her achievement" to advance their own particular agendas.[1] In a sense, he is right, but his criticism is less profound and less damaging than he thinks. Some degree of "distortion" is a necessary part of any criticism: Bell Gale Chevigny's work on Fuller, for example, is informed and enriched by her principled feminism, and any "distortion" that this ideological position produces is amply balanced by the insights it generates. The question to ask of it is not "does this account of Fuller's work match the plain, undistorted truth?" but rather "how does this account of Fuller's work help us understand that work, its author, and its historical moment?" With this in mind, I propose in what follows not to debunk all previous treatments of Fuller or to present a definitive, "undistorted" version of her life and work, but rather to show how any understanding of her European experience should be influenced by a historical and generic reading of her travel writing, a reading that emphasizes the polyvocality of the genre as well as the multiplicity of her own beliefs and feelings.

Unlike her mentor Emerson, Fuller was both a passionate traveler and a professional journalist. Her travel writing reflected the pleasure and excitement of her journeys and provided a conventional generic framework for her political, moral, and aesthetic reflections. A new reading of this body of work will demonstrate the capaciousness of the travel-writing genre and its adaptability to a wide range of authorial purposes while linking Fuller's literary practice to a set of generic conventions and helping to account for the undeniable inconsistencies in her themes and in her style.

Versions of Fuller's Europe

Every new view of Fuller's life and work must pay close attention to her European sojourn, which began in 1846 as a pleasure tour, ended with her shipwreck off Fire Island in July 1850, and included her love affair with (and perhaps marriage to) Giovanni Ossoli, the birth of her child, and her political and humanitarian engagement in the Roman revolution of 1848–49.[2] The first, and most notorious, (re)conceptualization of Fuller's life, the *Memoirs of Margaret Fuller*, collected and edited by Ralph Waldo Emerson, W. H. Channing, and James Freeman Clarke, responded to the political and social radicalism of Fuller's Roman years with a kind of defensive panic. Whereas Fuller had struggled for much of her life to assume, in Ann Douglas's terms, a "historical" persona, to take significant action in the world,[3] Clarke and his associates cast her as a brilliant but comfortingly ineffectual bluestocking. "The picture that emerges from the *Memoirs*," writes Paula Blanchard, "is of a tender-hearted, passionate woman, fitfully strong but very much at the mercy of her emotions and subject to frequent attacks of the vapors."[4] "Where Fuller's individuality seemed to threaten deep-seated cultural, social, and political norms," Bell Gale Chevigny argues, "the editors tempered or obscured it."[5] Rather than represent their radically disturbing, nonconforming subject as she was, they fitted her to the mold of a previously existing literary and cultural stereotype.

Not surprisingly, the Margaret Fuller of the *Memoirs* provided ample material for popular biographers, who emphasized the romantic and erotic aspects of her European experience to create even more conventional tales of gratified desire. "Imperfect as love might be," writes Madeleine Stern about Fuller's relationship with Ossoli, "she suffocated without it. . . . There were no books that could give her the stimulus that his presence did; his dark hair and olive skin, his handsome, youthful form attracted and charmed her. Now at last, after having searched so long for love, it was joy to be sought after, to be loved."[6] "Perhaps . . . ," writes Joseph Jay Deiss about Fuller's longing to be in Rome, "perhaps she knew intuitively that *amore*, like Rome itself, was eternal . . . and awaited there."[7] For these writers, Fuller's story fitted the still-familiar plot of the repressed woman humanized through passion.[8]

Other biographers have told Fuller's life as a version of a different, psychoanalytically oriented plot. Katharine Anthony's brief "Psychological Biography" is remarkably clear and evocative, but it emphasizes Fuller's successful attempt to construct a personality in the face of social and psychological repression rather than her achievement of any less personal work in the world. According to Anthony, Fuller had "a neurotic constitution." "The source of her hysteria was a secret which she kept from herself." "As Margaret kept the date of her marriage a secret to evade the social censor, she had in earliest childhood undertaken a far more dangerous concealment, the concealment from the inward censor of an erotic element in her love for a deeply reverenced father."[9] Fuller diagnosed was Fuller naturalized, Fuller reduced to case history, Fuller tamed. The psychoanalytic mode, comfortingly scientific and conveniently distancing, persisted in what became the standard midcentury biography, Mason Wade's tellingly subtitled *Margaret Fuller: Whetstone of Genius*, which perpetuated the theme of "frustrated femininity" as the underlying cause of her political activism.[10]

If Margaret Fuller's life and works lent themselves to use as vehicles for romantic fantasy and psychoanalytic narrative, they were also perfectly suited for, and perhaps best understood by, the new feminist and political criticism of the 1970s and 1980s. No fewer than five major feminist treatments of Fuller appeared between 1976 and 1979,[11] effectively claiming her as a model for engaged, intellectual feminism and plotting her story as a kind of bildungsroman, a tale of intellectual, emotional, and political growth and progress, of movement from various versions of New England idealism and repression to political realism and emotional and sexual exploration and fulfillment, first in New York and later in Europe. Ann Douglas sees Fuller's career as a quest for authentic engagement with the real life of the contemporary world, an engagement made difficult if not impossible by her culture's simultaneous idealization and marginalization of women. "[Her] life can be viewed as an effort to find what she called her 'sovereign self' by disavowing fiction for history, the realm of 'feminine' fantasy for the realm of 'masculine' reality."[12] She achieved this engagement first as a journalist in New York, then as an observer of class oppression in England and on the Continent, and finally as a participant in and chronicler of the Italian revolution of 1848. Douglas sees her Italian writings as, among other things, an effort to reclaim Italy from the aesthetes and the dilettanti, "to translate Italy from the realm of literature back into the realm of history."[13] This account of Fuller's life and career is an essential element in any understanding of its subject, but it is perhaps a little too literary in its plot structure, too neat in its tale of progress, too good, in a word, to be true.

Margaret V. Allen's much longer account affirms Douglas's interpretation of Fuller's European experience and provides a more thorough and less linear reading of Fuller's oeuvre. Instead of viewing each stage of Fuller's career as marked by a definitive rejection of what went before, Allen sees her work as more cumulative and catholic. In Allen's view, history does not cancel fiction for Fuller, and life does not cancel art. Throughout her career, "Margaret Fuller knew the power of art, how human potential is realized through it, and how necessary courage is to artistic and intellectual leadership."[14]

Two more recent essays demonstrate the power of the linear plot to influence individual readings of Fuller's work. In his book *European Revolutions and the American Renaissance,* Larry J. Reynolds provides a fine close reading of the letters from Italy. In the absence of any parallel reading of her earlier travel writing, however, his assertions that these late letters "display more artistry and power than any of her other writings" and that her "new sociopolitical concerns, which supplanted her interest in art, resulted, paradoxically, in the best writing she ever did"[15] seem to be the product of an assumption about biographical plot structure rather than the result of a comparative reading of texts.

Bell Gale Chevigny attempts to correct the linear view by positing a "centrifugal trajectory" for Fuller's career, a Whitmanesque impulse toward inclusion resulting from "the largeness of her curiosity" and "her several kinds of incompleteness" rather than a more properly transcendentalist desire to exclude certain kinds of experience as unworthy of consideration.[16] At the same, time, however, Chevigny wants to see Fuller's late Roman letters as exclusively political. "She cared no longer to write about art, 'famous people,' or 'magnificent shows and palaces,'" Chevigny tells us. "The 'inward life' had been the very name of Emerson's greatest gift to her: then it was informed by the desire for transcendence; now it is informed by the desire for immersion in experience."[17] In the broadest sense, Chevigny is right: Fuller had rejected frivolous aesthetic and social sightseeing in favor of political action and subordinated her contemplative impulses to her desire for political engagement. The enjoyment of art, however, is not limited to gaping at "'magnificent shows and palaces.'" "Immersion in experience" does not necessarily exclude aesthetic appreciation. Chevigny has reduced Fuller's catholic eclecticism to what she had called in her earlier book the "modern radical analysis toward which she was moving when her life ended."[18] She recognizes the decentered nature of Fuller's writing but replots her career as a standard story of education and maturation.

Despite their limitations, Reynolds's and Chevigny's works are essential for a contemporary understanding of Margaret Fuller: they are reductive for a purpose and give us a strong, vivid view of one aspect of her career; they create literary versions of Margaret Fuller to match their own theories of personal and political development; and their texts help readers understand both Fuller and the philosophy and ideology of patriarchal New England Protestantism. In the process, however, they necessarily reduce a complicated and often contradictory life to a somewhat simpler life story. My understanding of Fuller's career is also generic, and probably reductive as well, but it is historically plausible, I think, and it has the added virtue of inclusivity. It is capable, in other words, of incorporating several simple plots and characters, it places Fuller's European writings in the generic context in which they originally appeared, and it provides a more complicated account of her uses of Europe.

POLYVOCALITY IN AMERICAN TRAVEL WRITING

Fuller's first original book was an extended account of a trip to Wisconsin and the Great Lakes in 1844; her last published works were her letters from Europe. Like many of her contemporaries, Fuller used travel writing as both a convenient money-earner and a vehicle for serious thought. Like many others, too, she made the most of the opportunities the genre provided to speak in a number of voices, male and female, marked and unmarked, real and fictional, without establishing a hierarchy among them or a sense of progress from one to another. She used the conventions of travel writing to create a kind of discourse and a kind of textuality that allowed her to sound various voices and maintain a disparate set of interests and personas without abandoning her identity as their ultimate source. Rather than repress one aspect of her experience—the conventionally female sensitivity, say, or the conventionally male political enthusiasm—in order to represent the other in as pure a form as possible, she was enabled by this technique to affirm them all.

Travel writing was neither a particularly masculine mode nor an exclusively feminine domain when Fuller came to it in the mid-1840s,[19] but a genial form of narrative that served as a meeting place for various voices, literary styles, levels of speech, and kinds of subject. Bakhtin coined the term "heteroglossic" for such narratives and used it to describe his version of the dynamics of the novel. The typical novel, he argues, combines several modes of discourse to create a "dialogic" tension, which in turn helps generate "the higher unity of the work as a whole."[20] Nineteenth-century travel writing employed all of Bakhtin's narrative modes and incorporated guidebook copy, poetry, folktales, and sermons. It tended to remain heteroglossic instead of becoming dialogic, however, combining disparate voices and modes of discourse without necessarily generating tension among them or forging them into a "higher unity." Travel books were more casual than novels, with no necessary form other than that of the journey they purported to describe, and no necessary single purpose more important than the various purposes of their various parts and voices.

The conventional heteroglossia of travel writing may be seen very clearly in Irving's *Sketch Book* and Sigourney's *Pleasant Memories*, and in two lesser-known works, one by Emma Willard and the other by Zachariah Allen. Irving's *Sketch Book* presents itself as a collection of disparate prose pieces strung like beads on the string of the narrator's travels. Irving's narrator describes the passing scene, quotes poetry, and tells stories. He allows himself to speculate in good romantic-sentimental fashion on the fate of men and ships lost at sea. He poses as a moral biographer in a short sketch of Roscoe, the Liverpool banker, poet, and philanthropist, and then sets up as a poetic social commentator in an essay entitled "The Wife." He throws in the story of Rip Van Winkle, then an essay on the low opinion of America held by English writers, then a description of rural life in England. He takes on the voices of the German romantic storyteller in "The Spectre Bridegroom" and of "an independent gentleman of the neighbourhood" (970) in a description of the Little Britain district of London. He is Geoffrey Crayon in the famous description of Stratford-upon-Avon, but he becomes the sober historian of the American Indian in "Traits of Indian Character" and "Philip of Pokanoket." He describes an old fisherman, tells the Legend of Sleepy Hollow, and concludes with an "Envoy" acknowledging his work's heterogeneity and "requesting the reader . . . to rest assured" that everything he likes in the book "was written expressly for intelligent readers like himself" and that anything he dislikes was "one of those articles which the author has been obliged to write for readers of a less refined taste" (1090). The tone is relaxed, eclectic, pluralistic. The voices speak for themselves; their juxtaposition creates no particular narrative tension. They are all male, it is true, but they are otherwise genuinely different, not the same male voice repeated over and over again, but a collection of voices assembled for the reader's pleasure by a genial master of ceremonies.[21]

Irving's heteroglossia persists in Sigourney's combination of anecdotes, quotations, and guidebook copy with personal observations, but instead of preserving the various voices these forms might suggest, Sigourney subsumes them all in the single recognizable voice of the genteel female poet. This is not the productive tension of Bakhtinian dialogism, but rather a kind of imperialistic heteroglossia in which the dominant voice speaks in forms and patterns appropriated from the subordinate discourses. This dominant voice is always sweetly superior. In the conventional self-deprecatory preface, Sigourney (writing of herself in the third person) makes a virtue of her willed narrowness: "The writer has not sought to dwell upon the dark shades of the countries that it was her privilege to visit [but] has preferred rather to press the flower than to preserve the thorn" (iv). The literary flowers she proffers are all eminently correct and maintain some vestige of their generic origins, even when pressed in Sigourney's fervid and sentimental prose or verse. The subject of Sigourney's second poem, for example, is the Sunday service at sea, a common theme of early transatlantic travelers.

> Upon the sheltered deck
>   Was held a sacred rite,
> The worship of old Ocean's king,
>   The Lord of power and might[.]
>
>   .   .   .   .
>
> High words of solemn prayer
>   Each listening spirit stir,
> And by the fair young babe knelt down
>   The bronzèd mariner[.]
>
>   .   .   .   .
>
> Poor Erin's ardent sons
>   Up from the steerage came,
> And in their rude response invoked
>   Jehovah's awful name[.]   (7–8)

This is followed by a sentimental tale of a child's death at sea ("Happy shall we be, if in the closing of our frail life, we, like this trembling voyager, leave behind a gleam of light and consolation, as the olive-leaf above the flood, or the dove whose last act was peace, ere it entered rejoicing into the ark, to be a wanderer no more" [17]), a pious account of narrowly averted shipwreck, a visit to a charitable institution in Liverpool, and a quick transition from unadulterated guidebook material ("Chester has a Castle where a garrison is stationed, and a Cathedral erected in the fifteenth century, which is 350 feet in length, by 75 in breadth, and the altitude of the tower 127" [38]) to superior Sigourney pontification:

> During our ride of ten miles from Chester to Eastham . . . we had delightful views of the blossomed hedges and cottage-homes of England. And as whatever we see of surpassing excellence in a foreign country, we are naturally desirous of transplanting to our own, we could not avoid wishing that our agricultural friends at home, who are such models of industry and domestic virtue, would be more careful to surround their dwellings with comfortable and agreeable objects. (39)

As the references to various subordinate groups and individuals suggest (the bronzèd mariner, Erin's ardent sons, inmates of charitable institutions, agricultural friends), Sigourney's social and political opinions are as homogeneous as her tone and as complacent in their support of all that is most moral and most repressive in the status quo. The "perfect subordination" of the poor boys in the Blue Coat Hospital in Liverpool seems to her most appropriate in children and paupers, and she comments with profound poetic approval on the benefactions of Mrs. Fry, the volunteer chaplain of Newgate, whose purpose seems to be to reconcile deportees to their fate and transform them into obedient servants. She is always careful, too, to keep her upper-middle-class female readers in mind and tune her song to their ears, as the following passage from her poem on Kenilworth most strikingly testifies:

> It seems like an illusion still, to say,
> I've been at Kenilworth. But yet 'tis true.
> And when once more I reach my pleasant home,
> In Yankee land, should conversation flag
> Among us ladies, though it seldom does,
> When of our children, and our housekeeping,
> And *help* we speak, yet should there be a pause,
> I will bethink me in that time of need
> To mention Kenilworth, and such a host

> Of questions will rain down, from those who read
> Scott's wizard pages, as will doubtless make
> The precious tide of talk run free again.   (192–93)

The author of these lines uses her European experience as a source of conversational gambits for those moments when even the servant problem begins to pall as a subject for discussion and to distinguish her from other "ladies" in "Yankee land" as the source of privileged information about and vicarious contact with literary genius.

Sigourney's book was directed to a feminine—and "feminized"—audience. Her purpose was to produce, display, and foster a respectable combination of piety, gentility, and literary pleasure. Zachariah Allen's *Practical Tourist* was written for an audience of men, and his purpose was to convey practical information. In his preface he adopts (proleptically, to be sure) a voice very much like that of Dickens's Thomas Gradgrind and subordinates the text's other voices to it. "The principal design of the following pages," he writes, "is to record useful facts."[22]

The primary facts he has in mind consist of the details of every industrial process he can lay his eyes on, together with the economic system that supports them, and his primary narrative voice is that of an inquiring reporter in the service of manufacturers and employers back home. His accounts of the procedures adopted by employers of labor and deployers of capital in the booming British industrial system are straightforward, technical, and admiring. He describes everything from coal mining, shipbuilding, and the various aspects of textile production to "the manufacture of pins" (61) in great detail. He quotes with admiration such regulations as the twelve-hour day for children and the prohibition of mill work for any child under nine years old, "except in silk mills, where they may be employed at 7 years of age," and attributes them without a trace of irony to the care exercised by "humane English Statesmen to protect children from being overworked" (150).

Even when Allen takes on the role of the conventional sightseer or the sentimental tourist, he improves the frivolous hour by making it an occasion for the communication of more facts. His paragraph on the first landfall in England begins with the conventional comments on "our old home," on the "verdure" of "refreshing landscapes," moves on to "the gleaming lights of various light-houses, sprinkled along the headlands of the coast," and then jumps with relief to an account of the colored glass and clockwork rhythms that distinguish one light from another (19). Describing his first visit to the English countryside, he bows briefly in the direction of aesthetic appreciation and goes on to a long disquisition on the competing merits of stone fences and hedges (47–49). When he waxes lyrical, it is over the not very bucolic view from the battlements of Dudley Castle, near Birmingham, a view of "tall chimneys of numerous iron furnaces . . . gilded on one side by the last rays of the setting sun" (66–67). He combines a romantic regard for nature with an industrial utilitarian vision of progress but subordinates them both to his practical Yankee concern for how to do a job efficiently.

Both Sigourney and Allen make limited use of the conventional heteroglossia of travel writing: Sigourney uses all the voices she collects to amplify her own sweet gentility; Allen subordinates the various voices of his narrative to his practical purposes. Another writer, Emma Willard, develops the form of travel narrative in a different direction by bringing various voices to life and allowing them a certain independence while maintaining their clear relationship to a central thematic concern and authoritative discourse.

Willard is as practical as Allen, but her subject is different. Allen reports on industrial processes and managerial techniques to ambitious and presumably male entrepreneurs; Willard reports on foreign customs in meticulous detail for the benefit of the female pupils in her school at home. Willard moves freely from one distinct voice to another, using the traveler's privilege of combining impressions, opinions, reportage, and paraphrase to convey cultural and historical information, points of etiquette, and domestic tips to her audience. In the guise of a teacher of domestic economy, for example, she describes her writing table and the red-and-blue cloth that covers it, the parquet floor and the technique the servants use to keep it clean. On other occasions she copies what sounds like a tour guide's patter into her letters and combines it with practical hints worthy of a more modern guidebook.

> By the way—I have a substantial pair of leather shoes which I bought at Havre, suitable to French mud. . . . I assure you, that the sound judgment of my countrywomen, is absolutely called in question by foreigners, on account of the manner in which they expose their health by wearing, in all weathers, thin shoes to walk in.
>
> Our feet, being well guarded, we will go forth in grand procession to see Paris, and get an idea of its most celebrated places. Our starting point is the Palais Royal, with which you are doubtless acquainted. I will conduct you in the first place to the Louvre, which may be considered as the very heart of Paris.[23]

What is more, the several voices Willard uses in her pedagogical role do not exhaust her store. She was a theorist of women's education as well as a teacher, and she describes her visits of inspection to educational institutions in the voice of the serious professional.

> I had before told her, why I was so deeply interested in female schools,—I was myself devoted to the cause of female education. In America, we were comparatively a recent people, and hoped to learn much, from their skill and experience. I then asked her, if it would be consistent with their usages, that I should be allowed to peruse the rules and regulations of the institution. (117)

She also led an active social life in Paris, and in the letters to her sister included in the volume she exults in the attention paid her by General Lafayette and relishes the necessity of sending for a "*marchande des* [*sic*] *modes*" to consult on "the important affair of head-gear" (43).

Willard's voices are neither strictly consistent nor mutually contradictory. She is frivolous and serious by turns and gives equal space to what now seem trivial and important matters. The result is an artless but revealing depiction of her character and the breadth of her interests. The job of synthesizing the apparent disparities in the text as a whole and of constructing a conceivable speaker for them all falls to the reader.

The writers I have been discussing exemplify three narrative variations on the polyphonic model of travel writing. Irving seems to abdicate his position of narrative authority by presenting his readers with chapters purporting to issue from various pens and record various voices. Lydia Sigourney and Zachariah Allen, in contrast, appropriate the voices of others and subsume them in their own pleasantly pious or unrelentingly practical discourse: every word is clearly theirs and openly serves their purposes. Emma Willard takes up a more boldly, or perhaps more naively, eclectic position, assuming a number of voices, giving them room to speak, as it were, in her narrative, and giving the reader the opportunity to evaluate their relative claims to her attention and approval.

Fuller's Travel Writing

It would be handy at this point if I could argue that Margaret Fuller's travel writing progressed from the simplest to the most complex of these narrative modes, and that her European experience made it possible for her to adapt them all into a grand and triumphant synthesis, but I do not believe this is the case. Fuller wrote at every stage of her career, but she produced no masterpiece. She did leave behind an impressive amount of finely crafted, tightly argued, and rhetorically effective prose, much of it governed by the loose conventions of the travel narrative, which allowed her to express in a single context the disparate aspects of her consciousness: the appreciative and the analytic, the intellectual and the aesthetic, the conventionally masculine and feminine. Her only completed travel book, *Summer on the Lakes,* and her posthumously collected letters from Europe to the *New-York Tribune* sound a variety of voices that are sometimes attributed to others, sometimes derived from generic conventions and models, and sometimes clearly Fuller's own. At its best, Fuller's travel writing makes all of these voices interact, thus expressing a subtle, complicated understanding of American and European politics and culture.

Summer on the Lakes is in many ways a conventionally eclectic travel book, tracing Fuller's 1843 journey to Niagara Falls, the Great Lakes, and the Illinois prairie. It contains transcendental musings,[24] Wordsworthian aspirations,[25] reactions to famous scenes,[26] and such illustrative material as the anecdote of the man who spat into the falls (6) and the description of the eagle chained up for the amusement of Niagara tourists (8–9). It contains also, in the first few pages, a philosophical dialogue on the four elements (14–17), some well-known comments on the narrowness of New Englanders moving west (18), the touching story (told by a fellow passenger) of an unfortunate gentleman ruined by a vicious wife (19–26), a paragraph deploring the "'go-ahead'" "mushroom growth" of Western towns (28), and several critical summaries of books on Indians (30–33). These pages are vigorous, witty, and charming, full of competing voices, all monitored by a woman with her own intellectual, spiritual, domestic, and social concerns.

The tone, the technique, and the purposes remain similarly mixed throughout the book: Fuller includes more anecdotes, original poems, conventionally rhapsodic appreciations of scenery, critical observations of Western life, and long interpolated tales, all held together not by a single voice or subject, but by the simple fact that they coexist in the same text and the same consciousness. This does not make every page of the book compelling and indispensable, nor does it ensure that every sequence and passage comment neatly on every other. At the very least, however, Fuller's book reminds the reader that conventional aesthetic responses to nature, love of landscape and of wildflowers, concern for women's education, and outrage at white settlers' treatment of Indians are not mutually exclusive, and in its most effective passages it institutes a real dialogue among its various voices.[27]

Such a dialogue is established, for example, among the generically distinct voices that Fuller uses in her discussions of frontier women. The first and most conventional of these is the idealizing literary voice that uses the sights of the prairie as raw material for pastoral scenes and neat rhetorical conceits. Look, for example, at Fuller's simultaneously serious and amused account of some cheerful and accomplished young ladies of Illinois, who refused to allow their irrelevant education to interfere with their important economic and domestic tasks. In this passage, the contrast between the young ladies' useless "accomplishments" and their newly acquired practical skills is tidily ironic, as a simple comparison of the nouns and verbs in the two sentences demonstrates.

> The young ladies were musicians, and spoke French fluently, having been educated in a convent. Here in the prairie, they had learned to take care of the milk-room, and kill the rattlesnakes that assailed their poultry-yard. (38)

The nouns in the first sentence (*ladies, musicians, French, convent*) bespeak an urban world of shelter, privilege, and high culture; those in the second sentence (*prairie, milk-room, rattlesnakes, poultry-yard*) describe an uncultivated rural setting, a place of hard work and real danger. The verbal elements of the first sentence are gentle, descriptive, and passive (*were, spoke, having been educated*); those in the second are vigorous and active (*had learned, take care of, kill, assailed*). The rest of the passage develops the conceit by adducing several additional versions of the basic contrast— indoors/outdoors; young (American) ladies/Norwegian peasants; wild roses/blue spiderwort; civilized regions/western place; Europe/ America; sweet, wild beauty/the vulgarities of city "parties."

> Beneath the shade of heavy curtains you looked out from the high and large windows to see Norwegian peasants at work in their national dress. In the wood grew, not only the flowers I had before seen, and wealth of tall, wild roses, but the splendid blue spiderwort, that ornament of our gardens. Beautiful children strayed there, who were soon to leave these civilized regions for some really wild and western place, a post in the buffalo country. Their no less beautiful mother was of Welsh descent, and the eldest child bore the name of Gwynthleon. Perhaps there she will meet with some young descendants of Madoc, to be her friends; at any rate, her looks may retain that sweet, wild beauty, that is soon made to vanish from eyes which look too much on shops and streets, and the vulgarities of city "parties." (38–39)

The passage as a whole represents Fuller at her most self-consciously literary, constructing appealing structures of words, images, and ideas to convey a striking contrast to her readers.

Fuller uses this voice and this technique frequently in *Summer on the Lakes*, but she also treats similar subjects in the mode of logical argument rather than rhetorical description.

> The great drawback upon the lives of these settlers, at present, is the unfitness of the women for their new lot. It has generally been the choice of the men, and the women follow, as women will, doing their best for affection's sake, but too often in heartsickness and weariness. Beside it frequently not being a choice or conviction of their own minds that it is best to be here, their part is the hardest, and they are least fitted for it. The men can find assistance in field labor, and recreation with the gun and fishing-rod. Their bodily strength is greater, and enables them to bear and enjoy both these forms of life.
>
> The women can rarely find any aid in domestic labor. All its various and careful tasks must often be performed, sick or well, by the mother and daughters, to whom a city education has imparted neither the strength nor skill now demanded. (61)

Fuller is here constructing a case rather than describing a piquant contrast. The first sentence introduces her opinion: "The great drawback" in these settlers' lives "is the unfitness of the women for their new lot." The rest support that opinion with facts and logical conclusions. Women are unfit for several reasons, Fuller declares: they were reluctant to move west in the first place but had no choice but to follow their men; unlike the men, who can fish and hunt, they left all sources of enjoyment and recreation behind them; unlike the men, they can find no hired helpers to ease their toil; their "city education" did not prepare them for a frontier life. These two paragraphs introduce a longer section, whose purpose is to argue for the practical education of Western women. "Instruction the children want," she concludes, "but methods copied from the education of some English Lady Augusta, are as ill suited to the daughter of an Illinois farmer, as satin shoes to climb the Indian mounds" (63). The voice is still literary, as the comparison that ends this sentence shows, but its literariness is no longer its purpose: it aspires instead to a broader social utility.

A third voice and a third generic mode are evident in the tale of a Creole girl named Mariana, whose school experience, temperament, and genius resemble Fuller's own. The tale is conventionally romantic. Mariana is a highly colored and tragic character, "a strange bird . . . a lonely swallow that could not make for itself a summer" (81). She gives "her heart capable of highest Eros" "to one who knew love only as a flower or plaything, and [binds] her heartstrings to one who parted his as lightly as the ripe fruit leaves the bough" (95). She wishes to open her heart to her husband in fervent conversation; he desires only "an indolent repose." "In fine, Sylvain became the kind, but preoccupied husband, Mariana, the solitary and wretched wife" (97). The substance of the tale could be drawn from Irving's *Sketch Book* (compare, for example, the chapter called "The Broken Heart"), and the tone is reminiscent of de Staël's *Corinne*. Its conclusion, however, is pure Fuller, an emotional rather than a strictly logical lesson this time, but still consistent with her position in the preceding passage.

> It marks the defect in the position of woman that one like Mariana should have found reason to write thus. To a man of equal power, equal sincerity, no more!—many resources would have presented themselves. He would not have needed to seek, he would have been called by life, and not permitted to be quite wrecked through the affections only. But such women as Mariana are often lost, unless they meet some man of sufficiently great soul to prize them. (102)

A fourth and final example demonstrates yet another of Fuller's voices and exhibits a polyvocality of its own while adding another dimension to her discussion of women in the West. Her celebrated description of the Indian encampment at Mackinac combines her own observations, reports of her conversations with Indian women, imagined speeches of Catholic missionary priests and Indian skeptics, and several long passages from other writers. She is particularly interested in the status of Indian women, but she also uses the white women's voices she hears or imagines to add critical depth to her previous comments on their condition.

> I have spoken of the hatred felt by the white man for the Indian: with white women it seems to amount to disgust, to loathing. How I could endure the dirt, the peculiar smell of the Indians, and their dwellings, was a great marvel in the eyes of my lady acquaintance; indeed, I wonder why they did not quite give me up, as they certainly looked on me with great distaste for it. "Get you gone, you Indian dog," was the felt, if not the breathed, expression towards the hapless owners of the soil. All their claims, all their sorrows quite forgot, in abhorrence of their dirt, their tawny skins, and the vices the whites have taught them.
>
> A person who had seen them during great [*sic*] part of a life, expressed his prejudices to me with such violence, that I was no longer surprised that the Indian children threw sticks at him, as he passed. A lady said, "do what you will for them, they will be ungrateful. Bring up an Indian child and see if

you can attach it to you." The next moment, she expressed, in the presence of one of those children whom she was bringing up, loathing at the odor left by one of her people, and one of the most respected, as he passed through the room. When the child is grown she will consider it basely ungrateful not to love her, as it certainly will not; and this will be cited as an instance of the impossibility of attaching the Indian. (183)

Here Fuller writes in the voice of the engaged reporter, quoting her sources and commenting in what we take to be her own voice on what she observes. The tone is again ironic; the irony, however, is not formal, conventional, and literary, as it was in the first passage, but bitter and deeply felt. Fuller refers to the Indians as "owners of the soil" and attributes their ill-treatment in part to the white women's "abhorrence of their dirt"; she describes a white woman's open expression of "loathing at the odor left by" a passing Indian and this same woman's outrage at the ungratefulness of dependent Indian children. The voices that Fuller sounds and the voice that she adopts in this passage speak to and comment upon earlier voices in the text, reminding her readers that the genteel ladies of the Illinois prairie were also racist usurpers of the property of "the owners of the soil," and that their correspondent is not only a lady herself and an observer of middle-class culture, but also a true democrat and an engaged social critic.

The voice and the tone of this passage represent not a goal achieved once and for all, however, but one of a number of alternative modes available to Fuller as a writer of travel narratives. Fuller does not abandon her concern for the domestic affairs of frontier women or her appreciation for the beauty of their gardens because she disapproves of their relations with the Indians. All of the passages I have analyzed exemplify Fuller's concern for the condition of women; together with many other passages in the book, they help map out a complicated position from which Fuller can adopt variously descriptive and analytic, humorous and sentimental, critical and supportive voices. Some of these voices could be called masculine, either because of their conventional points of view or because of their actual sources, others feminine, and others unmarked. They all help define Fuller's stance as a writer and as a thinking, acting person.

Fuller used her experience of the upper midwestern frontier to help formulate and then to help illustrate her views on the proper role of "woman in the nineteenth century," to use her own later formulation. In *Summer on the Lakes* she uses the conventions of the travel book to speak with a number of voices, recount pleasant visits, repeat interesting stories, and observe unfamiliar customs. She does not reduce all these elements to a single, consistent narrative, but she does put them together and give her reader the opportunity to hear them talk to each other.

Fuller's European experience and her *Tribune* letters present a more complicated picture to the interpreter of her life and work. Europe for Fuller was the object of constant longing, the goal of oft-deferred ambition. Its meaning in her thinking and yearning changed several times before she reached its shores, her conception of it shifted from the fantasy kingdom of childhood to the home of artists, writers, and elegant, sophisticated intellectuals to the setting of social and political developments, without ever settling on a single, exclusive understanding of the Old World. Similarly, as I have suggested, Fuller's experience of Europe can be organized into a number of conventional biographical plots, all of which I believe were unrolling simultaneously in her life and her complicated consciousness, all influencing her understanding of Europe, and all suggesting ways for her to use her European experience to promote personal growth and develop political and intellectual understanding.

Her letters to the *Tribune* reflect Fuller's sense of herself as a tourist, a thinker, an appreciator of art, a writer, a political activist, and even, indirectly, a lover, yet they always cater on some level to the needs and the tastes of her New York readers. They are not in any proper sense a single text at all, but rather a collection of journalistic pieces, commissioned by Greeley, paid for at the rate of ten dollars apiece, and collected into a volume only after Fuller's death. They are consistent neither in style nor in originality nor in the interest they hold for modern readers: some are mere catalogs of obligatory sights, parrotings of the voices of a hundred other such letters, and testimony to Fuller's perpetual need for the money they would bring in rather than to her experience of Europe; others are skillful, even passionate amalgams of several of Fuller's voices, testimony to the variety of her experience and to her belief in the ultimate unity of that variety, of the compatibility, indeed of the necessary coexistence of the personal, the emotional, the aesthetic, and the political.

Although it is indisputably true that Fuller's emphasis changes, that her voice gains force and confidence as she commits herself to the republican cause in Rome, it would be a mistake to read this change as a total conversion, the triumphant final stage of a linear process of maturation, the predestined *terminus ad quem* of Fuller's intellectual, political, and personal life, superseding, even canceling, all that came before. Fuller's last letters from Rome, which her brother chose not to reprint, are moving evidence of her engagement in political struggle, of her continuing commitment to the personal dimension of this struggle, of the continuing utility of the conventional polyvocality of travel writing, and of the multiple meanings of Europe for a brilliant, complex, and multifaceted American woman.[28]

The *Tribune* letters are full of lively, excerptible bits: the story of Fuller's near death on Ben Lomond; her accounts of George Sand, Mickiewicz, and Mazzini; her discussions of Americans abroad; her descriptions of public washing establishments and American sculptors in Florence; her eyewitness reports of the birth and death of the Roman Republic. Instead of looking at any of these relatively familiar passages, I will examine in some detail Fuller's first letter from Europe and the letters her brother refused to reprint, in order to show how all of them exploit the heteroglossic conventions of travel narrative to present the writer's beliefs and opinions in a rhetorically effective setting. Without denying the very real changes that took place in Fuller's writing and thinking between 1846 and 1850, I will emphasize the continuing advantages of polyvocal writing for her political and rhetorical project.

The first letter begins with the obligatory account of the crossing in the *Cambria*, together with a moralizing comment and a conventional metaphor that could have been penned by practically any member of the domesticated, genteel class of travelers and writers: "Our ship's company numbered several pleasant members, and that desire prevailed in each to contribute to the satisfaction of all, which, if carried out through the voyage of life, would make this earth as happy as it is a lovely abode" (39). A more distinctive voice emerges in Fuller's comments upon the awe a number of the passengers feel in the presence of Lady Falkland, the illegitimate daughter of King William IV and "the celebrated Mrs. Jordan," and her mockery of the fact that this feeling is the result of "her left-handed alliance with one of the dullest families that ever sat upon a throne" rather than her "descent from one whom Nature had endowed with her most splendid regalia" (40). Fuller goes on in this same voice to praise the *Cambria*'s captain, who, on an earlier crossing, had insisted that Frederick Douglass be "admitted to equal rights upon his deck with the insolent slaveholders, and assumed a tone toward their assumptions, which, if the Northern States had had the firmness, good sense and honor to use would have had the same effect, and put our country in a different position from that she occupies at present" (40). A voice very much like that of Emma Willard is heard in an account of English travel arrangements ("The dinner if ordered in time, is cooked properly, and served punctually" [41]), and Allen's can be heard in a description of the Mechanics Institute at Manchester, where, "for a very small fee the mechanic, clerk, or apprentice, and the women of their families can receive various good and well-arranged instruction" (41).

In addition to assuming various voices herself, Fuller quotes, and even invents, the voices of others. When the director of the Liverpool Institute ("a very benevolent and intelligent man") quotes "our Boston 'Dial'" on the subject of self-improvement, she quotes him quoting it (42). The discovery in Bradshaw's Railway Guide of a set of quotations from Charles Sumner and Elihu Burritt on the subject of peace gives rise to an imaginary dialogue between Fuller and her English acquaintances, who are happy to be at peace with the United States but quick to celebrate their military victories in China and Ireland. "'You are mightily pleased,'" Fuller imagines herself saying, "'and illuminate for your victories in China and Ireland, do you not?' and they, unprovoked by the taunt, would mildly reply, 'We do not, but it is too true that a large part of the nation fail to bring home the true nature and bearing of those events'" (43).

Fuller then describes in her own voice some aspects of working-class self-education, telling how the young women in a certain unnamed town cut out passages from books and pamphlets and newspapers "on the great subjects of the day," "which they send about in packages, or paste on walls and doors," and how Joseph Barker, "a working-man of the town of Wortley, publishe[s]" improving tracts "through his own printing-press" (44). This leads to a glimpse of one of her less conventional modes of touring and a passage that would be surprising from anyone but the author of *Woman in the Nineteenth Century*.

> How great, how imperious the need of such men, of such deeds, we felt more than ever, while compelled to turn a deaf ear to the squalid and shameless beggars of Liverpool, or talking by night in the streets of Manchester to the girls from the Mills, who were strolling bare-headed, with coarse, rude, and reckless air through the streets, seeing through the windows of the gin-palaces the women seated drinking, too dull to carouse. (47)

Here Fuller's voice changes in a single sentence from that of a detached, generalizing observer of conditions to that of an engaged witness of, almost a participant in, a specific, sordid street scene. She goes on to refer with ironic emphasis to England's much-touted domesticity and suggest that it cannot long coexist with the deplorable condition of the women she has just observed.

> The homes of England! their sweetness is melting into fable; only the new
> Spirit in its holiest power can restore to those homes their boasted security
> of "each man's castle," for Woman, the warder, is driven into the street, and
> has let fall the keys in her sad plight. (47)

Immediately after making this bold political statement, however, Fuller
becomes the conventional tour guide once more, listing in the same paragraph such curiosities as "the statue of Roscoe by Chantrey" and the funeral of an infant, "borne to the grave by women" (48). She gives a brief
account of Chester, the site of the conventional American's first glimpse
of Old England, calling it "a *tout-ensemble* highly romantic in itself and
charming, indeed, to trans-Atlantic eyes" (48), and concludes with a comment on the availability of bathing facilities in English hotels and the
American traveler's unfortunate habit of generalizing from inadequate
experience (49).

The letter as a whole shows Fuller using the polyvocal travel-writing
tradition to create a complex persona of her own out of several different
voices. The writer of these letters is clearly a woman of independent mind
and advanced opinion, who is yet not above attention to the always fascinating details of travel or excitement at the experiences it offers, however
conventional they may have become. She is well read; she is politically,
socially, and historically alert; she is bold enough to converse with stroll-
ing mill girls at night and confident enough to comment on the lineage
of royal bastards. She has a practical streak and a sense of humor. The fact
that she can combine evidence of all these characteristics into a single
letter, make it speak with several voices, and insist that these voices, however disparate, are not inconsistent demonstrates her mastery of the conventions of travel writing and her ability to use them for her own ends.

This same mastery is evident in her last two letters from Italy, which
appeared in the *Tribune* on January 9 and February 13, 1850 but were
omitted from the posthumously published *At Home and Abroad,* and
until recently were available only in the pages of the *New-York Tribune.*
These letters are more single-minded than the earlier ones, it is true, and
focus more directly on current events, but they also make effective use of
the conventional polyvocality of travel writing, combining such elements
as personal narrative, genre paintings of Italian life, and comments on
American behavior abroad with an account of the political situation in
various parts of Italy and two impassioned perorations advocating social
justice and political freedom.

In the letter printed on January 9 Fuller speaks in the voices of the

political reporter, the private individual subjected to the trials of this unsettled time, and the committed socialist. She tells of protests in Rome
and of the behavior of the Austrian occupiers of Florence. She recounts
her own depression and the comfort she takes in nature and in art: "I gaze
on the beauty of nature, and seek thus to strengthen myself"; "I look
again upon art, and solace myself in its calm" (317). She waxes fervent and
optimistic in her hope for a socialist future.

> I believed before I came to Europe in what is called Socialism, as the inevi-
> table sequence to the needs and wants of the era, but I did not think these
> vast changes in modes of government, education, and daily life, would be
> effected as rapidly as I now think they will, because they must. The world
> can no longer stand without them. (320)

The letter printed on February 13 begins with a conventional interpretation of the weather and its relation to human events, and the kind of
domestic genre scene familiar from the writings of Emma Willard.

> Last winter began with meteors and the rose-colored Aurora Borealis. All
> the winter was steady sunshine, and the Spring that followed no less glori-
> ous, as if Nature rejoiced in and daily smiled upon the noble efforts and
> tender generous impulses of the Italian people. This winter, Italy is
> shrouded with snow. Here in Florence the oil congeals in the closet beside
> the fire—the water in the chamber—just as in our country-houses of New-
> England, as yet uncomforted by furnaces. (320)

Fuller goes on to moralize the scene still further, and to move away from
the conventional traveler's voice by undercutting her own easy use of the
pathetic fallacy.

> Thus Nature again sympathizes with this injured people, though, I fear me,
> many a houseless wanderer wishes she did not. For many want both bread,
> and any kind of shelter this winter, an extremity of physical deprivation
> that had seemed almost impossible in this richest land. It had seemed that
> Italians might be subjected to the extreme of mental and moral suffering,
> but that the common beggar's plea, "*I am hungry*," must remain a mere
> poetic expression. 'Tis no longer so. (321)

Then she moves, and this is the astonishing part, and doubtless the reason her careful brother chose not to reprint the letter, from description of
conditions to a prescription for their correction and takes on in the process a new voice, rare among detached nineteenth-century travelers but

existing in productive relation to her other, more conventional voices.

> The next revolution, here and elsewhere, will be radical. Not only Jesuitism must go, but the Roman Catholic religion must go. . . . Not only the Austrian, and every potentate of foreign blood, must be deposed, but every man who assumes an arbitrary lordship over fellow man, must be driven out. It will be an uncompromising revolution. England cannot reason nor ratify nor criticize it—France cannot betray it—Germany cannot bungle it—Italy cannot babble it away—Russia cannot stamp it down nor hide it in Siberia. The New Era is no longer an embryo, it is born; it begins to walk. . . Men have long been talking of a transition state—it is over—the power of positive, determinate effort is begun. . . . God be praised! (321–22)

This is clearly the voice of a revolutionary, a voice that violates the canons of gentility with its inflammatory rhetoric and its political message. In an era when women did not address mixed public gatherings on any subject, let alone revolution, it is also a conventionally masculine voice. It is not, however, a voice that Fuller adopted in any final way; it did not replace her other voices, any more than her experience of motherhood replaced her concern for the Roman poor or her interest in American sculpture or her enthusiastic friendships with Mazzini and Mickiewicz. It coexisted, in this letter and in Fuller's consciousness, with the voices of the sensitive and vulnerable observer who found solace in nature and art and of the practiced writer, maker of metaphors and evoker of domestic scenes.

The significance of Fuller's life and thought does not lie in some inexorable progress, in which the errors of one stage are constantly being replaced by the truths of a new one. Although she was "radicalized" by her engagement in Italian political struggles, this fact cannot adequately describe or explain the power of her example and of her work. These are better understood by reference to the scope of her interests in these last letters, the compendiousness of her sympathies, the power of her convictions, and especially her ability to incorporate the domestic, the compassionate, and the revolutionary in a single text, a single discourse, and a single life, to deny the conventional limitations of femininity, in other words, without for a moment abandoning her identity as a woman. Her argument from the very first had been that women should have the same opportunities for self-fulfillment as men, that they should be sea captains if they wished, or journalists, or efficient household managers, without ever repressing anything truly womanly in their characters. Fuller's life would have exemplified this inclusiveness if she had never written a line of traveler's prose. It is also fair to say that we would have known far less about it if she had not discovered and made use of the polyvocal conventions of nineteenth-century American travel writing.

Europe evoked Fuller's strongest emotions and helped produce some of her most focused, passionate writing. Just as Fuller was always many women at once—activist, intellectual, tourist, lover, journalist—so Europe remained for her many things at once—the scene of political commitment, sexual fulfillment, motherhood, aesthetic pleasure, and ordinary curiosity. Of all the writers in this book, she made the most intense and varied use of Europe, cultivating a broader understanding of European society than even Henry James would achieve and a deeper, more sympathetic understanding of European politics than Adams ever cared to develop.

CHAPTER SEVEN

The Innocents in Europe: Twain, Travel Humor, and Masculinity

During that memorable month I basked in the happiness of
being for once in my life drifting with the tide of a great popular
movement. Every body was going to Europe—I, too, was going
to Europe. Every body was going to the famous Paris Exposition—I, too, was going to the Paris Exposition. The steamship
lines were carrying Americans out of the various ports of the
country at the rate of four or five thousand a week, in the aggre-
gate. If I met a dozen individuals, during that month, who
were not going to Europe shortly, I have no distinct
remembrance of it now.
(*Mark Twain*, The Innocents Abroad)

Yet notwithstanding it is only a record of a pic-nic, it has a
purpose, which is, to suggest to the reader how *he* would be
likely to see Europe and the East if he looked at them with
his own eyes.
(*Mark Twain, Preface to* The Innocents Abroad)

The *Innocents Abroad* is certainly the best-known American travel book
of the nineteenth century. It is the work of a pilgrim to the shrines of
Europe, like Emerson, Sigourney, Fuller, and George Palmer Putnam,
and a citizen of a strikingly modern world of railroads and steamships,
grand hotels, telegrams, and package tours, like James, Adams, and the
author of *Morford's Short-Trip Guide*. Like the antebellum travelers and
travel writers, Twain saw his first European tour as an occasion for pleasure and instruction, a chance to demonstrate his independence and his
authority, and an opportunity to act out his own proper relation to everything that Europe had come to stand for. Like the travelers of the gilded
age, however, he also recognized that he was a participant in "a popular
movement" and, willy-nilly, a tourist. In his excellent essay on *The Inno-*

cents Abroad, Leslie Fiedler argues that it is "not a 'travel book' at all . . . but a chronicle of tourism at the precise point when the Puritan aristocrat abroad is giving way to the Puritan plebeian on tour."[1] I would add that one of Twain's purposes in the book was to describe for a new mass audience what had been an elite-identified experience, to provide the readers of the San Francisco *Alta California* and the customers of the American Publishing Company with an account of the grand tour that would amuse and instruct them without intimidation or pretentiousness. Another purpose, at least as important from Twain's point of view, was to consolidate his position as a writer by developing his voice and his persona and finding a place for himself in a rapidly changing literary culture.

In many ways Twain's task was unique to his peculiar position in history and in society. It may be useful, however, to think of it as a version of three projects that had been motivating American travelers for two or three generations by the time the *Quaker City* cast off for Europe. Americans from Emerson to Adams used European travel as an occasion for establishing a relation to historical and cultural authority, to the "noble," the "high," the "artful," the "beautiful," the "venerable," to everything, in short, that Hawthorne found missing from American experience when he wrote his preface to *The Marble Faun* ("no shadow, no antiquity, no mystery, no picturesque and gloomy wrong")[2] and that James most famously enumerated in his study of Hawthorne.[3] In addition, traveling Americans like David Dorr, Margaret Fuller, Bayard Taylor, and Henry Adams used Europe as a stage to create and perform themselves both as individuals and as men or women, intellectuals or artists, patricians or plebeians, Americans, African Americans or displaced Europeans. For Twain, furthermore, as for many of his male compatriots, these projects were part of the wider task of finding a way to be a man and a writer in a society that labeled artistic and intellectual pursuits effeminate.[4] Emerson and Brown had responded to this challenge by emphasizing the inherent importance of their work, whether as "manly" thought or as moral and political action. Taylor and Willis had joined the male-identified commercial mainstream by turning art into business. Dorr (like many others, as we will see) had acted out his manhood in pranks and bravado. Throughout the nineteenth century, male writers of personal travel narratives, and travel humorists as well, suggested ways for commonsensical American men to deal with art, with Europe, and with "the feminization of American culture." None of them succeeded in discovering a perfectly comfortable role for the American male traveler, artist, and appreciator of art, but Twain certainly provided his readers the opportunity to think about appropriate responses to cultural authority and to judge male roles and male behavior as they are represented by the "boys," the "pilgrims," and his own narrative and dramatic persona.

TRAVELERS, FUNNY MEN, AND ART

Despite the easy stereotype of successful nineteenth-century American men as bold and glamorous loners in the wide, hostile world and undisputed patriarchs in the well-ordered home, we have been learning in recent years that the definition of masculinity raised serious problems for nineteenth-century American culture in general and for certain categories of men in particular. Building on the work of feminist critics and historians such as Ann Douglas, Nancy Cott, and Carroll Smith-Rosenberg, a number of (male) critics have been exploring the relations between the historically problematic class and gender identity of certain nineteenth-century men on the one hand and their choice of a literary career and the strategies they employed as literary artists on the other.

In *Manhood and the American Renaissance* (1989), for example, David Leverenz suggests that the status of "bookish" men in the antebellum period was gravely threatened, and their masculinity called in question, by a change in available models for manly success brought on by social and economic developments in the rapidly expanding United States. According to Leverenz, two "paradigms" of masculine respectability, the "patrician" and the "artisan," were challenged in the nineteenth century by a third, more contentious version of masculinity, endorsed by the growing middle class. "Patricians" owed their prestige and their sense of self to heredity, "property ownership, patriarchy, and republican ideals of citizenship." "Artisans" prided themselves on their independence, their crafts and skills, and their citizenship ("to a lesser degree," according to Leverenz) but questioned the value of "patriarchal deference." The new class of entrepreneurs valued successful competition over inherited advantages or traditionally acquired skills; their standard of success was based not on a stable, independent identity, but on a relative position, achieved in competition with others and vulnerable to competition from others. "Middle-class American males at mid-century" were constantly compelled not only to defend their economic position but at the same time and in the same way to assert their masculinity, to claim and reclaim their identity as "real men."[5] Among the results of this compulsion, Leverenz suggests, were public bluster and braggadocio (87), private, compensatory assertion of "patriarchal" privilege (165), and the generalized suspicion that men who kept aloof from the battles of politics, commerce, and the active professions were hardly men at all, but docile allies of the ladies, inhabitants of the "woman's sphere" of life. Male writers responded to this imputation directly, by asserting the manliness of their moral and intellectual concerns, or indirectly, "by transforming feelings of unmanly deviance into strategies of [literary] deviousness" (172).

As its title suggests, Leverenz's study concentrates on the literary culture of the 1840s and 1850s. To follow the fate of embattled manhood into the gilded age, we can turn to Michael Davitt Bell's *The Problem of American Realism*. Bell argues that the genteel, "popular" moralism of such Brahmin writers as Longfellow, Lowell, and Whittier, the serious, engaged realism of their anointed successor, William Dean Howells, and the self-consciously antigenteel naturalism of Norris, Sinclair, and, later, Lewis can all be seen as claims to masculine prestige by members of a marginalized, feminized class and profession. Reacting against the pejorative connotations of the "artist type," for example, Longfellow explicitly proclaimed himself a "masculine," "useful" poet.[6] A little later, Howells would declare that realist fiction was no mere aesthetic amusement, but an important tool for understanding society and living an enlightened, moral life. If art and other forms of materially nonproductive intellectual work were by definition womanly, then the realist had to claim that *his* version of art was different, that *he* was not spending his life on trivial matters that could just as well be handled by women. "To claim to be a 'realist' in late nineteenth-century and early twentieth-century America," Bell suggests, "was among other things to suppress worries about one's sexuality and sexual status and to proclaim oneself a man" (37).[7]

The set of ideas that Douglas, Cott, Smith-Rosenberg, Leverenz, and Bell put forward is by now fairly familiar. My purpose in reviewing it is not to suggest that what Nina Baym has called the "melodrama of beset manhood"[8] is a "universal" feature of "American" experience, but rather to argue that the particular challenge that nineteenth-century economic and social developments posed to American male writers and intellectuals made them vulnerable to accusations of "effeminacy" in an era when the constructed difference between the genders was at least as stark and as detrimental to women as it ever has been. This vulnerability encouraged them to engage in various forms of self-defense, from Emerson's assertion of the manliness of powerful thinking to the clubby superiority of the Brahmin writers, the literary evasiveness of Melville, Poe, and Hawthorne, the righteous moralism of the realists, and the bad-boy bluster of

Twain. It also complicated their relations with high culture in general, with the visual arts of the European tradition, and with Europe itself, all of which were conventionally coded womanly.

As Alfred Habegger has pointed out, one place where this combination of masculine defensiveness and self-assertion has manifested itself is in humorous writing. I want to suggest that Europe and European travel provided midcentury male humorists with the chance to act the part of "bad boys defying a civilization seen as feminine,"[9] to combine "masculine" (or, more often, boyish) common sense, high spirits, and defiance with "feminine" sensitivity and aesthetic appreciation. Other critics have established Twain's general debt to earlier humorists;[10] I propose to show how a number of male humorists used Europe for their own purposes, and how Twain in *The Innocents Abroad* provided a definitive, but still quite uneasy, representation of the uses of Europe for a middling range of American men, neither boors nor aesthetes, neither plutocrats nor workers, but common-sense middle-class democrats determined to see and judge the Old World for themselves and to act out their senses of themselves and of their place in their society and culture.

The Innocents Abroad is in many ways a hybrid text, owing as much to the tradition of the travel chronicle as it does to that of American humor. Like a number of its predecessors, it is a revised version of letters originally dispatched from Europe to an American newspaper, combining the illusion of spontaneity that on-the-spot reporting provided with the sense of continuity and wholeness that leisurely revision afforded. Twain had been familiar with the travel chronicle tradition at least as early as his days on the Hannibal *Journal*, where he typeset pirated passages from such writers as N. P. Willis and Bayard Taylor.[11] He had also written travel chronicles himself in his dispatches from the Sandwich Islands to the *Sacramento Union*. Before I turn to humorous travel writing, therefore, I want to look briefly at four male travel chroniclers, to see how they reconciled their sense of themselves as men with an appreciation of Europe, of high culture, and especially of the visual and plastic art of the European masters.

We have already seen how Bayard Taylor, William Wells Brown, and David Dorr used travel and the travel chronicle as occasions to define themselves as belonging to categories of men worthy of masculine respect, the first as a self-sufficient adventurer, the second as a knowledgeable gentleman-reformer, and the third as a sophisticated man-about-town, after his own lights. This could be done in other parts of the world—in Douglass's Maryland, Parkman's West, or on Dana's high seas[12]—without reference to high culture, but European travelers almost always felt obliged to take some account of the commonly recognized monuments and masterpieces of architecture, painting, and sculpture. In fact, Taylor, Brown, and Dorr all confronted European high culture and used the confrontation to help construct their ideal (male) writing and narrating personas.

Taylor used his frequent visits to museums and monuments to establish his credentials as a sensitive, educated traveler and a moralist in the fashionable, sentimental vein of Irving, Willis, Mitchell, and Curtis.[13] Having demonstrated his rugged masculinity by traveling in the steerage and making his way across the Continent primarily on foot, often in the company of tramping German students and apprentices, he was eager to claim a place in the company of respectable magazine moralists and popular poets who made their living by their pens. Relatively secure in his sense of himself, his way of dealing with the "feminized" intellectual establishment was to join it and exploit it to advance his own career.

One way of doing this was to invite the reader to participate in a sympathetic, sentimental way in some classic aesthetic experience. In Leipzig, for example, Taylor goes twice to see "Raphael's heavenly picture of the Madonna and Child," reports on the growth of his admiration for the painting, and suggests, by his use of the third person "one," that his reader would experience it in a similar way. The painting is disappointing at first, Taylor reports. It has faded over time and is protected by a distracting sheet of glass. These obstacles to appreciation disappear, however, as the viewer is taken up by the picture's magic, and transported to realms of spiritual and sentimental bliss.

> After I had gazed on it a while, every thought of this vanished. The figure of the Virgin seemed to soar in the air, and it was difficult to think the clouds were not in motion. Two divine cherubs look up from below, and in her arms sits the sacred child. Those two faces beam from the picture like those of angels. The dark, prophetic eye and pure brow of the young Jesus chain one like a spell. There is something more than mortal in its expression—something in that infant face which indicates a power mightier than the proudest manhood. There is no glory around the head; but the spirit which shines from those features, marks his divinity. In the sweet face of the mother a sorrowful foreboding mingles with its tenderness, as if she knew the world into which the Saviour was born, and foresaw the path in which he was to tread. It is a picture which one can scarce look upon without tears. (199–200)

In this passage Taylor parades his sentimental sensibility and courts the reader by assuming that (s)he, too, would yield to involuntary tears in the presence of this religious masterpiece. Instead of denying the association of high art with womanly feeling, he uses it to help him claim a place in the genteel, established, "feminine" magazine culture of his day.

Another typical response to art is a little more intellectual, leading the reader to a profound truth rather than a transcendent religio-aesthetic frisson. After contemplating (and displaying) the treasures of Florence, Taylor treats his readers to a defense of the practical and spiritual value of art. In the first place, he opines, art pays big dividends for a long time. "The spirits of the old painters, living still on their canvas, earn from year to year the bread of an indigent and oppressed people. This ought to silence those utilitarians at home, who oppose the cultivation of the fine arts, on the ground of their being useless luxuries" (354–55). Furthermore, art ennobles and sanctifies.

> Nothing is useless that gratifies that perception of Beauty, which is at once the most delicate and the most intense of our mental sensations, binding us by an unconscious link nearer to nature and to Him, whose every thought is born of Beauty, Truth and Love. I envy not the man who looks with a cold and indifferent spirit on these immortal creations of the old masters— these poems written in marble and on the canvas. They who oppose every thing which can refine and spiritualize the nature of man, by binding him down to the cares of the work-day world alone, cheat life of half its glory. (355)

If the passage on the Raphael *Madonna* flatters the reader by assuming a shared aesthetic response, this passage continues the process by identifying reader and writer as among those superior beings who have been improved by art and rumors of art. Taylor sees no reason to challenge the social and aesthetic assumptions that underlie the valuation of European art. On the contrary, his personal, cultural, and professional purposes are very well served by the idea of the enshrined, transcendent masterpiece, the appreciation of which validates his own taste and the discussion of which helps establish his own cultural authority. Taylor's hardy young man "a-foot" in Europe is also a respectable belletrist in training, out to claim a prominent position in the "feminized" clerisy of journalists and litterateurs without giving up his central, powerful position as a male in a patriarchal society.

William Wells Brown's position as an author and a man of consequence in the liberal pacifist-abolitionist political world was well estab-

lished by the time he sailed for Europe as a delegate to the World Peace
Conference in Paris. His sense of himself as a man, furthermore, had
everything to do with his experiences as a slave and a fugitive. As I argued
in chapter 4, however, one of the effects, if not one of the conscious
purposes, of Brown's European sojourn was to establish his credentials as
a cultivated gentleman, and one necessary element of this project was a
relationship with European art.

Unlike Taylor, Brown was no aesthete in training, and his comments
on art suggest that he valued it as a practical source of knowledge and
moral inspiration without denying its power to stimulate erotic fantasy.
So, for example, he writes that some statues in the British Museum "are
of great value as works of art, and more so as a means of enlightening
much that has been obscure with respect to Lycia, an ancient and celebrated country in Asia Minor."[14] His favorite picture at the Royal Academy is the unattributed (by him) "'Dante meditating the episode of
Francesca da Rimini and Paolo Malatesta, S'Inferno [*sic*], Canto V'"
(133), which prompts the moral reflection that "no one can be a great poet
without having been sometime during life a lover, and having lost the
object of his affection in some mysterious way" (134). He also comments
that it is "an excellently painted piece" (135), but his further characteriza-
tions of it ("The delineations are sublime, the conception is of the highest
order, and the execution admirable" [135]) fairly exhaust his store of aesthetic judgments. Still, he is often thrilled by music and moved by poetry
and admits to being captivated in a dreamily erotic fashion by a statue of
Venus.

> Venus, seated and smelling a lotus-flower which she held in her hand, and
> attended by three Graces, put a stop to the rapid strides that I was making
> through this part of the hall. This is really one of the most precious produc-
> tions of the art that I have ever seen. . . . I wandered to another part of the
> building, but only to return again to my "first love," where I remained till
> the throng had disappeared, one after another, and the officer reminded me
> that it was time to close. (113–14)

All three of these uses of art, as a stimulus to moral meditation and a
source of both information and crypto-erotic pleasure, are perfectly compatible with Brown's sense of himself as a moralist, a thinker, and a practical man of the world, as well as a "normally" susceptible heterosexual
male.

Art clearly had its place in Brown's experience of Europe, then, and he certainly felt called upon to report on his experience of art to his readers. He does not, however, rely on art as Taylor does, to provide him with authority and status. The position of authority to which Brown aspired was moral and political rather than cultural and aesthetic. It went without saying that a gentleman in such a position was aware of and responsive to the world of art, and Brown was careful to demonstrate this aspect of his character in his *American Fugitive in Europe*, but it played a less than central role in his construction of self and his quest for power.

Dorr's relation to art is simpler than either Taylor's or Brown's but not for that reason any less important. I have suggested that Dorr's primary purpose in writing *A Colored Man Round the World* was to try out for himself the most attractive free male persona available to him, that of the young New Orleans dandy and bon vivant. Such young men do not seem, in Dorr's experience, at least, to have spent much time at the Louvre or to have felt the lack of the polish and cachet conferred by an acquaintance with the old masters. Unlike Taylor and Brown, they had no public reputations to make, relying instead on their inherited positions as wealthy white slaveowners for status and self-esteem. But Dorr was neither wealthy nor white nor a slaveowner, and his very brief treatments of art confirm its association with prestige and respectability.

For Dorr, art is primarily embodied in architecture, whose two main duties are to be splendid and to evoke history. The Cathedral of Notre Dame, in Paris, "that Venerable old monument of reality and romance" (33), lures him with its literary associations ("I approached it like a timid child being baited with a shining sixpence" [33]) and keeps his interest with its "magnificent aisles," "magnificent pictures," "golden knobs," "gorgeous" furnishings, and royal tombs (34). St. Mark's, in Venice, is "magnificent," too, with its precious mosaics and alabaster pillars, and all the more interesting as the burial place of Mark the Evangelist, as well, he seems to think, as the emperor Alexander (145). Where the authority of architecture is really important to Dorr, though, is in Egypt, where he claims kinship with the builders of the great monuments and ancient cities, citing Homer as his authority for describing them as "men with wooly [sic] hair, thick lips, flat feet, and black" (134). He finds the paintings at Luxor "as bright today as any modern painting I have seen in the Louvre, at Paris" (175), and is "confounded and awe struck" by the pyramids (169) and fascinated by the "tall columns of the Memnonian" (175). His pride in the assumption that all of these monuments were the work of "colored" men like himself is only a more explicit version of the pride

Anglo-Americans took in the works both of their English ancestors and of the Romans from whom they traditionally claimed their political institutions descended.

Taylor, Brown, and Dorr used their European trips in very different ways to help establish themselves as very different kinds of respectable, independent men. For each of these writers, art played a role in the process, whether as a central concern, an inescapable presence, or a vehicle for racial pride.

Art also played an important part in the European experience of Theodore Witmer, a young American who published his chronicle of European travel in Philadelphia in 1853, under the title *Wild Oats, Sown Abroad; or, On and Off Soundings, Being Leaves from a Private Journal By a Gentleman of Leisure*. Like Dorr, Witmer uses Europe as a stage upon which to act out, presumably in life, but certainly in the imagination and on paper, the part of a dashingly independent young dandy. Like Taylor, though without his professional motivation, Witmer becomes more and more interested in art as his trip goes on and engages with it in a serious and extended fashion. In addition, and here is where the relation to Twain becomes even clearer, Witmer indulges in a certain amount of conventional humor, occasionally takes an ironic position in respect to his own persona, and even anticipates a number of the attitudes and opinions expressed in *The Innocents Abroad*.

Witmer's first concern in his narrative is to project an image of himself as a devil-may-care boy's man and a knowledgeable rake. In his preface, he compares his chronicle to a schoolboy's prank and pretends to believe that he "deserve[s] just as severe a flogging" for publishing his book "as [one such prank] called forth."[15] Early in his first sketch, he characterizes himself as the idle, private gentleman of the title, taking his ease and his pleasure in Europe, with no thought for fame or reputation. "Let your warriors and your statesmen take their airing from the tops of marble monuments and in dignified silence greet the rising sun—they were born for such a purpose—while we were predestined to the quiet enjoyment of a Louis Quatorze [cigar], and the sweet oblivion of a 'siesta'" (9). Later in the book he refers to himself as a "'refined loafer'" (75), and all the way through he spends time describing the readily available delights of the barroom (37–43) and the dance hall (62–63).

Much of the pleasure he takes in travel is clearly erotic. He sets the tone in the second letter, in describing his flirtation with "Mrs. N," who "once dared the hazard of as ugly a nightcap as I could find. I put a red flannel one upon her head. She tossed the nasty thing racily upon one side 'a la Grec' [*sic*]—pulled the tassel over her left eye, jumped up, kissed me, and looked too sweet for earth" (17). Later he describes an encounter with a courtesan ("'I hate a mercenary woman as I do the devil,'" he tells her. "'Who asked you for money?'" she replies. "'I told you I liked your face'" [35–36]) and theorizes on the proper strategies to be used with "Grisettes" and "Lorettes."

> The Lorette dresses with great care and finish. Her toilet is a sort of "pro-spectus" for the passing speculator to invest at his peril. The dividend is very uncertain. With the Grisette the prospectus is plainer, but there is less to lose for the installments are lighter. With your Grisette it is your first kiss—with the Lorette it is your first dinner. . . . Ask her for a small favor, and she treats you as the Athenians did Aristides; seize her as Napoleon did Venice, and the key of her possessions is in your hand. (66)

In Genoa, he nearly falls victim to "one of those amorous brokers," the "mercantile Cupids" who frequent the piazza in front of the Exchange (93–94), but the merchandise turns out to be otherwise engaged ("Cupid return[ed] to announce that Aspasia was engaged with some happier Per-icles" [95]), and he escapes without being "murdered in a low bawdy house" (94) and vilified as "a 'bad young man'" (95) in the newspapers.

In addition to posing as a sly rogue and a man of the world, Witmer fancies himself a writer, in a dilettantish if not a professional way, and is eager to show off his skill as a wordsmith. He writes, he declares, because it is in his nature to do so, and he enjoys the products of his pen as an owl enjoys its shrieks or a donkey its braying. "Man, though more rational, is not less vain of his production [than the owl or the jackass], and so long as it tickles his ear, will indulge in the luxury, and will never cease to wonder why others are not equally delighted" (7). Witmer accordingly sounds off in a series of purple passages ("In that blue strip which hangs like a cloud upon the horizon sleep all my memories—in its embrace lie triumphs and defeats—from this far-off point I see the specula—the phantom of my past life" [10]) and shows off in aggressively fancy diction ("Did the slightest vapor of a culinary preparation waft itself towards us, immediately the peristaltic motion became excessive, and we were forced to surrender!" [12]).

Travel and travel writing give Witmer the chance to parade himself as a winning (he thinks) "bad boy," an erotic adventurer, and the possessor of an impressive vocabulary. He could be all of these things, however, without leaving North America. What distinguishes his European tour from a journey to New York, Quebec, Havana, or New Orleans is the necessity for coming to terms with art. Witmer rises unexpectedly to this challenge, convincingly adding the role of art lover to the other personas he develops in the course of his travels but inflecting it as an appropriate role for a sensible man of independent taste and judgment, willing to learn to admire what seems to him admirable but unwilling to submit blindly to cultural authority.

Witmer's first comments on art contain the familiar combination of insecurity and independence. "I know nothing about painting or sculpture," he begins, ". . . and when I stroll through the galleries of the Louvre, I invariably find myself admiring some outlawed effort of genius, which the arbitrary taste of the connoisseur has criticised down to the marshy district of mediocrity" (58). This passage could well introduce a variation on the defiantly philistine theme of "I don't know much about art but I know what I like." In Witmer, however, it introduces the first of a series of earnest attempts to come to terms with European art and art criticism without abandoning the right of personal aesthetic judgment. Witmer reports that he is reading art criticism and discovering a few solid principles amid a great deal of cant. So far, he says, he can recognize two principles of excellence in art, "the close imitation of the natural, and the natural idealized" (58). Of "mysticism," "allegory," and "deep design" he remains happily ignorant; he wonders if his trip to Italy will provide him with greater insight, but he does not hesitate to list his favorite artists from among those represented in the Louvre, nor to characterize them in perfectly reasonable ways.

> At present I see in Raffaelle [sic] the most beautiful of all creators; in Correggio the most attractive; in Guido, all that is silvery and soft. . . . In Salvator I have no difficulty to mark the gloomy; in Rembrandt, the dignified; in Van Dyke the polished, and in Reubens [sic] the coarse, clumsy, flashy, and dashing spirit of self-confidence and genius. (59–60)

In Nîmes a few weeks later, Witmer has what he calls his "first lesson in taste," by which he means his first lesson in the construction of aesthetic pronouncements based on ignorance, brashness, guides, and guidebooks. A true understanding of "ruins," for which he has already evinced a passion (9), would require "as much study . . . as there is in the acquisition of a language." Instead of undertaking this study, however, the tourist "stands by the side of a half shattered edifice, ignorant of its architecture, and indifferently versed in its era and history," listens to "an even more ignorant guide," and pronounces it "beautiful" if it pleases him or "picturesque" if it has "the stoop of age—the melancholy shroud of ivy." "If I were asked for a receipt to make an amateur," Witmer concludes, "I should prescribe one-third Murray to a full dose of brass" (85–86). Witmer's scorn is palpable, but it extends only to the false connoisseur, not to the work of art or to genuine learning. Rather than dismiss the Maison Carrée as a fraud, ineradicably contaminated by its canting admirers, he looks it over, "admires" it himself, and resolves to take *it*, rather than Murray or the nattering local guide, as his "instructor" (86).

Witmer's disdain for potted art appreciation and his openness to art itself bear fruit in Italy, where he feels confident enough to express independent opinions without apology. He admires the mythological paintings of Titian and Correggio, for example, but finds the latter's depictions of passion more natural if perhaps less elegant than the former's.

> Titian [he aptly remarks] invariably has an eye to a handsome yet oftentimes artful distribution of the person. Correggio idealizes the shape, but retains its natural play. . . . The Danae of Correggio is a perfect picture of its kind; so is Io embraced by the Cloud. . . . There is a soft, half-bewildered, deep enjoyment upon Danae's face, which reveals bliss more potently than ever canvass [*sic*] yet accomplished; and there is a wild, fitful abandonment in Io's limbs which speaks an ecstasy no other pencil has yet portrayed. (134)

Like Brown, Witmer uses his comments on art, here and elsewhere, to underline his own male heterosexuality, his "appreciation" of passion and the female form. He never becomes a great connoisseur; he does not turn himself into a James Jackson Jarves, Charles Eliot Norton, or Bernard Berenson. He does, however, achieve a comfortable, confident relationship with European art, which resists both the easy dismissiveness of the philistine and the equally easy formulaic smarm of the guidebook devotee. He knows what he likes and why he likes it, having learned taste from art itself, rather than from authorities, and become a genuine, not an artificial, art lover.

There is one further role that Witmer takes on in the course of his travels, and it links him to the tradition of travel humor. Witmer was not primarily a humorist, any more than he was a professional connoisseur, but his chronicle combines a taste for the comic anecdote and a sense of ironic narration that link it to the writings of Haliburton, Browne, Curtis, DeMille, and Twain.

As we have seen, Witmer describes himself in his preface as a joker and compares his book to an elaborate pleasantry. Like Twain's "sinners," he is fond of a witty remark, or a prank. When, for example, one of his dimmer countrymen asks him whether "this Magdalen that I see painted so often in these galleries" is "Mrs. Christ," he says no, she is "the mistress of one of the old saints, I forget which" (132). When one of his companions sets his coat on fire by putting an unextinguished half-cigar in his pocket for safekeeping in a church and then smells smoke, Witmer tells him not to worry, it is just the incense (163–64). He satirizes ignorant, mercenary guides ("I could have murdered my guide without the slightest remorse." "These English guides are more annoying than a host of Orleans musquitoes [*sic*]" [27]), and doses an unsuspecting old gentleman with American snuff, leaving him "sneezing in the depot at Padua amid continued effort to tell me at parting that America must be an extraordinary country, and that he owed to me the most delicious moment of his life" (198).

In addition, and unlike Dorr, for example, Witmer maintains a certain distance from all his pranks and pronouncements, which begins to suggest the complicated narrative strategies Twain will use some fifteen years further on to qualify the ideals of masculine selfhood he espouses in *The Innocents Abroad*. We can see him standing back, watching his own aesthetic education, for example, or his noninitiation into the mysteries of the Genoan bordello, and realize that one of the reasons that Taylor's version of American manhood, and Dorr's, and maybe even Brown's seem inadequate or simplistic when compared with Twain's is that Twain, like Witmer, combined the devices of irony and humor with the conventions of the travel chronicle.

Not all travel humor is as complex as Twain's, though, and a look at some earlier humorous works will demonstrate the originality of *The Innocents Abroad* as a piece of humor and as a stage for enacting a version of nineteenth-century masculinity. Thomas Chandler Haliburton's *The Attaché; or, Sam Slick in England* (1843–44), George William Curtis's *The Potiphar Papers* (1853), Charles Farrar Browne's *Artemus Ward in London* (1867), and James B. DeMille's *The Dodge Club; or, Italy in 1859* (1867) all depict American men in a European setting and propose relations to Europe, and in some cases to art, for their characters and their male narrators.

Thomas Haliburton was a staunch Tory loyalist from Nova Scotia, whose Yankee character, Sam Slick, of Connecticut, is both a buffoon and a democratic-liberal foil for the conservative good sense and good manners of his creator, represented in the texts by a narrator known as the Squire and his traveling companion, the Reverend Mr. Hopewell. In Leverenz's terms, we could say that Haliburton assumes a "patrician paradigm" of (masculine) respectability and uses his character's foolish behavior to demonstrate the legitimacy of his assumption. The prestige of the Squire and the clergyman is guaranteed by their standing in the (presumably) stable social order of old England, which they praise whenever they can, and underlined by the Yankee democrat's buffoonery. Slick combines features of the yokel, the slick Yankee peddler suggested by his name, and, believe it or not, the stereotyped blackface buffoon of the minstrel shows. When they first sight land off the coast of England, Slick celebrates by cutting a caper and reliving the Battle of New Orleans.

> He then uttered the negro ejaculation "chah!—chah!" and putting his arms a-kimbo, danced in a most extraordinary style to the music of a song, which he gave with great expression:
>
> > "Oh hab you nebber heerd ob de battle ob Orleens,
> > Where de dandy Yankee lads gave de Britishers de beans;
> > Oh de Louisiana boys dey did it pretty slick,
> > When dey cotch ole Packenham and rode him up a creek.
> > Wee my zippy dooden dooden dooden dooden dooden day,
> > Wee my zippy dooden dooden dooden dooden dooden day."[16]

When he visits a country house, Slick is so resourceless that he seeks out the stable boy for conversation and then cannot understand the dialect he speaks (41). He finds that the ancient parish church where the Reverend Mr. Hopewell preaches one Sunday "ain't quite up to the notch, and is a leetle behind the enlightment of the age like, with its queer old fixin's and what not," but admits that it "looks solemcoly" (215), and somehow more appropriate for worship than a newly painted, sparkling white, clear-paned, New England meetinghouse (218). He is, of course, not a character at all, but a device. He has no mind or consciousness; his function is merely to demonstrate Yankee foolishness in the context of Old World superiority, in order to confirm his author's sense of his own superiority as a conservative patrician male.

The Potiphars play a similar role in George William Curtis's "The Potiphars in Paris." They are undereducated New York plutocrats and not Yankee bumpkins, however, and their pretentious vulgarity lacks the charm of Slick's good-humored gaucheness. Perhaps because he feels that they represent a real threat to the old-fashioned, established gentility of his own class, Curtis exposes their ignorance and criticizes their misuse of Europe in the directest possible terms. "'You understand life, my dear Mrs. Potiphar,'" says one of his characters, in a speech whose irony is almost too bitter to be humorous.

> Here you are, speaking very little French, in a city where the language is an atmosphere, and where you are in no sense acclimated until you can speak it fluently—with all French life shut out from you—living in a hotel—cheated by butcher, baker, and candle-stick maker—going to hear plays that you imperfectly understand—to an opera where you know nobody, and where your box is filled with your own countrymen, who are delightful indeed, but whom you didn't come to Paris to see—constantly buying a hundred things because they are pretty, and because you are in Paris—entirely ignorant, and quite as careless, of the historical interests of the city, of the pictures, of the statues, and buildings—surrounded by celebrities of all kinds, of whom you never heard, and therefore lose the opportunity of seeing them—in fact, paying the most extravagant price for every thing, and purchasing only the consciousness of being in Paris—why, who ought to be happy, and considered to be having a fine time of it, if you are not?[17]

Mr. Potiphar, even more ignorant than his wife, is naturally cheated on every hand. Like Twain in Gibraltar, he is royally duped by a mock-flirtatious young *vendeuse* who tells him he has "such a delicate hand" (181) as she helps him draw on a pair of gloves and sells him "piles of cravats, and gloves, and fancy buttons, and charms, until he was quite dizzy, and found that he hadn't money enough in his pocket to pay" (182). In *The Innocents Abroad* the glove-buying episode ends in good-natured mockery all around, as Twain and his comrades realize that they have been had (60). Mr. Potiphar, in contrast, never notices the game that has been played with him and leaves the shop basking smugly in what he thinks is the shop girl's admiration. "Poor French gentlemen!" the narrator remarks with undisguised sarcasm. "How they must be annoyed to see foreigners carrying off not only all the gloves, but all the smiles, of the beautiful Maries" (183).

Mr. Potiphar does no better in the art market, where acquisition, not appreciation, is his goal. He is taken by a picture agent to a grand old house, where an heirloom Poussin must be sold, in secret, to pay off the family's debts. "'To any one else, of course, in France,'" he is told, "'the price should be eleven thousand francs,'" but for him, since he is an

American, the family will let it go for ten (193). "You see clearly it's quite worth while coming to Paris to do this," Curtis's spokesman in the text sarcastically comments, "because, I suppose, there are not more than ten or twenty artists at home who could paint ten or twenty times as good a picture for a quarter of the price" (193–94). As in the Sam Slick series, the purpose of the humor here is to affirm the author's superior position by ridiculing the foolishness of his characters. Slick's and the Potiphars' misuse of Europe allows their creators to assert their own cultivation and instruct their readers on how best to enjoy and profit from the European experience.

Charles Farrar Browne's Artemus Ward, a character he both performed on the lecture stage and developed in print, is more complicated. In the first place, he is both identified with and distinguishable from his creator. His books are humorous, and they are written in the first person, but he is not a humorist. What the audience and the author recognize as funny, Ward presents straight-faced, as a simple report. The distance is emphasized by Ward's comic spelling, but most of the jokes would be just as funny without it. The following report, for example, depends for its humor almost entirely on the incongruity of its last word, an incongruity that is clearly a creation of the author for the amusement of the audience, conveyed through the unsuspecting medium of Artemus Ward:

> I like the Beefanham theatre very much indeed, because there a enthoosiastic lover of the theatre like myself can unite the legitermit drammer with fish.[18]

As an object of humor Ward is a direct descendant of Sam Slick and the Potiphars. As a narrator, though, as a canny Yankee, and as a common-sense critic of the European experience he is an immediate forerunner of Mark Twain and the boys in *The Innocents Abroad.* His appreciative report of his landlord's reaction to an exhibition of spiritualism, for example, directly anticipates one of Twain's travelers' favorite jokes.

> "He is one of these spirit fellers—he is a Trans-Mejim, and when he slings himself into a trans-state, he says the sperrits of departed great men talk through him. He says that tonight sev'ril em'nent persons will speak through him—among others, Cromwell."
> "And this Mr. Cromwell—is he dead?" said the lan'lord. (32)

His treatment of English policemen resembles Twain's travelers' treatment of guides, but it is both kinder and more practical.

"It's only a fit, Sir Richard," I said. I always call the perlice Sir Richard.
It pleases them to think I'm the victim of a deloosion; and they always treat
me perlitely. (35)

Unlike Haliburton and Curtis, who use their comic travelers to
demonstrate their own superiority of class and education, Browne associates himself with Ward, without becoming him completely. Like
Samuel Clemens, Browne began his career as a provincial journalist who
aspired to both fame and respectability. Artemus Ward served as both a
vehicle for Browne's humor and an alter ego, a voice in which he could
poke fun at respectability without abandoning it in his own person. This
is particularly clear in Ward's comments on museums, monuments, and
works of art, which allow Browne to allude to their importance, their
beauty, or their emotional effects without becoming pious or sentimental
himself.

"And this," I said, "is the British Mooseum! These noble walls," I contin-
nerd, punching them with my umbreller to see if the masonry was all right.
(75)

Once inside the museum, he is open to experience but joins many museum goers in finding "rayther too many 'Roman antiquity of a uncertin
date'" (77). This is a perfectly reasonable observation—who, faced with
case after case of figurines and potsherds, would not agree? Ward's explanation of his reaction, however, is a masterpiece of comic misprision. It
is not that he finds row on row of Roman jugs boring, it is that he misses
the date (and, to top it off, suggests an incorrect one).

I can cry like a child over a jug one thousand years of age, especially if it
is a Roman jug; but a jug of a uncertin date doesn't overwhelm me with
emotions. (77)[19]

Browne uses Ward in this passage to claim familiarity with the British
Museum, to acknowledge one of the hazards of museum going, and to
make fun of misplaced sentimentalism. In a subsequent description of a
young farmer's reaction to a famous sculpture, he has Ward testify to the
power of "Art" by providing a comic description of the young man's ordinary experience.

The statute of Apollo is a pretty slick statute. A young yeoman seemed
deeply imprest with it. He viewd it with silent admiration. At home, in the
beautiful rural districks where the daisy sweetly blooms, he would be

swearin in a horrible manner at his bullocks, and whacking 'em over the head with a hayfork; but here, in the presence of Art, he is a changed bein. (78)

Browne is saying that art has real emotional and spiritual effects while carefully distancing himself from their more foolish manifestations. Like Irving in *The Sketch Book of Geoffrey Crayon* and Twain in *The Innocents Abroad*, he approaches Europe, European travel, and art in a gingerly fashion, willing to acknowledge their benefits but careful to distance himself from a potentially foolish, because in some way feminine or sissyish, reaction to them.

One final example of European travel humor, in many ways quite similar to *The Innocents Abroad*, can be found in James B. DeMille's fictional narrative *The Dodge Club*, which began running in *Harper's New Monthly Magazine* just three months before the sailing of the *Quaker City*. DeMille's text tells the story of a group of grown-up American "boys" who have formed "a society for the purpose of going to Italy," called the Dodge Club, "because our principle is to dodge all humbugs and swindles, which make travelling so expensive generally."[20] Like Twain's merry party in an early portion of *The Innocents Abroad*, the club travels from Paris through Italy, flirting, playing pranks, and condescending to the French and the Italians for their venality (10–12), their "narrow-mindedness" (18), and their deficiency in "the leading element of the age," their failure to have "any idee [*sic*] of the principle of pro-gress [*sic*]" (16). Like Twain, DeMille uses the journey to criticize European customs and practices, to make fun of the rollicking American "boys," and to admire their high spirits and their refusal to be unduly impressed by obligatory sights and certified masterpieces.

The Dodge Club's adventures, however, add up to little more than a comic romp against a series of classic European backdrops. Their irreverence is not balanced by a serious regard for any aspect of European history or culture; their story is told in the third person, so there is no central consciousness to register the sights and experiences, and at least possibly to learn from them, and none of the narrative tension that animates both Artemus Ward's narratives and Twain's. Everything, instead, is the butt of parody; the boys' letters to local newspapers (56–57), their love affairs, their enthusiasms, and the treasures of art and antiquity are all subject to indiscriminate debunking. They parade across the European landscape criticizing the sights and having romantic adventures with mysterious ladies, brigands, and lazzaroni. The only chapter of the book that promises

THE DODGE CLUB; OR, ITALY IN MDCCCLiX.

THE DESCENT OF VESUVIUS.

"The Descent of Vesuvius," from De Mille's *The Dodge Club* (1869).

TRAVELLING IN ITALY.

"Travelling in Italy," from De Mille's *The Dodge Club* (1869).

to deal with art turns out to be nothing but an elaborate, parodic chapter heading followed by a long account in brackets of why the chapter itself was never written. Here is the part of the heading that deals with art, and a sample of the explanation that follows:

Remarks on Art.—THE RENAISSANCE.—THE EARLY PAINTERS: CIMABUE, GIOTTO, PERUGINO, RAFFAELE SANZIO, MICHELANGELO BUONAROTTI.—THE TRANSFIGURATION.—THE MOSES OF MICHELANGELO.—BELLINI.—SAINT PETER'S, AND MORE PARTICULARLY THE COLONNADE.—THE LAST JUDGMENT.—DANTE.—THE MEDIEAEVAL SPIRIT.—EFFECT OF GOTHIC ART ON ITALY AND ITALIAN TASTE.—COMPARISON OF LOMBARD WITH SICILIAN CHURCHES.—TO WHAT EXTENT ROME INFLUENCED THIS DEVELOPMENT.—THE FOSTERING SPIRIT OF THE CHURCH.—ALL MODERN ART CHRISTIAN.—WHY THIS WAS A NECESSITY.—FOLLIES OF MODERN CRITICS.—REYNOLDS AND RUSKIN.—HOW FAR POPULAR TASTE IS WORTH ANY THING.—CONCLUDING REMARKS OF A MISCELLANEOUS DESCRIPTION.

[There! as a bill of fare I flatter myself that the above ought to take the eye. It was my intention, on the departure of the Club from Rome, to write a chapter of a thoroughly exhaustive character. . . . I have finally decided to enlarge the chapter into a book, which I will publish after I have given to the world my "History on the Micmacs," "Treatise on the Greek Particles," . . . "Transactions of the Saco Association for the Advancement of Human Learning, particularly Natural Science" (consisting of one article written by myself on "the Toads of Maine") and "Report of the 'Kennebunkport, Maine, United Congregational Ladies' Benevolent City Missionary and Mariners' Friend Society,'" which will all be out some of these days, I don't know exactly when.] (88)

DeMille's strained wit reads in the long run like Twain without irony or tension, without the sense of a restless intelligence that animates the pages of *The Innocents Abroad*. His narrative provides an excellent idea of what an account of the *Quaker City* cruise might have been if it had been written by someone without Twain's skill and ambition.

By the time Twain came to write *The Innocents Abroad*, male American chroniclers and humorists had long been using the experiences of Europe and European travel as vehicles for working out independent relations with high culture and honorable positions in American society for men whose personal and professional choices distanced them from traditional male roles. Each of the writers I have examined in this section took on at least some portion of this task, but none of them with the long-term cultural effect of Twain in *The Innocents Abroad*. The reasons for this, I will argue, lie to some extent at least in Twain's ability to combine the techniques and concerns of the earlier chroniclers and humorists in a single text, to use Europe to inform and entertain his audience, and to provide them with several alternative versions of American manhood.

The Innocents Abroad

This book is the record of a pleasure trip. If it were the record of
a solemn scientific expedition, it would have about it that gravity,
that profundity, and that impressive incomprehensibility which
are so proper to works of that kind, and withal so attractive.
(*Twain*, The Innocents Abroad)

The first sentence of Twain's preface to *The Innocents Abroad* is straightforward and impersonal. It makes a modest documentary claim for the book, suggesting that it will be a "record of a pleasure trip," a testimony to a pleasant experience, a chronicle of leisure and enjoyment. The second sentence gradually introduces the narrator. The word *solemn* begins to suggest a wry judgmental voice; the highly rhetorical, self-important rhythm of the middle of the sentence ("that gravity, that profundity, and that impressive incomprehensibility"), which lists three abstract qualities and qualifies the last, eight-syllable one as "impressive," would carry a hint of self-mockery even if the final quality it mentions were actually desirable; the last four words, including the comically archaic *withal* and the incongruous and inappropriate *attractive*, confirm the narrator's impish tone by affirming a certain distance between him and his language, a necessary gap for the development of humor, whether parody, burlesque, or subtle irony.

Early reviews confirm the book's double identity as an innovative travel chronicle and a humorous work. "It is so different from any narrative of travel that ever was written before," opines the Buffalo *Express*, which could be expected to present Twain's own view of the matter, since he was one of its owners. "It would be a great mistake," the reviewer goes on to say,

> to suppose that the book is just a big package of Mark Twain's jokes, to be read with laughter, and for the sake of laughter. It is the panorama of Europe and the Holy Land as they were seen by one who went abroad with no illusions; who carried about with him a shrewd pair of American eyes, and used them to get his own impression of things, as they actually presented themselves, not as he had been taught to expect them; who bore with him, moreover, as acute an appreciation of sham and humbug as his sense of the humorous and ludicrous was keen.[21]

A more independent reviewer, in the Boston *Daily Evening Transcript*, had a similar reaction, remarking that it was "not . . . a merely funny book," but "a very full and matter-of-fact record of travel in Europe" by "a shrewd, quick-witted person, who . . . saw things as they were."[22] Bret Harte, in the *Overland Monthly*, was even more perspicacious about the book's multiple identities. The book comes, Harte writes, "like a joyous revelation" amid the ponderous tomes of the American Book Company. "Hardly a line . . . is not readable," and Twain's comic account has done "the suffering world" the further service of "chok[ing] off and prevent[ing] the enthusiastic chronicling of the voyage by any of his fellow-passengers, who may have been sentimentally inclined." Twain's humor is not merely lighthearted, however, nor is his tone consistent. Many of his comic passages are based on his speaker's "grotesque rage" at his shipmates, and the criticism that underlines them is often bitter. Furthermore, "when 'Mark Twain' is not simulating indignation, he is *really* sentimental," and when he is not mocking his fellow tourists he is himself following "his guide and guide-books with a simple, unconscious fidelity." It is the old Old Europe that he visits, the familiar sights that attract his scorn or his admiration. "His remarks," Harte concludes, "might have been penciled on the margins of Murray."[23]

Twain, in other words, had multiple agendas in *The Innocents Abroad*. As I have suggested, he wanted to consolidate his reputation as a popular writer, and at the same time move beyond the limitations of strictly Western humor. To accomplish this he set out to write an accessible and comic account of an elite experience for a wide audience that was predominantly provincial, and certainly not elite itself. In addition, as a Westerner and a humorist with aspirations to something like gentility, or at least to a close relationship with it, he needed to invent a role for himself that would allow him access to respectable drawing rooms and prestigious magazines without identifying him as a member of a genteel coterie of "feminized" artists and intellectuals. As a midcentury, middle-class American male, furthermore, he was anxious about retaining his boyish-manly identity. And finally, as an aspiring literary artist and a curious, inquiring intellectual he was eager to see the great works and sights of other times and places and ready to criticize or enjoy them or both, as his own honest judgment would dictate.

These agendas produced a work that has fascinated readers and critics since its publication. Unlike every other work in this study, it was an enormous popular success.[24] Unlike most of them, too, it has generated a great deal of first-rate critical commentary. Dewey Ganzel and Daniel Morley McKeithan have chronicled its genesis; Henry Nash Smith, James M. Cox, and Forrest Robinson, to name only the best of many, have studied its significance for Twain's development as a literary artist and a "consciousness" (Robinson's term); Richard Bridgman has supplemented the work of Twain's general biographers in his study of the place of travel and travel writing in Twain's sense of himself and his work throughout his career.

Because of these differences, my task in what remains of this chapter is rather different, too, from what I have done in other chapters. Readers of nineteenth-century American literature hardly need to be introduced to *The Innocents Abroad*; students of Twain do not need to be taken once more through arguments already made by other critics. What I propose to do, therefore, is to focus rather more narrowly here than elsewhere, to concentrate specifically on the European sections of the book and the ways in which Twain used his European experience to create a male persona and work out a relationship to art. Instead of providing an overview of Twain's life and his career, in other words, I will attempt to situate the larger part of an important text and two of the projects it embodies in the context of travel, travel writing, and American humor. The result should be a fuller sense than has previously been available both of how the text participates in its culture and of how Samuel Clemens's creation of Mark Twain as a public figure and a narrative voice was a historical and cultural as well as a formal and aesthetic act.

Despite the continuing popularity of *The Innocents Abroad*, we do not automatically associate the name of Mark Twain with the idea of Europe. Unlike Fuller or James, his early life was not dominated by European texts and images and the longing to visit the "sacred" works and sites of the Old World. Placed alongside Adams, Howells, and James, his contemporaries, or Wharton, his successor by a generation, he stands out as the plain American among quasi-foreigners, the creator of Tom Sawyer and Huck Finn, the evoker of Nevada, California, and the Mississippi, rather than Paris or Venice or Mont Saint-Michel. In his study of Twain and James, for example, Henry Seidel Canby characterized his two subjects as the "Turn West" and the "Turn East Americans."[25] In fact, Leslie Fiedler was closer to the truth when he suggested that Twain's "literary career [was] marked by an almost obsessive concern with Europe and the quest for American identity."[26] From *The Innocents Abroad* to *A Connecticut Yankee* and beyond, Twain's work is pervaded by the problem of Europe, whether it is embodied in contemporary Europe, in Scott-inspired Southern fantasies of chivalry and glamour,[27] in Malory's version of the Arthurian Middle Ages, or in Huck's "Duke" and "Dauphin." Like the chroniclers and humorists who preceded him, Twain felt compelled to confront Europe and empowered to use it for his own particular purposes. Like Taylor, Brown, Dorr, and Witmer, he used it as a stage for producing and performing a more-or-less fabricated, more-or-less ideal self; like Haliburton, Curtis, Browne, and DeMille, he took up a humorous attitude toward it and used this attitude to help him develop an ironic voice and a complex narrative persona.[28]

As I have suggested, one of Twain's purposes in combining generic features of the travel chronicle and travel humor was to imagine a specifically masculine version of the respectable, knowledgeable, and well-informed American writer as artist and to propose a reasonable relation to Europe for this figure.[29] He does this both negatively and positively in

The Innocents Abroad, following the humorists in making fun of inappropriate attitudes and using the conventions of the travel chronicle to demonstrate more acceptable ones.

Twain's shipmates provide the most obvious examples of undesirable roles and inappropriate relations to Europe. These include such buffoons as the self-miseducated "Oracle," who "reads a chapter in the guidebooks, mixes the facts all up, with his bad memory, and then goes off to inflict the whole mess on somebody as wisdom which has been festering in his brain for years, and which he gathered in college from erudite authors who are dead, now, and out of print" (56). If the Oracle uses his half-baked misconceptions of Europe to parade his own supposed erudition, the Interrogation Point makes a show of his ignorance and gullibility by posing innumerable questions and believing all the answers, no matter how inane. This ignoramus is also, appropriately enough, the ship's great patriot, bragging to the British that "a couple of" American "gunboats could come here and knock Gibraltar in to the Mediterranean Sea" (57). These two are joined by the uncommonly prolific "Poet Lariat," who writes execrable verses for every occasion and sends them to local notables, embarrassing the rest of the ship's company (57).

It is not only grotesques like these, however, whose attitudes Twain criticizes. The general run of his companions come in for their share of increasingly bitter derision as he comes more and more to resent their self-satisfied middle-class complacency. He describes them collectively and at a certain comic remove in his famous invention of the Pilgrim Bird at the Marseilles Zoo.

> This fellow stood up with his eyes shut and his shoulders stooped forward a little, and looked as if he had his hands under his coat tails. Such tranquil stupidity, such supernatural gravity, such self-righteousness, and such ineffable self-complacency as were in the countenance and attitude of that gray-bodied, dark-winged, bald-headed, and preposterously uncomely bird! (82)

And other, more differentiated travelers embody other attitudes and modes of behavior to be avoided. There is the loud American who orders wine "with a royal flourish," announces that he never dines without it "(which was a pitiful falsehood)," and "look[s] around upon the company to bask in the admiration he expect[s] to find in their faces" (81). There are the Old Travelers, who "prate and drivel and lie," "brag, and sneer, and swell, and soar," all on the strength of having "'been here before'" (89). And there are, finally, and most pitifully and tellingly, those poor Americans who take up foreign customs, pepper their conversation with

"POET LARIAT."

"Poet Lariat," from Twain's *The Innocents Abroad* (1869).

foreign phrases, and make themselves into "thing[s]" that are "neither male nor female, neither fish, flesh, nor fowl" (185).

These examples suggest that the American man who wished to cut a decent figure in Europe would need to avoid solemnity, braggadocio, and pretense of any kind; he would not make himself conspicuous by his ignorance or his arrogance; he would neither deny his nation nor boast of its superiority. So far this sounds like a recipe for unobtrusive, inoffensive traveling, for passing through Europe without raising a hackle or leaving a mark or asserting anything at all. This is not what Twain had in mind. The roles that he and his friends assume provide positive masculine alternatives to the foolishness and self-importance of the pilgrims and the buffoons. None of these roles is new; all of them were anticipated by the chroniclers and travel humorists who preceded Twain. Twain makes them his own by developing them with comic verve and by combining them in an uneasy, unsimplified tension.

The most conventionally Twainian of these roles, the one that dominates the first two-thirds of the book, is that of the grown-up boy on a lark, the commonsensical, no-nonsense, ordinary, red-blooded, American out to enjoy himself in foreign parts without compromising his masculinity or his Americanness by making any concessions to foreign values. Twain claims this role explicitly for himself and his friends, whom he calls "the boys" (60) or "the sinners," as if they were a gang of school friends or barroom cronies.[30] Their escapades combine boyish foolery with a kind of insouciant, unthinking sense of their "natural" superiority as white American males. They frolic in Tangier, for example, among picturesque and exotic "natives"—"stalwart Bedouins," "stately Moors," "Jews whose fathers fled hither centuries upon centuries ago," "original genuine Negroes," "howling dervishes and a hundred breeds of Arabs" (62). They comment on the age and the "orientalness" (62) of it all, on the "ugliness" of the women (69) and the "savagery" of all the inhabitants (69–70). They torment and patronize their guides and snicker among themselves like a gang of high school boys on a field trip (229–32).

Perhaps their greatest adventure comes when they defy a quarantine order in the Piraeus harbor, "[steal] softly ashore in a small boat" (270), and set out overland to visit the Acropolis, stealing grapes along the way. They reach their goal at last, attempt to break down the gate and then to climb it, but are reduced to bribing the guards to admit them. Once inside, they are genuinely moved by the ruins: Twain meditates on the great heroes who preceded him here, follows consciously in the footsteps of the apostle Paul, and allows himself some romantic description of the Parthenon by moonlight. They are not classical scholars or pedants, however, and Twain is careful to note that they did not know the names of the buildings until a guide told them what they were (273). On the way back to the ship they steal more grapes and variously confront and dodge a number of guards and sentinels. Twain's comments on these events foreshadow those he will attribute to Huck or Tom later in his career. "I was not afraid," he writes. "I only felt that it was not right to steal grapes. All the more so when the owner was around—and not only around, but with his friends around also" (277). Finally, "just as the earliest tinges of the dawn flushed the eastern sky and turned the pillared Parthenon to a broken harp hung in the pearly horizon," they reach the harbor, board the ship, and begin gloating about their adventures (278).

Taking into account both the escapade and the text that describes it, we can see Twain claiming a complex role combining the high-spirited, devil-may-care, and lawbreaking youth; the travel chronicler; the humorist; and the educated writer. He enjoys the adventure, describes parts of it with a certain comic irony and others with something approaching reverence. His description of the return to the harbor uses Homeric allusion to bow in the direction of high culture; his exultation at successfully dodging the police and managing to see the most important monument of ancient times "in its most attractive aspect" (278) asks the reader to admire his boldness and his touristic dedication. All of these gestures and attitudes combine with Twain's treatment of the Portuguese in the Azores, the mixed population of Tangier, as well his fellow tourists and the guides and hotel keepers of France and Italy, to project a persona made powerful and prestigious by his race, gender, class, and nationality.

The rest of the text reinforces this persona by adding several other roles, as well as several dimensions to those of the boy, the chronicler, the humorist, and the professional writer. In the set pieces on Abelard and Héloïse, Petrarch and Laura, for example, as well as many passages on the Catholic church, Twain can be seen as a supporter of common-sense middle-class Protestant American family values, as opposed to ritualistic mumbo jumbo, or "the nauseous sentimentality that would enshrine for our loving worship a dastardly seducer like Pierre Abelard" (117). In the legend of Count Luigi (165–69), the "newspaper" account of an evening at the Coliseum with the gladiators, Christians, and lions ("The whole to conclude with a chaste and elegant GENERAL SLAUGHTER!" [221]) and many other passages he shows himself a master of the familiar midcentury genres of literary parody and burlesque.[31] In a famous comparison of Italy and the United States, he turns social critic, imagining a Roman peasant marveling at the fact that in America a rich man may become "a legislator, a governor, a general, a senator, no matter how ignorant an ass he is" (211). And in an infamous interval in Paris he offers near-rapturous praise of "Napoleon III, Emperor of France!" (101).

Like other male chroniclers, Twain uses Europe as material for writing, as a context for developing ideas and values, and as a stage upon which to create and perform versions of himself as an American man. Like the humorists, he also uses European travel as an occasion for satire and social commentary, as well as an opportunity to mock false values and praise true ones. The only problem with all of this, and a very fruitful problem it turns out in the end to be, is that the roles that Twain invents and enacts as traveler, chronicler, and humorist are not all easily compatible. We have seen a number of male travel chroniclers and humorists responding in different ways to the challenge of inventing a masculine role for the midcentury American writer and/or intellectual. Taylor and Brown, for example, opt for different versions of professionalism;

DeMille glorifies the carefree prankster, and Dorr and Witmer modify this persona with their serious comments on art and history; Haliburton, Curtis, and Browne all create comic travelers who help define proper roles and decent behavior at least in part by contrast. What we have not seen until Twain is the way in which all these roles necessarily contaminate each other in experience, how none of them, in other words, can be played out in total isolation from the others.

Take, for example, the passage quoted earlier, in which the narrator describes the foolishness of the Oracle and the Interrogation Point. Here it is clear that he is a sensible, superior person, in a perfect position to mock and criticize these ineffectual men. As soon as he is through describing the Interrogation Point, however, the narrator goes on to recount the beginning of his own excursion to Tangier in terms that seem to me slightly equivocal and self-mocking. This tone is derived from Twain's juxtaposition of the vocabulary of vacation with that of military prowess. "Nothing can be more absolutely certain than that we are enjoying ourselves," he writes as he and his friends "speed . . . over these sparkling waters, and breathe . . . the soft atmosphere" (58). It is a tourist dream, interrupted only when they steam "recklessly" past "the frowning fortress of Malabat," whose parading troops cause them nary "a twinge of fear." "I suppose we really do not know what fear is" (58), Twain remarks, so grandly that he can only be making small fun of his party's smugness. This mocking tone becomes even more evident when thoughts of the martial reputation of the chief of the Malabat garrison remind Twain of his own reputation for gallantry with the ladies and induce him to tell the story of his glove purchase in Gibraltar. Here, as is well known, Twain comes off looking every bit as foolish as the Oracle or the Poet Lariat, discarding the overpriced, ill-fitting, and shoddily made gloves he had been lured into buying by the assiduous personal attention of the charming Gibraltar shop girl. In the course of a couple of pages he has depicted himself as a mature traveler, the sophisticated critic of some of his more foolish shipmates, as a smug and perhaps overconfident tourist, and as a would-be Lothario who was sold a bill of goods in the shape of a shoddy pair of gloves.

Similar modifications of persona occur at the beginning of the journey, when Twain smugly watches a succession of other passengers lurch from the cabin to the rail to relieve their seasickness, only to be scolded himself by several of the ship's "captains" for smoking in the wrong place, meddling with sensitive instruments, and being generally underfoot in a troublesome boyish way. They are repeated in the opposite direction in chapter 13, when a comic sequence involving the guide Billfinger, dubbed Ferguson, is followed by the genuinely solemn comments on the greatness of Napoleon III, issuing from an authoritative narrative voice.

Perhaps the most comic concatenation of roles, though, occurs when the presumably democratic pilgrims are introduced to the autocratic Tsar of Russia and find themselves awed, impressed, and instinctively deferential. Twain is as impressed as the others by the Tsar's power ("a man who could open his lips and ships would fly through the waves, locomotives would speed over the plains, . . . and a countless multitude of men would spring to do his bidding" [312]), the tastefulness of his palaces, and the friendly condescension of the grand duke and the royal ladies. He modifies his awestruck attitude in three ways, though. First, he pretends to a kind of comic oh-gosh Tom-Sawyer ignorance: "I supposed that Emperors were terrible people. I thought they never did any thing but wear magnificent crowns and red velvet dressing-gowns with dabs of wool sewed on them in spots, and sit on thrones and scowl at the flunkies and the people in the parquette, and order Dukes and Duchesses off to execution" (315–16). Second, he provides a commentary on his own sedate behavior in his character as one of the boys. "If this man sprained his ankle," he marvels, "a million miles of telegraph would carry the news . . . if he dropped lifeless where he stood, his fall might shake the thrones of half a world!" But then he slyly goes on, "If I could have stolen his coat I would have done it. When I meet a man like that, I want something to remember him by" (312–13). Finally, he describes the company's solemn address to the Tsar, written with great care by a committee of which he was a member, and beginning: "We are a handful of private citizens of America, traveling simply for recreation—and unostentatiously, as becomes our unofficial state" (320). If the address is painfully correct and perhaps even embarrassingly self-abasing in its development, its use by the *Quaker City* crew is both hilarious and not-so-subtly critical of their bosses, the passengers, including Twain. First they put on a mock visit to the court, repeating the address, which the mock Tsar finds ridiculous ("'Then what the devil did you come for?'" he asks after they've told him they are only "private citizens" [321]). Then they repeat its words in all manner of incongruous settings.

> Grimy sailors came down out of the foretop placidly announcing themselves as "a handful of private citizens of America, *traveling simply for recreation* and unostentatiously," etc.; the coal passers moved to their duties in

the profound depths of the ship, explaining the blackness of their faces and their uncouthness of dress, with the reminder that *they* were "a handful of private citizens . . . traveling simply for recreation," etc. (321)

What Twain accomplished by all this slipperiness is something I would call a rhetoric of noncommittal enthusiasm.[32] Twain's way of being a man and a writer, a cigar-smoking, cussing "sinner" and a respectable bourgeois husband, father, and dinner guest was to keep his audiences and his constituencies guessing by playing every role with brief, sincere commitment and then undercutting the commitment, the sincerity, and the role itself. Lesser writers and lesser artists, like Taylor and Browne, and men whose agendas differed from Twain's, like Brown and Dorr, chose simpler figures to emulate, simpler personas to write themselves into. By inventing a male narrator and protagonist who was at the same time enthusiastic and skeptical, boyish and mature, scornful of pretense but sensitive to what he considered genuine feeling and beauty, self-assertive in a "manly," "American" way but also quick to recognize the foolishness of some of his own actions and attitudes, Clemens/Twain created a slippery social and rhetorical position that could not be dismissed by either the businessmen, patriots, and farmers who patronized the American Book Company or the aesthetes and intellectuals of the more conventional literary establishment.

European travel and the challenge that European high culture represented tended to make American men feel insecure. Travel itself was an unproductive activity; many of the diversions European travel offered were female coded. Twain took advantage of this insecurity to explore and criticize the ways in which American men responded to cultural pressures. In this sense Europe was as much a convenience for him as it was a cultural imperative: it provided ideal conditions in which to develop an effective literary and social persona.

In theory, then, Europe was simply the most suitable, serendipitously available setting for an intellectual and a social project that Twain very much needed to complete if he was to become a successful writer. If the *Quaker City* had never sailed, he might well have carried it out in reports and stories of life in New York, Boston, Newport, or Saratoga. What Europe had that these places lacked, however, what *did* impose itself on Twain as it had on earlier chroniclers and humorists, was art. How was the American male to take honest account of European art without caving in to the authority of tradition, experts, and guidebook writers?

European art was a hard nut for Twain to crack, and it is fair to say that his solution to the problems it posed was less original than his response to the threat posed by the European experience in general. Twain's early reports on art in New York suggest that he was receptive to the charms of painting. Church's *Heart of the Andes*, for example, takes a strong hold on his imagination. "I have seen it several times," he writes to his brother Orion, "but it is always a new picture,—*totally* new—you seem to see nothing the second time which you saw the first."[33] There were a number of obstacles, however, to his parallel enjoyment of art in Europe. First, there was the association of art with a social system repugnant to any right-thinking democrat. Twain admitted that some of the "miles of paintings" in the Louvre were "beautiful," but their beauty was spoiled for him by the social structures they reflected.

> They carried such evidences about them of the cringing spirit of those great men that we found small pleasure in examining them. Their nauseous adulation of princely patrons was more prominent to me and chained my attention more surely than the charms of color and expression which are claimed to be in the pictures. (109)

The painters, in other words, were not "manly" in the independent American sense, but were "cringing" dependents of the hereditary aristocracy.

Worse still, the whole art establishment appears to have been subservient to the Roman Catholic church, one of the great demons of Twain's and many other Americans' conception of Europe. Not only were the subjects religious ("We have seen thirteen thousand St. Jeromes, and twenty-two thousand St. Marks, and sixteen thousand St. Matthews, and sixty thousand St. Sebastians" [188]), but the paintings themselves, together with countless other art treasures, usually belonged to the church if not to some member of the aristocracy and were therefore in a sense contaminated by the massive immorality represented by the contrast between ecclesiastical wealth and widespread misery among the people.

In addition to these political and moral factors, there was the problem of the art appreciators. Twain suspected them first, and doubtless correctly, of parroting the cant phrases of the guidebooks. "It vexes me," he writes, "to hear people talk so glibly of 'feeling,' 'expression,' 'tone,' and those other easily acquired and inexpensive technicalities of art that make such a fine show in conversations concerning pictures" (152). He was also impatient with what we would nowadays call the undecidability of art interpretation and took the fact that two people might have incompatible interpretations of the same painting as a sign of the essential dishonesty of interpretation itself, since it cannot be counted upon to produce the single, reliable truth (153). Finally, Twain deplored the role of fashion in judgments of art. With typical overstatement, he writes that actually liking a painting was an infallible sign that it was "*not* a beautiful picture" by current standards, and a pretty good sign that it was a product of the discredited Renaissance, a term always pronounced with a sneer by guides and "used to signify what was at best but an imperfect rejuvenation of art" (189). "The Renaissance pictures suit me very well," he goes on, "though sooth to say its school were too much given to painting real men and did not indulge enough in martyrs" (189).

How, then, to respond honestly and independently to works of art that are almost inextricably bound up with a deplorable history and a set of social arrangements one finds unacceptable and that tend to elicit from their viewers the callow cant of fashion and received opinion rather than any honest reaction? The answer is implied in the question. One should simply look at them with unprejudiced American eyes and trust one's "natural" judgment. Tradition and reputation will necessarily have a role in what one sees and where one sees it, but the act of judging should be independent. Twain remembers Raphael's *Transfiguration* partly because of its reputation as "the first oil painting in the world," partly because of its placement in a room by itself, and "partly because it was wonderfully beautiful."

> The colors are fresh and rich, the "expression," I am told, is fine, the "feeling" is lively, the "tone" is good, the "depth" is profound, and the width is about four and a half feet, I should judge. It is a picture that really holds one's attention; its beauty is fascinating. (239)

Twain suggests in this passage that although he can deploy cant phrases (and judge dimensions) with the best of them, his valuation of the picture rests neither on jargon nor on measurement but on its indescribable power over his "attention." This is the usual, common-sense solution to the problem of art appreciation, and as a response to guidebook-parroting tourists it is not a bad one. Rather than coming to terms, however, with the questions of history and authority posed by European art in particular, it tends to equate art with nature and treat paintings as if they were actual landscapes or people.[34]

The Innocents Abroad does a brilliant job of creating a protean narrative persona, "a consciousness," as Robinson puts it, "irremediably at odds with itself, moving at great speed between mental states, struggling quite in vain to find a comfortable point of vantage on a deeply unsettling experience."[35] It is just this lack of comfort, I would argue, that gives the book its bite, its edge, and its advantage over the chronicles and humorous works that preceded it. Twain's narrator thinks he knows who he is (one of the "boys") and who he does not want to be (one of the "pilgrims"), but his categories keep slipping. The boys can be foolish and even occasionally cruel, as jingoistic as the Interrogation Point and as self-satisfied as any pilgrim. The pilgrims, however, are certainly dignified and respectable, but joining them would mean denying his own high spirits and sacrificing most of his pleasure for the sake of their version of spiritual and intellectual "improvement." The great strength of *The Innocents Abroad* is precisely that it did not define a single masculine persona who would reconcile the contradictory exigencies of independence, respectability, authorhood, industry, leisure, and work. Instead, Twain suggested that the only way that a male artist in his culture could avoid the eventual sanctimoniousness of a Howells or a Taylor on the one hand and the triviality of *The Dodge Club* on the other was to embody these contradictions. Rather than opting for the serious purposefulness of the realists, as Bell describes it, in other words, Twain in *The Innocents Abroad* preferred to develop the rhetorical deviousness that Leverenz finds in Emerson and Whitman. He stumbled into conventionality only when confronted with European art. Faced with "masterpieces," he did not learn from them, like Widmer, but judged them according his own "natural" criteria, implying that his good old Western American taste was as good as any canting connoisseur's. In a sense it was: taste follows fashion, and the history of taste shows that the treasures of one generation often become the kitsch of another. In another, equally important sense, however, it was not: taste is learned; beauty is not a natural category but a cultural product, so to claim that one can perceive beauty with the uneducated "natural" eye is simply to deny the education that that natural eye has already received. It is a fruitful contradiction, and one that Twain unfortunately missed his chance to incorporate into his account of his European experience in *The Innocents Abroad.*

Epilogue: After the Innocents in Europe

The Innocents Abroad does not end in Europe, nor do Mark Twain's travels end with *The Innocents Abroad.* Despite a number of memorable set pieces in the last section of the book and in *A Tramp Abroad,*[36] however, the important work of Twain's travel writing was done in his descriptions of the innocents in Europe.

As Leverenz and Bell have demonstrated, the task of reconciling con-

"American Men in Europe," from Twain's *The Innocents Abroad* (1869).

ventional "manliness" with a literary vocation was a daunting one all
through the nineteenth century. In Twain's generation James sidestepped
it by retreating to Europe, Howells succumbed to it by turning himself
into the ultra-respectable "Dean" of American letters, and Adams dealt
with it, as we will see, by a series of moves that repeatedly placed him on
the privileged margins of influence and power. Among the poets, Whitman, sixteen years older than Twain, exploited the challenge to best advantage, and among prose writers Twain responded in the most productive way by creating a series of not necessarily compatible personas and a
prose style that jumps from mode to mode with such agility that it is
impossible to pin it down. He accomplished this by exploiting the multiple voices available to the travel writer, as Fuller had done, and by following a whole line of male travel chroniclers and humorists in using the
experience of Europe as an occasion for staging a series of alternative and
experimental selves.

CHAPTER EIGHT

Henry James, or
The Merchant of Europe

It's a complex fate, being an American, and one of
the responsibilities it entails is fighting against a
superstitious valuation of Europe.
(*Henry James*)

HOW MANY New Englanders may not have been brought to the Old World by the limpid, beautiful and delightful phrases of what we now call the early James?" Ford Madox Ford wondered in 1915. "What may not *Daisy Miller, The Four Meetings, A Passionate Pilgrim, Roderick Hudson,* or, for that matter, *The Spoils of Poynton,* have done to swell the receipts, in the 80s and the 90s, of the American touring agencies?"[1] Henry James as huckster? The Master, the supreme literary artist, the founder of high modernism, writing copy for American Express? It may sound unlikely, but James was in effect if not in intention a skilled practitioner of what his own Chad Newsome called "the art of advertisement."[2] His European "wares"[3] fueled his customer-readers' desire to travel and offered them the opportunity to buy into a version of cultural and social distinction that included not only familiarity with Europe but also the refined sensibility, the highly developed consciousness of James's traveling and writing persona. Selling his work helped pay James's bills; selling his point of view, persuading others to adopt his values and aspire to his heightened consciousness, helped confirm his distinguished cultural and social status and ratify the superiority of his class. James had an important personal and professional stake in one of the major projects of the nineteenth-century U.S. bourgeoisie, the conversion of earned or inherited liberal-republican economic privilege into class-based superiority justified by such intangible features as sensibility, good taste, and savoir faire.

Veblen analyzed the dynamics of this complex transaction in *The Theory of the Leisure Class,* arguing that modes of behavior and sets of values motivated by the privileged classes' need to convert excess time and money into prestige become standards of "decency" for entire cultures.[4] This is precisely what happened to Europe in the nineteenth-century

United States as the social benefits of "honorific waste" were added to the very real personal pleasures and satisfactions of European travel. The trip to Europe, a luxury made possible by the accumulation of excess capital, became a token of bourgeois respectability; travel abroad became a quest for social superiority, inadequately (but necessarily) represented by sheafs of souvenir photographs, samples of Italian silk and Parisian couture, and increased familiarity with art, music, and theater.

What James famously "inhaled" on his arrival in Europe, then, what he "appropriated" from his European experience (*L* 1:484), and what he sold to his readers was a version of what Pierre Bourdieu calls distinction. Following Veblen,[5] Bourdieu argues that the work of high- and even middle-brow culture is simultaneously to produce and to ratify social distinctions. A "taste" for the disinterested pleasures of art and literature, he believes, marks the social difference between people who have achieved a certain elegant distance from the demands of economic necessity and people whose time and attention are entirely absorbed by mercenary or domestic labor.[6] It masquerades as a personal characteristic, a distinguishing attribute of an individual, but it is in fact the product of cultural work, the effort of a socioeconomic class to perpetuate itself and to justify its privileges by acquiring what looks like a natural, inborn grace. This so-called grace manifests itself as knowledge, as sophistication, and, in the best of cases—in James himself, in some of his characters, and in his most appreciative readers—as heightened moral and aesthetic consciousness, all of which contribute to the production of class-based cultural power. What James and his contemporaries meant when they spoke of Europe, then, was a continent and a string of cities and landscapes and works of art, but also and perhaps most importantly a sense of cultural legitimacy, an opportunity to turn economic power into cultural power, to run dollars through the machinery of the tourist infrastructure and convert them into cultural capital.[7]

So Ford was right: James in his travel writing, and in the international fiction that grew out of it, helped perpetuate the idea that Europe could provide Americans with a certain distinction unavailable on these shores. This idea helped sell copy to magazines, magazines to readers, boat tickets, hotel rooms, and a wide range of travel products and services to an ever-increasing number of Americans.

But this is a far too simple account of James's relations to Europe, to travel, and to writing. James was a sincere, enthusiastic sharer of Europe's pleasures, as well as a frank exploiter of its literary and commercial potential. He loved Europe and travel with an unfeigned if not uncomplicated passion; he sincerely admired and deeply responded to European art, architecture, and landscape; he invested time and money in his European experience with the expectation of making it pay dividends; he transformed that experience into prose and often into art and sold it; he promoted the superstitious valuation of Europe even while, and sometimes by, criticizing it.

James did all this in two overlapping stages. In his early years in Europe, between 1872 and 1884, he published approximately seventy-five European travel sketches and notes in American magazines and newspapers. He was at first very pleased to find a market for these products; his earliest travel sketches bear the marks of his fullest attention and care. As time went on, however, and James established himself as a writer of fiction and an artist, he grew "weary of writing articles about places, and mere potboilers of all kinds" (*L* 2:150–51). In early 1884 he declared that his travel sketches belonged "to a class of composition which I have left behind me today" (*L* 3:33). Between that time and his death, in 1916, he published only six more European sketches and nine very brief "Notes from London."

James's evaluation of his early travel writing in the light of his growing fame (and, I would wager, of his recent, rather dreary, little tour in France)[8] is perfectly understandable if a little unfair. Travel sketches might have boiled the pot in 1872 and 1873, but from 1874 on James made far more money from his fiction.[9] Furthermore, James's fiction shared a marketable subject with his travel writing. Between "Chester" (1872) and the last installment of "En Province" (1884), James was developing the international theme in some seventeen short works of fiction, including the epoch-making *Daisy Miller* (1878),[10] and three full-length novels: *Roderick Hudson* (1875), *The American* (1878), and *The Portrait of a Lady* (1880).

In what follows I will first look at the place of travel and of Europe in James's experience and then discuss his participation in the production and marketing of Europe as it manifests itself in his travel writing and his fiction, focusing on the way he both constructs and represents a particular American experience and trying to tease out some of the meaning, for Americans, especially, of European travel and tourism toward the end of the nineteenth century.

JAMES IN EUROPE

Henry James, Jr., was genuinely moved by those European scenes and objects which his status as a "native" of the James family, a highly Eurocentric unit of a Eurocentric class, had prepared him to appreciate. Of all the James children, it was he who drank most deeply of the "sense of Europe" that permeated his boyhood home, he who most fervently believed in "our constant dream of 'educational' relief, of some finer kind of social issue, through Europe," he who learned most thoroughly the lesson that "in Europe . . . there was Art."[11] His early, personal conquest of Europe and his "reeling," "moaning" arrival in Rome on his first visit in 1869 (*L* 1:160) prefigure a lifelong relationship compounded of manifest pleasures, latent satisfactions, and professional exploitation.

The student of James's life and letters is struck again and again by his zest for travel and his wholehearted enjoyment of the European scene. A stroll through the Oxford colleges in the spring of 1869, for example, lives up so well to James's expectations that he reports it to his brother William in near-Blakean terms.

> It was a perfect evening and in the interminable British twilight the beauty of the whole place came forth with magical power. There are no words for these colleges. As I stood last evening within the precincts of mighty Magdalen, gazed at its great serene tower and uncapped my throbbing brow in the wild dimness of its courts, I thought that the heart of me would crack with the fulness of satisfied desire. (*L* 1:110)

His descent into Italy from the heights of the Simplon Pass a few months later becomes, in a letter to his sister Alice, "a rapturous progress thro' a wild luxuriance of corn and vines and olives and figs and mulberries and chestnuts and frescoed villages and clamorous beggars and all the good old Italianisms of tradition," which he caps off in a conventional, banal, and totally satisfying manner by checking into "a vast, cool, dim, delicious hotel," bathing in a "great marble tank," "touch[ing] up [his] toilet," hiring a little boat with a striped awning, and stretching "out at my length" to be rowed "out to these delicious absurd old Barromean [*sic*] Islands" (*L* 1:128–29).

In both of these passages James is reveling in classic tourist experiences (and perhaps making gentle fun of himself for doing so). Communing at twilight with the beauty and the ghosts of an Oxford college or descending Goethe-like from "Northern" Switzerland into warm, noisy, fruitful, luxurious Italy were conventional elements in the tourist's dream of Europe, recommended by guidebook writers from Putnam to Allen and described in countless travel narratives throughout the century.[12] Such scenes were predictably thrilling to the susceptible twenty-six-year-old, and they continued to charm James all his life. He was just as thrilled by the Bay of Naples, seen from Sorrento ("like a vast pale-blue floor") in 1880 (*L* 2:282), and the pleasures and surprises of "a wondrous and absolutely incessant motor-tour" with Edith Wharton in the south of France in 1906 (*L* 4:444) as he had been by the classic moments of his first independent European tour.

In addition to such travel-poster satisfactions, James relished the sense of personal independence that his journeys provided. Freud suggests that much of the pleasure of travel derives from "early wishes" to escape from the pressures of family life and is therefore tinged with the sense of both empowerment and guilt associated with independent adulthood.[13] Dennis Porter explores this connection, suggesting that "most forms of travel . . . seem to promise or allow us to fantasize the satisfaction of desires that for one reason or another is denied us at home. As a result, not only is travel typically fueled by desire, it also embodies powerful transgressive impulses."[14] To travel is to escape, even to subvert, the authority of the father; it is to declare one's independence from the family and to establish one's personal authority on the basis of experience.

There can be no doubt that travel played all these roles for James. It clearly represented the explicit, literal consummation of long-cherished desires; it served as a vehicle for the young man's claim to personal independence and the feelings of guilt that so often accompany that claim, complicated in James's case by his continuing financial dependence on his parents; it symbolized and indeed continued throughout his life to create a feeling of artistic independence that fostered his imagination and stimulated his writing.

On his first independent trip to Europe he is happy, guilty, homesick, and self-assertive by turns. Many of his letters from this period begin by emphasizing his own faithfulness as a letter writer, underlining his connection to the distant family, and implicitly forestalling accusations of inattentiveness.[15] He alludes frequently to his homesickness but prides himself, too, on overcoming it. He appears to be suffering from chronic constipation, and he uses his recovery from this ailment as an index of his growing independence. His digestive complaints seem to be symptoms of the trauma of separation, and their disappearance coincides with his new-found sense of himself as an adult, running his own life without apology or guilt-induced somatic consequences. "There is no sudden change," he writes euphemistically to his sister, "no magical alleviation; but a gradual and orderly recurrence of certain phenomena which betray slow development of such soundness as ultimately may be my earthly lot" (*L* 1:96). "When a *man* [my emphasis] is able to breakfast out," he tells his brother

William a little self-consciously, "to spend a couple of hours at the British Museum and then to dine out and go to the play, and feel none the worse for it, he may cease to be oppressed by a sense of his physical wretchedness" (*L* 1:99).

To his siblings, then, James presents himself as a young man well on the way to healthy, independent maturity. His contemporaneous letters to his parents suggest somewhat slower progress in the same direction. Guilt is the central focus of these letters, and illness here functions as both an excuse for staying in Europe (at parental expense) and an index of filial piety.

> I feel very guilty and selfish in entertaining any projects which look in the least like extravagance. My beloved mother, if you but knew the purity of my motives! Reflection assures me, as it will assure you, that the only economy for me is to get thoroughly well and into such a state as that I can work. (*L* 1:124)

"To have you think that I am extravagant with these truly sacred funds sickens me to the heart," he writes to his father, and then suggests that he is treating both his (guilt-induced?) heartsickness and his (psychosomatic?) physical symptoms by spending his father's money as prudently as possible.

> My constant aim is to economise and make my funds minister, not to my enjoyment—which may take care of itself—it wasn't assuredly for that I came hither—but to my plain physical improvement, for which alone I live and move. . . . I have quite got my £25's worth of flexibility in the back, of experience and insight into my condition. (*L* 1:115)

By the time he reaches Switzerland, some three months later, this strategy has worked: his health is much improved, and his sense of self is somewhat sturdier. He revels in good weather and physical exercise and boasts of walking thirty-three miles over the Simplon Pass.

The great pleasure, conscious and presumably unconscious, that James took in his European travels derived in part from the satisfaction of seeing long-dreamed-of classic works and scenes and in part from the exhilaration of establishing himself as an independent adult. It was augmented by the related opportunity travel provides for role-playing and the adoption of consciously constructed points of view. To be a traveler is necessarily to play a role, and James used his travels to experiment with a range of personas, from the "puling pining Yankee"(*L* 1:137) to the "critical amateur," the "cold-blooded stranger," the "brooding tourist," and the "sensitive stranger."[16]

At the age of sixteen he was already exploiting the freedom this experimentation entails. His correspondence with Thomas Sergeant Perry in 1859–1860 gave the young traveler the chance to write himself into several conventional roles and to practice seeing Europe from several conventionally defined positions. In his first letter from Geneva he is the sophisticated traveler, reporting briefly on a rough crossing and a brief sojourn in Paris, which he "devoted to the revisiting of certain familiar spots" (*L* 1:7). Later letters show him as the blasé and superior youth enduring the indignities of dancing school,[17] the well-traveled man of the world addressing a provincial stay-at-home,[18] the intrepid mountaineer crossing the Mer de Glace (*L* 1:22–24), the burlesque author ("'Arry Jeames") of travel romances ("High into the vast unclouded vault of Heving rose the Awb of Day. . . . Nowhere shone it brighter than on thy banks O! lovely Rhine!" [*L* 1:27]), and the serious writer of the kind of descriptive prose he would soon be incorporating in his short stories and travel sketches.[19] In a letter to his mother ten years later, he is still experimenting with personas and viewpoints, depicting himself as the enthusiastic appreciator of the "exquisite unutterable beauty" of painting in Florence, explaining Raphael's "three manners" and the paradox of the hint of ugliness in "M. Angelo's" sublime figures, while at the same time maintaining enough ironic distance to describe himself as a "poor vulgarian, catalogue in hand," and to ridicule the pleasure he takes in his own self-congratulatory connoisseurship: "Two of the other things that I most enjoy at the Uffizi are a magnificent Albert Dürer and a most celestial Memling or Hemling—or whatever it may be. I enjoy immensely standing before them murmuring invidiously, 'Ah que c'est bien Allemande [*sic*]—que c'est bien Flamand!'" (*L* 1:150–51).

James's pleasure in assuming and manipulating conventional roles does not diminish with age and fame. Thirteen years after playing the tourist-connoisseur in Florence, he savors the extraordinary privilege of the early-middle-aged writer commissioned to make a "little tour in France" and luxuriates in the traveler's power both to arrange scenes and experiences and to criticize them for not coming up to his expectations.

I came away [from the convent at Villeneuve-lès-Avignon], and wandered a little over the base of the hill, outside the walls. Small white stones cropped through the grass, over which low olive-trees were scattered. The afternoon had a yellow brightness. I sat down under one of the little trees,

on the grass—the delicate grey branches were not much above my head—
and rested, and looked at Avignon across the Rhône. It was very soft, very
still and pleasant, though I am not sure it was all I once should have expected of that combination of elements: an old city wall for a background,
a canopy of olives, and, for a couch, the soil of Provence.[20]

And at the end of his career he cultivates the last best (double) pose of all,
that of the Master, recalling in his prefaces the earnest young writer, la-
boring picturesquely in a series of perfect European rooms to create those
works for which he fervently hopes to be remembered.

> A benediction, a great advantage, as seemed to me, had so from the first
> rested on them, and to nurse them along was really to sit again in the high,
> charming, shabby old room which had originally overarched them and
> which, in the hot May and June, had looked out, through the slits of cool-
> ing shutters, at the rather dusty but ever-romantic glare of Piazza Santa
> Maria Novella.[21]

> My windows looked into the Rue de Luxembourg—since then meagrely
> re-named Rue Cambon—and the particular light Parisian click of the small
> cab-horse on the clear asphalt, with its sharpness of detonation between the
> high houses, makes for the faded page to-day a sort of interlineation of
> sound. (1058)

In the prefaces James claims the privilege of displaying his younger
creative self enjoying the sights, the sounds, the air, "the very odour"
of a densely "European" scene while distilling them into works of art.
The sweet, sad nostalgia of these scenes, associating the glamour of distant places and times with the prestige of successful creative work, projects a double image of their author as a working artist and a successful
writer and associates the privileged perspective of the occupant of
"rooms" in foreign cities with the authority of the Master surveying his
accomplishments.

Travel, travel writing, Europe, and the description of European experience provided James the occasion to cast himself in various roles, to try
himself out as various characters. If Europe provided a stage for James's
dramatic imagination, it also served as a field for the essentially economic
activity that Jean-Christophe Agnew calls acquisitive cognition, the accumulation of cultural, aesthetic, and spiritual capital.[22] In fact, James habitually described his travels as occasions to acquire large stocks of material at a good price and lay them by for future literary processing and
distribution. "I have spent little more than was needful for the full and

proper fruition of my enterprise," he wrote to his mother from Italy in 1879, and added that he had "got a great deal" in exchange. "Wait till I get home," he went on,

> and you behold the glittering treasures of my conversation—my fund of anecdote—my brilliant descriptive powers. I assure you, I'll keep the table in a roar. Your guests will forget to eat—and thus you'll get back your money.—To say nothing of my making your universal fortunes by the great impetus with which I shall have been launched into literature. (*L* 1:197)

James's early travels taught him to treat his disparate experiences and impressions as an ever-accumulating fund of intellectual and aesthetic capital, to be managed like an investment to produce the highest possible return. "I have quite given up the idea of making a few retrospective sketches of Italy," he wrote to his brother William. "I had far rather let Italy slumber in my mind untouched as a perpetual capital, whereof for my literary needs I shall draw simply the income" (*L* 1:208). And to the same correspondent, thirty-three years later, he made the implausible claim that he had "never travelled at all," and was not about to begin, since

> now, more and more, all such adventures present themselves in the light of mere agreeable *luxuries*, expensive and supererogatory, inasmuch as not resolving themselves into new material or assimilating with my little acquired stock, my accumulated capital of (for convenience) "international" items and properties. (*L* 4:271)

"Capital," "stock," "items," "property"—James never stopped thinking of his impressions of Europe as money in the bank. In the book he was working on when he died, *The Middle Years*, he persisted in describing the sights of London as so many negotiable securities.

> The great sought-out compositions, the Hampton Courts and the Windsors, the Richmonds, the Dulwiches, even the very Hampstead Heaths and Putney Commons, to say nothing of the Towers, the Temples, the Cathedrals and the strange penetrabilities of the City, ranged themselves like the rows of great figures in a sum, an amount immeasurably huge, that one would draw on if not quite as long as one lived, yet as soon as ever one should seriously get to work.[23]

So travel was delightful for James, it was instructive, and it was profitable. It made him happy, it gave him the opportunity to practice detached observation and construct various seeing and speaking personas for himself, and it provided him with a store of literary raw material. Travel has other, equally seductive, attractions, of course, including the irresponsible feeling of being on the move, the sense of doing something without in fact getting anything done, and the freedom to comment on the passing scene without taking the slightest responsibility for improving it.

All of these factors contributed to James's enjoyment of travel and of Europe, to his highly developed sense of place and his intense appreciation for both locatedness and displacement. "For there was the pattern and measure of all he was to demand," he wrote of himself; "just to *be* somewhere—almost anywhere would do—and somehow receive an impression or an accession, feel a relation or a vibration."[24] Like the true traveler, however, the constant if sublimated refugee from the demands and the expectations of familial—and national—authority, he liked places best when they were *somewhere else.* "He liked being 'away'—from wherever," Edwin Fussell tells us, "then he could feel homesick; so long as he was homesick he knew himself in good shape."[25] "The solution," he himself writes, "is . . . not to live, in short, where one *does* live! . . . I can work better in other places (especially abroad)."[26] He loved Europe—loved "abroad"—as a destination and as a refuge, a set of places with deep artistic, historical, and social roots where he could play the part of the rootless transient observer. He also loved the idea of himself in Europe, of the pleasures, the freedom, the privileges, and the cachet associated with aesthetic travel in the glory days of the high bourgeois Anglo-American gentry. The pleasures of Europe were heightened for James by his sense of it as an elsewhere, a "not-home" where he was not dominated by considerations of conventional and familial duty, and his sense of himself as being "in" a European setting and at the same time, at least until the crisis of World War I, resolutely not "of" it. Any sense of guilt that this irresponsibility may have engendered was offset by his sense that his experience of Europe was a valuable investment, acquired at great cost, which must be made to pay appropriate dividends. Europe for James, then, was never merely a place but always also a phantasm, a stock in trade, the ideal setting for his own imaginative life, to be sure, but also a commodity that he helped manufacture, promote, and sell.

THE MERCHANT OF EUROPE

Richard Brodhead has recently suggested that "the articulation of a new-style 'high' social class" in the years following the Civil War encouraged "the regimen of the upper-class vacation," the proliferation of "touristic or vacationistic prose," the heightened prestige of aesthetic experience, and a new understanding of "art" and "art appreciation" as self-justifying, autonomous activities.[27] James's central participation in the last two of these projects is universally acknowledged; his early production of "vacationistic prose" underlines the connection Brodhead proposes between the consumption of travel, the generation of social distinction, and the new prestige of art.

James's first travel sketches can be read both as superior visitors' guides to a string of North American resorts and attractions and as occasions for studied, "literary" composition. The very first of them exploits its readers' putative desire to learn about life at Saratoga while adopting a superior attitude toward its "shops," "sidewalks," "loafers," and "'boarders'" and indulging in passages of finely wrought, self-consciously artistic prose ("a region of shady forest drives, with a bright, broad-piazzaed hotel gleaming here and there against a background of mysterious groves and glades"; "The horizon undulates with an air of having it all its own way").[28] James's first sketches from Europe carry out a similar program, promoting at one and the same time their author's professional standing and cultural authority and their readers' sense of cultural and social prestige.

The speaker of James's first two European travel sketches is a connoisseur of landscape and architecture and an expert creator and packager of aesthetic experience. It is too bad, he writes, that Chester comes so early in the typical English itinerary, "for it is so rare and complete a specimen of an antique town, that the later-coming wonders of its sisters in renown . . . suffer a trifle by comparison."[29] Still, he goes on, "the first impressions of an observant American in England—of our old friend the sentimental tourist—stir up within him . . . a cloud of sensibility" (TS 7).

These sentences establish the speaker's authority as a knowledgeable traveler, and the actual situation of James's text in an American magazine suggests three overlapping roles for the reader, who is free to imagine him/herself as the intimate and experienced interlocutor implied by the word "our"; as the newly arrived "sentimental tourist," "observant," open to impressions, but lacking experience and perspective; or as the homebound reader.

In his travel sketches James creates a privileged relationship with Europe for each of these textual personas, endowing them with their own peculiar kind and degree of distinction. The speaker assumes the prestige of authority and experience, which he shares with his mute and complaisant addressee; the newly landed "sentimental tourist" is being introduced to Europe, thus gaining the status of an initiate; the reader is invited to envy the first-time traveler's opportunity to visit Europe and at the same time to adopt the superior attitude of the speaker and the addressee. All of these textual personas share and value the aura of distinction that the speaker creates through his language, his assumption of wide knowledge and education, and his detached view of the European scene.

The language of these sketches is consciously artful: their vocabulary and style claim distinction for their author and reader alike. The speaker assumes that his readers will savor a nice figure and a neat turn of phrase. He asks us, for example, to imagine "the civic consciousness" of Chester "sunning itself on the city's rim, and glancing at the little, swarming, towered and gabled town within" (*TS* 8). He describes the city's famous wall as "the gentlest and least offensive of ramparts" (*TS* 9) and its streets as constituting "a perfect feast of crookedness" (*TS* 10) and invites his readers to understand and enjoy phrases like "superincumbent veranda" (*TS* 13), "nether integuments" (*TS* 15), "*gros Jean comme devant*" (*TS* 25), and "*Stat magni nominis umbra*" (*TS* 11), recognize literary allusions ("the passing tribute of a sigh" [*TS* 13]), and make sense of references to Dickens, Eliot, Edgeworth, Kingsley, and Dr. Johnson.

If the speaker's language lays claim to the distinction associated with an artful prose style, a large vocabulary, and a wide range of reference, his whole attitude toward the European scene assumes a certain superior detachment. England is old, he writes, and "foreign," and by implication somewhat primitive. It is "a crowded country," with low roofs and not much "elbow-room" (*TS* 14). When it is not quaintly and conveniently embodying a type, the "population" can impinge unpleasantly on the tourist's aesthetic sensibilities, spoiling an otherwise pleasing scene.

> The English landscape is always a "landscape with figures." And everywhere you go, you are accompanied by a vague consciousness of the British child hovering about your knees and coat-skirts, naked, grimy, and portentous. (*TS* 15)

The speaker and the addressee in this passage are figures from another world, to whom the grimy "British child" is a vague annoyance, an unwelcome reminder of potential social unrest. So little does the speaker concern himself with the pressing problems of English politics, in fact, that they become for him a matter of aesthetics and taste rather than justice or conviction.

> Conservatism here has all the charm, and leaves dissent and democracy and other vulgar variations nothing but their bald logic. Conservatism has the cathedrals, the colleges, the castles, the gardens, the traditions, the associa-

tions, the fine names, the better manners, the poetry; Dissent has the dusky
brick chapels in provincial by-streets, the names out of Dickens, the uncertain tenure of the *h*, and the poor *mens sibi conscia recti*. (*TS* 17)

The speaker here invites his American friends to distinguish themselves
from their English cousins by virtue of their spacious homeland, where
the naked children of the poor do not dirty the coat skirts of the sentimental tourist, and from their American compatriots by virtue of their
aristocratic preference for the charm of conservatism over the vulgar,
shabby rectitude of democracy.

James's traveler acts out his privileged position, then, by maintaining
an aesthetic detachment from and a proud nationalistic superiority to the
social and political concerns of "foreign" peoples. He assumes, furthermore, that the primary purpose of Europe is to be at his own particular
disposal, to provide occasions for self-conscious meditation, self-important observation, and carefully constructed aesthetic experience.

Attending services at Chester Cathedral, for example, turns out to have
nothing to do with worship, prayer, or the affirmation of international
Christian community. Instead it provides the speaker with an opportunity to relate his refined feelings and sensations to his superior understanding of ecclesiastical history.

> English cathedrals, within, are apt at first to look pale and naked; but after
> a while, if the proportions are fair and the spaces largely distributed, when
> you perceive the light beating softly down from the cold clerestory and your
> eye measures caressingly the tallness of columns and the hollowness of
> arches, and lingers on the old genteel inscriptions of mural marbles and
> brasses; and, above all, when you become conscious of that sweet, cool
> mustiness in the air which seems to haunt these places, like the very climate
> of Episcopacy, you may grow to feel that they are less the empty shells of a
> departed faith than the abodes of a faith which is still a solid institution and
> "establishment." Catholicism has gone, but the massive respectability of
> Anglicanism is a rich enough substitute. (*TS* 16–17)

Like millions of tourists before and after him, James here treats the cathedral and its ceremonies as curious phenomena available for delectation
and analysis; he turns the church into a museum of art and history and
makes himself and his readers into detached flaneurs rather than earnest
worshipers.

Just as the cathedral provides matter for meditation, so the whole foreign scene provides occasions for aesthetic "composition"[30] and imagina-

tive adventure. A walk on Chester's ancient wall offers an excellent opportunity for James to compose a view of the cathedral which reveals its
architectural distinctiveness and makes it a figure for the structure of medieval English society and experience, and then to move on to paint a
modest mental watercolor of two picturesque towers whose juxtaposition
seems "designed" to attract the sensitive stroller's attention (*TS* 11). While
exploring Lichfield Close, James anticipates Proust's Marcel in composing an aesthetic experience for himself by observing the spires from different angles, and then uses the experience as the occasion for some finely
honed descriptive prose.

> You have not seen [all of Lichfield] till you have strolled and restrolled along
> the close on every side, and watched the three spires constantly change their
> relation as you move and pause. Nothing can well be finer than the combi-
> nation of the two lesser ones soaring equally in front, and the third riding
> tremendously the magnificently sustained line of the roof. At a certain dis-
> tance against the sky, this long ridge seems something infinite, and the great
> spire to sit astride of it like a giant mounted on a mastodon. Your sense of
> the huge mass of the building is deepened by the fact that though the cen-
> tral steeple is of double the elevation of the others, you see it, from some
> points, borne back in a perspective which drops it to half their stature, and
> lifts them into immensity. (*TS* 24–25)

In his sketch of Haddon Hall, a few pages later, James appropriates the
romantic precincts of the great house as the scene for a carefully contrived
aesthetic adventure, suggesting in the process that the really distinguished
pleasures of travel must be boldly sought and ruthlessly seized. The traveler in this passage is a hunter, a warrior, or even a sexual assailant; his
superiority partakes pretty clearly of male-coded power.

> To walk in quest of any object that one has more or less tenderly dreamed
> of, to find your way, to steal upon it softly, to see at last if it is church or
> castle, the tower-tops peeping above elms or beeches,—to push forward
> with a rush, and emerge, and pause, and draw that first long breath which
> is the compromise between so many sensations,—this is a pleasure left to
> the tourist even after the broad glare of photography has dissipated so many
> of the sweet mysteries of travel. (*TS* 25)

The traveler's quarry in this passage, the "object" of his "quest," is no
unsuspecting "native" village or rich pedestrian, but a perfect aesthetic
moment, to be translated into charming descriptive prose.

But I achieved my own sly pilgrimage in perfect solitude; and as I descried the gray walls among the rook-haunted elms, I felt, not like a tourist, but like an adventurer. I have certainly had, as a tourist, few more charming moments than some—such as any one, I suppose, is free to have—that I passed on a little ruined gray bridge which spans, with its single narrow arch, a trickling stream at the base of an eminence from which those walls and trees look down. (*TS* 25–26)

The effect of the language in these two passages is to conflate "charming moments" and forceful conquest and to glamorize both in the process. The dominance of the traveling class is acted out; the reader is invited to associate the passive appreciation of a perfect moment with the satisfactions of conquest. That James is being gently ironic does not completely negate his flattering suggestion that travel is an adventurous and heroic activity, offering important challenges and rewards.

This dynamic of genteel conquest is made explicitly sexual in James's writings on Italy. His first essay on Venice, for example, develops the conceit of a male traveler whose initial indifference to tawdry Venice warms to attraction as he learns its charms. "The creature varies like a nervous woman," James writes, "whom you know only when you know all the aspects of her beauty" (*IH* 6). "Tenderly fond you become. . . . The place seems to personify itself, to become human and sentient and conscious of your affection. You desire to embrace it, to caress it, to possess it; and finally a soft sense of possession grows up and your visit becomes a perpetual love-affair" (*IH* 6–7).

Like many successful lovers, furthermore, James's speaker is eager to discredit his rivals and to idealize the object of his affection. On one hand he characterizes his fellow tourists as "barbarians" and cringes fastidiously as the "terrible brassy voice" of the "valet-de-place" "resounds all over the place" (*IH* 7), "savage Germans" fill "the Ducal Palace and the Academy with their uproar," and the French "tak[e] very long repasts at the Caffè Quadri," which luckily keep them "out of the way" for hours at a time (*IH* 7). Actual Venetians, on the other hand, may "never have enough to eat," but they "lie in the sunshine," "dabble in the sea," "wear bright rags," "fall into attitudes and harmonies," "assist at an eternal conversazione," and so contribute to "the spectacle" and add to "the pleasure" of the "thorough-going devotee of local colour" (*IH* 3). Venice is a source of exquisite pleasure for those who know how "to follow the example of these people and make the most of simple pleasures" (*IH* 4).

James's Venice-lover expresses his devotion by composing charming scenes and experiences for himself and his beloved, being careful to eschew the commonplace and avoid crowds. He visits the obligatory attractions "at one o'clock, when the tourists have flocked off to lunch" (*IH* 23), and floats out to the cockneyfied Lido alone, returning at sunset in order to savor the exquisite beauty of "that glowing hour." He ends his day, or imagines ending it, by participating in a scene that could come from a travel poster or an illustrated advertisement for some five-star hotel or expensive product.

> If you are happy you will find yourself, after a June day in Venice (about ten o'clock), on a balcony that overhangs the Grand Canal, with your elbows on the broad ledge, a cigarette in your teeth and a little good company beside you. The gondolas pass beneath, the watery surface gleams here and there from their lamps, some of which are colored lanterns that move mysteriously in the darkness. There are some evenings in June when there are too many gondolas, too many lanterns, too many serenades in front of the hotels. The serenading in particular is overdone; but on such a balcony as I speak of you needn't suffer from it, for in the apartment behind you—an accessible refuge—there is more good company, there are more cigarettes. If you are wise you will step back there presently. (*IH* 30)

In this ideal scene James's privileged tourist has all the pleasure of the slightly vulgar Venetian scene without the necessity of excessive mingling or participation. He can withdraw at will into the salon behind his balcony for the "good company" of other superior beings and the solace of a luxury only hinted at by the assurance that "there are more cigarettes." The scene is enormously appealing; it encourages the reader to identify all that is elegant and desirable with a privileged figure on a Venetian balcony. There is no way to calculate its effect "on the receipts of the American touring agencies," yet it is hard to imagine reading it and *not* wanting to drop everything and book a first-class cabin to James's Europe.

The mood of the commercial travelogue persists in James's last major piece of European travel writing, the series of sketches published in *The Atlantic* from July 1883 to May 1884 under the collective title "En Province," and collected in the 1884 volume, *A Little Tour in France*. If these sketches lack the intensity of some of James's earlier travel writing, they make up for it by their *désinvolture*, their air of assured, relaxed enjoyment. James's introduction to the first edition refers all self-deprecatingly to "these light pages" and introduces what I reckon to be the series' most frequent qualifier, "charming" (*LT* 1). *A Little Tour in France* shows us the Jamesian tourist as a frank seeker and maker of impressions and experiences, a man of the world it may be, but also a connoisseur of charming surfaces and not-too-hidden depths. In an 1877 essay, "Italy Revisited," James suggested that the detachment of the traveler resembled that of the theatergoer and added that there was "something heartless in stepping forth into foreign streets to feast on 'character'" (*IH* 116); in *A Little Tour in France* he adopts the spectator's role wholeheartedly, drifting like a pair of disembodied eyes and a mind through a landscape not unpeopled, to be sure, but in which people are seen as scenery rather than centers of consciousness or objects of exploitation.

The charm of the text is especially evident in James's descriptions and constructions of ideal scenes and experiences. This is James in the high aesthetic vein, "composing" moments that may not burn with a hard gemlike flame but certainly glow with their own pleasure and offer a portion of it to the reader in a lush prose that invites both sympathetic pulsation and critical judgment. He concludes his description of the abbey at Marmoutier, for example, by evoking a perfect moment, alluding to the conventional Anglo-Saxon distrust of Catholicism, and asserting the tourist's right to compare sights and attractions.

> The modern buildings (of the Sacred Heart), on which you look down from these points of vantage, are in the vulgar taste which seems doomed to stamp itself on all new Catholic work; but there was nevertheless a great sweetness in the scene. The afternoon was lovely, and it was flushing to a close. The large garden stretched beneath us, blooming with fruit and wine and succulent vegetables, and beyond it flowed the shining river. The air was still, the shadows were long, and the place, after all, was full of memories, most of which might pass for virtuous. It certainly was better than Plessis-les-Tours. (*LT* 21)

In other passages throughout the *Little Tour* he sketches ideal confluences of scene and air, weather and light, and even complaisant celestial bodies, all composing themselves in the consciousness of the sensitive visitor to such standard tourist attractions as Chenonceaux, Carcassonne, and the Pont du Gard. Like the very best travel posters, these passages please the eye and evoke the would-be traveler's envious fantasy. Their effect is to reproduce a series of classic experiences, to offer the reader a distilled essence of Europe, which reinforces the idea that the Continent's great purpose is to provide exquisite moments for the thoughtful, sensitive traveler. James shows the tourist how to get the best views and construct the most valuable experiences; he reinforces even the nontraveling reader's sense of his/her place in a world apparently dedicated to providing pleasing and improving moments for superior Anglo-Saxon readers.

This effect is reinforced by James's treatment of the people who inhabit his scenes: like the Venetian poor, their whole purpose seems to be to provide the tourist with a little local color or perhaps an occasion for some brief moral reflection. He invariably characterizes the guides and *gardiens* who show him the churches and great houses with a condescending adjective or two: "a very genial old sacristan" (*LT* 13); "this little trotting, murmuring, edifying nun" (*LT* 20); "a small, shrill boy" (*LT* 28); "a highly respectable person" (*LT* 33); "a very tidy little portress" (*LT* 40); "a worthy woman" (*LT* 43); "a talkative lodge-keeper" (*LT* 47); "an extraordinarily typical little Frenchman" (*LT* 142). These are not people but servants; if they have a little more place in James's travel narratives than the all but invisible servants in his novels it is because they are mildly exotic and remind the reader and the traveler the s/he is not at home. Local people who do not serve travelers are even more objectified; when they are not models for sketches, they are like the figures a sketcher of landscapes might include in the middle distance to indicate the historical period and nationality of the scene. An old woman in Tours, cleaning a pot in a doorway, near "a little dark window decorated with homely flowers, . . . would be appreciated by a painter in search of 'bits'" (*LT* 15). The "small stony, whitewashed streets" of Aigues-Mortes are "very still and empty," "tenanted" only "by a stray dog, a stray cat, a stray old woman" (*LT* 167). The shops in Toulouse "are probably better" than those in Turin, he remarks, "but the people are not so good" (*LT* 125). The laundresses of Langeais are among "the usual embellishments of a French village: little ponds or tanks, with women on their knees on the brink, pounding and thumping a lump of saturated linen; brown old crones, the tone of whose facial hide makes their nightcaps (worn by day) look dazzling; little alleys perforating the thickness of a row of cottages, and showing you behind, as a glimpse, the vividness of a green garden" (*LT* 62).

If one word for *A Little Tour in France* is "charming," then others, depending on the position of the speaker, might surely be "cold," "supercilious," and "condescending," or "commercial," "class-ridden," even in some sense "imperious." In all of his travel writing, from *Transatlantic Sketches* (1875) to the late essays on Italy included in *Italian Hours* (1909), James performs the travel writer's conventional tasks with aplomb, participating in what Dean MacCannell calls "sight sacralization"[31] by reinvesting classic "attractions" with the aura of his artistic prose and his aesthetic sensibility and treating "typical" scenes as "examples" of themselves, in

Jonathan Culler's formulation, signs of their own authenticity and of the authenticity of their observer's experience.[32] James also reaffirms the superiority of his own class, nationality, and frequently gender by treating indigenous populations as part of the scenery, "naturalizing" them, in Mary Louise Pratt's term,[33] or treating them as commodified, consumable "others," as John Frow suggests tourists typically do.[34] He reenacts, finally, the archetypal tourist-imperialist moment, what Pratt calls "the monarch-of-all-I-survey scene," in which the landscape and all it contains are presented to the traveler and represented to the reader to be enjoyed, interpreted (or, rather endowed with meaning), and mastered.[35]

James's travel writing had more work to do than Ford imagined. It certainly helped promote the nascent tourist industry, but it also encouraged its culturally elite readers to think of themselves as comfortably, naturally superior to foreigners, to vulgar tourists, and most of all perhaps to those compatriots who neither traveled abroad nor read the *Atlantic*, to that poor, unlettered herd for whom allusions to Fiesole and Florian's evoked neither fond memories nor fond longings, but just an ignorant, unsophisticated blank. One of its chief tasks, in other words, was to help create its own audience by promoting the social and aesthetic satisfactions that were available primarily if not exclusively to members of the "new-style 'high' social class" taking shape in the latter years of the nineteenth century.

TRAVEL AND EUROPE IN JAMES'S FICTION

Of course James was not primarily a travel writer, and it would be a mistake to expect his travel sketches to contain his final word on any subject, even travel. His complex understanding of the meaning of European travel and tourism for Americans, of what was seriously at stake in them, and of what the traveler had to gain beyond the pleasure of the moment and to lose beyond money and time is best set forth in his international fiction.

In an 1878 *Nation* essay James declared that Americans abroad "are ill-made, ill-mannered, [and] ill-dressed." They are ignorant, too, he went on, but unlike the general run of Europeans, they "have a certain amount of imagination."[36] In the fiction of 1876–1880, he made superior fun of undereducated, vulgar Americans on their travels, but he also admired their innocent boldness and criticized their supersophisticated, ineffectual, and amoral critics.

Pure satire is quite rare in James, shading off as a rule into sly sympathy and admiration for a Daisy Miller on the one hand and serious moral criticism of a Gilbert Osmond on the other. In between, the butts of satirical fun tend to be either hopelessly vulgar, like the shop-haunting Mrs. and Miss Ruck of "The Pension Beaurepas" ("They're awfully restless," Mr. Ruck remarks. "It takes the form of shopping"),[37] terminally snobbish, like *Daisy Miller's* Mrs. Costello, or irredeemably solemn, like *The American's* Benjamin Babcock. James neither criticizes these characters in any serious way nor sympathizes with them, but instead holds them up as comforting examples of how some people—not his own readers—act in Europe.

His genuine compassion and his serious criticism focus on characters like Caroline Spencer, of "Four Meetings" (1877), Daisy Miller, and the narrators of their stories, whose behavior has important personal and moral consequences. Spencer is a classic victim of the "superstitious valuation." An impoverished New England schoolteacher who has dreamed of Europe all her life, she saves her money, gets Byron by heart, and is made feverish by looking at European photo albums at an afternon tea party. Her obsession amounts to "a kind of craziness,"[38] she says. "It kills any interest in things nearer home" (233). She has worked herself into such a state that "a great friend of [hers]" tells her "she guessed I'd go crazy if I didn't sail, and yet certainly I'd go crazy if I did" (232). "You've the great American disease," the narrator says, "and you've got it 'bad'" (233). As a more sophisticated fellow sufferer, he knows that this illness is self-defeating and incurable: it devours time and imaginative power; the hours spent dreaming of Europe and its treasures actually diminish their power—the best they can do is to live up to the "terrible mirage" of the fevered fancy; the worst is to prove a terrible disappointment—and yet, he concludes, "I'm going back there—one *has* to" (234).

The narrator loves Europe with a controlled, detached passion; he "has to" return, but he knows how to use Europe for his own pleasures and purposes when he does so. Miss Spencer's passion for Europe, in contrast, controls her. When she finally sails, she spends the whole crossing at the ship's rail, staring eastward toward her imagined goal. When she lands at Le Havre, she is "intensely happy" (237) simply to sit on the terrace of a little café. "I feel so much in a dream," she says. "I've been sitting here an hour and I don't want to move. Everything's so delicious and romantic" (238). The innocuous "craziness" that makes her delight in this little bit of certified, classic Frenchness turns dangerous, however, when her rapacious cousin—an "art student" in Paris, who has met her ship—uses a yarn straight out of sentimental operetta to relieve her of her savings. It seems he has secretly married a Provençal *comtesse*, a great heiress, cast off by "her great-aunt, the old Marquise," because "she *would* have him, poor gifted young American art-student though he simply was, because she just adored him" (249). He needs his cousin's money—all of it—as a loan to tide him over until he finishes his great painting. Once it is done he will be rich and famous, all will be well, and Miss Spencer "will come back . . . to stay with them" (249).

What actually happens is the reverse of this starry-eyed scenario. The cousin dies in Paris, and the "comtesse" shows up one day on Miss Spencer's doorstep, penniless but indisputably "European," using her position as the poor but noble relative to swindle the poor woman once again. The spurious countess can be seen as embodying the idea of Europe as it afflicts so many Americans. She seems glamorous and exotic to naive Miss Spencer and to some, at least, of her North Verona neighbors, but to the more knowing narrator she is clearly a fraud.

> She was very strange, yet I was at once sure I had seen her before. Afterwards I rather put it that I had only seen ladies remarkably like her. But I had seen them very far away from North Verona, and it was the oddest of all things to meet one of them in that frame. To what quite other scene did the sight of her transport me? To some dusky landing before a shabby Parisian *quatrième*—to an open door revealing a greasy ante-chamber and to Madame leaning over the banisters while she holds a faded wrapper together and bawls down to the portress to bring up her coffee. (257–58)

The gullible, Europe-mad Miss Spencer is last seen in her New England dooryard serving morning coffee and brandy to a Parisian bawd. "As I went back past the Baptist church," the narrator concludes, "I could feel how right my poor friend had been in her conviction at the other, the still intenser, the now historic crisis, that she should still see something of that dear old Europe" (267).

Miss Spencer is pathetic but uncorrupted. Her superstitious valuation of Europe is wrongheaded, and she suffers for it, but it does no one else any harm. Europe itself, as embodied in the "comtesse," is to blame, but so, in part, is the worldly-wise narrator, who perpetuates the myth without succumbing to its power, who patronizes Miss Spencer without doing her any good. He is the real tourist of the story, detached from everything and everyone he sees and visits. Miss Spencer was to him "a touching specimen of a type" (227). She "was not quite a beauty, but was none the less, in her small odd way, formed to please." "Her eyes were perhaps just too round and too inveterately surprised, but her lips had a certain mild decision, and her teeth, when she showed them, were charming" (228). She was, in other words, a "sketchable bit," a piece of local color, the raw material for a wry and knowing narrative. The narrator of "Four Meetings" has a little too much in common with the speaker in James's travel sketches: in the story, however, James at least implies some criticism of the tourist role; in the sketches he adopts it more or less uncritically for himself.

This pattern repeats itself in the better-known *Daisy Miller*, whose central consciousness, Mr. Winterbourne, "felt he had lived in Geneva so long as to have got morally muddled"[39] and whose central figure suffers from his touristic, almost clinical interest in her "case." The story has often been taken as an exposé of the vulgar, undereducated, and over-rich "American girl," and Daisy has been considered a merely admonitory character, an example, like Babcock or Sophy Ruck, of how not to behave in Europe.[40]

Daisy *is* vulgar. Her clothes are expensive and elaborate, but they want "finish" and "form" (10). "She was composed . . . of charming little parts that didn't match and that made no *ensemble*" (9). What is worse, she thinks nothing of picking up strange men in hotel gardens and complaining to them of the lack, in Europe, of something she calls "society," by which she means mixed evening parties with plenty of free "gentlemen." In Europe, she complains, "there ain't any society—or if there is I don't know where it keeps itself." "In New York," she goes on, "I had lots of society," and concludes, "I've always had a great deal of gentlemen's society" (14).

Daisy is also undereducated. Her ideas of Europe are limited by her very narrow experience. She feels at home in Europe because even in Schenectady "she had had ever so many dresses and things from Paris" and "felt as if she were in Europe" "whenever she put on a Paris dress" (14). Her only original remark on the European scene is that it appears to be full of hotels. "I ha[ve] never been in so many hotels as since I came to Europe," she remarks. "I've never seen so many—it's nothing but hotels" (13). Her "superstitious valuation" of Europe has everything to do with purchases and amusements and nothing to do with "culture": in contrast to the Byronizing Miss Spencer, she refers to the Château de Chillon as "that old castle" (15, 18) and has not the slightest interest in its historical or literary associations, using it only as the backdrop for her flirtation with Winterbourne (35–36).

As is well known, Daisy pays for what others consider her vulgarity with her life, contracting malaria on a brash unchaperoned moonlight visit to the Coliseum with little Mr. Giovanelli, her constant Italian companion. For all that, she is far from the least appealing figure in her story and certainly not the only object of James's disapproval. Mrs. Walker and Mrs. Costello, the Europeanized grandes dames, are cruel while Daisy is only foolish: they treat her as beneath contempt; she treats them as amusingly "exclusive" (25) and annoyingly meddlesome (54). Winterbourne, like the narrator in "Four Meetings," is notably cold, indifferent to her apparent infatuation with him, and more interested in dealing with her as a phenomenon than as a person. His response to her forwardness is carefully calculated; he proposes to accompany her to Chillon only after satisfying himself as to her motives and classifying her once and for all. "Was she simply a pretty girl from New York State—were they all like that, the pretty girls who had had a good deal of gentlemen's society? Or was she also a designing, an audacious, in short an expert young person? . . . He must on the whole take Miss Daisy Miller for a flirt—a pretty American flirt. . . . Winterbourne was almost grateful for having found the formula that applied to Miss Daisy Miller" (15). As the story goes on, he falls in with the general condemnation of Daisy's conduct (75–78), ready to assume "the worst" of her until Giovanelli assures him at her very funeral that "she was the most beautiful young lady I ever saw, and the most amiable. . . . Also—naturally!—the most innocent" (79–80). Only then does he understand the meaning of her final message to him—she insisted three times in the course of her illness that Winterbourne be told she was not "engaged" to Giovanelli (79)—and realize that, as he puts it, "she would have appreciated one's esteem" (81). But the episode is by this time over, and Winterbourne returns to Geneva, whence the narrator hears "a report that he's 'studying' hard—an intimation that he's much interested in a very clever foreign lady" (81). Winterbourne condemned Daisy for appearing to do vulgarly what he was doing discreetly. James deplores the sophisticated expatriate's attitudes and behavior far more than the vulgar ingenue's.

In these two tales and many others James manages both to celebrate European tourism and to criticize it. The Europe that entices Caroline Spencer is genuinely attractive: Italy charmed James every bit as much as it charms the characters in this story; the stops on Miss Spencer's projected itinerary, dream cities whose names she "told over . . . as solemnly as a daughter of another faith might have told over the beads of a rosary" (241), were real places offering real pleasures to travelers and dreamers alike. The poignancy of her story depends in large part on the reader's sense that she has really missed something, that her gullibility, engendered in part by her romantic, bookish preconceptions about European life and people, has deprived her of a genuinely valuable experience. It is also true that entrancing itineraries like Caroline Spencer's may engender pleasing experiences that bear the same relation to actual European life as Miss Spencer's cousin's romantic tale of the "comtesse" and the "old marquise" bears to his commonplace affair with a vulgar *Parisienne*. And it is further and even more importantly true that the experience of touristic expatriation can produce such chronically detached, self-centered characters as the narrator of "Four Meetings," *Daisy Miller*'s Winterbourne, and the consummately sinister Gilbert Osmond.

James elaborates on the pleasures and dangers of tourism in two later, longer works as well. In both *The Princess Casamassima* and *The Ambassadors*, European travel is a transformative but not necessarily, and in any case not simply, a redemptive activity. The protagonists of both novels find European travel intensely pleasurable and deeply important for their sense of how life can and ought to be lived, but for both of them it raises problems for which neither they nor their author has a solution, problems that challenge the reader to reeexamine the very valuation of European experience which the texts seem also to be promoting.

Hyacinth Robinson, the central character of *The Princess Casamassima*, the English son of an unhappy Frenchwoman imprisoned in London for murdering the English lord who may have been her son's father, has been brought up by a friend of his mother's, a cockney seamstress who prizes his putatively noble blood and encourages his aesthetic sensibilities. Unlike the typical Jamesian protagonist, he is European and poor; like Caroline Spencer, Isabel Archer, Lambert Strether, and many others, however, he has been deprived of the pleasures of Continental travel for which his temperament and upbringing have peculiarly suited him. Although *The Princess Casamassima* is not, therefore, the story of an American in Europe, it does explore James's sense of the moral effect of European tourism on a susceptible sensibility.

When the main part of the story opens, young Hyacinth is a member of the proletarian elite, a skilled bookbinder who is being recruited into political activism by his fellow worker, the anarchist and ex-Communard Eustache Poupin. The political and social landscape of the novel is complicated by the presence of several type characters, including Hoffendahl, the anarchist ideologue, Paul Muniment, the ambitious worker-politician, his sister Rose, a Dickensian invalid, Lady Aurora, a do-gooding noblewoman, and the princess herself, the same Christina Light who had helped destroy Roderick Hudson and is now dabbling in left-wing politics. Hyacinth's character is complicated by his mixed class and national origin (James was more influenced here than in any other novel by Zola and the naturalists) and by his sense of himself as an aesthete and an artist as well as a poor man and a worker.

Like James, Hyacinth has always had a tourist's temperament, roaming the streets of his native London, absorbing the sights, the sounds, the very odors of the town. Since he is a perfect example of that most Jamesian artist figure, the "youth on whom nothing was lost,"[41] his observations have naturally fostered his desires to know and to experience; since he is also, however, a poor artisan, his anonymous examination of the privileged few has confirmed his sense of exclusion.

> Sometimes, of a Saturday, in the long evenings of June and July, he made his way into Hyde Park at the hour when the throng of carriages, of riders, of brilliant pedestrians, was thickest; and . . . a tremendous little drama had taken place, privately, in his soul. He wanted to drive in every carriage, to mount on every horse, to feel on his arm the hand of every pretty woman in the place. In the midst of this his sense was vivid that he belonged to the class whom the upper ten thousand, as they passed, didn't so much as rest their eyes on for a quarter of a second . . . they only reminded him of the high human walls, the deep gulfs of tradition, the steep embankments of privilege and dense layers of stupidity, which fenced him off from social recognition. (119–20)

Hyacinth gets a first taste of the beauties and pleasures he has missed when he visits the princess in her rented country house (256–83); he gets a chance to sample them further when his guardian dies, leaving him thirty-seven pounds and the "particular wish" that he "should go to Paris" (334). To Paris he goes, and also to Venice; in both he soaks up "impressions" (336) and reflects on his personal connection to history, to art, and to civilization. In Paris he is "proud to be associated with so much of the superb, so many proofs of a civilisation that had no visible rough spots" (337). Reminders of the revolution confront him, but he is struck not so much by its destructive force as by the creative energy it so evidently unleashed, by life, not death, and "a sense of everything that might hold one to the world, of the sweetness of not dying, the fascination of great cities, the charm of travel and discovery, the generosity of admiration" (350–51). In Venice he moves even further away from anarchism and gloom, rejecting Schopenhauer's pessimism and his "musty misogyn[y]" (351) to observe the life and particularly the women of the *campi* and to give himself over to worldly and aesthetic pleasures. To the princess he writes:

> I smoke cigarettes, and in the pauses of this composition recline on a faded magenta divan in the corner. Convenient to my hand, in that attitude, are the works of Leopardi and a second-hand dictionary. I am very happy—happier than I have ever been in my life save at Medley—and I don't care for anything but the present hour. It won't last long, for I am spending all my money. When I have finished this I shall go forth and wander about in the splendid Venetian afternoon; and I shall spend the evening in that enchanted square of Saint Mark's, which resembles an immense open-air drawing-room, listening to music and feeling the sea-breeze blow in between those strange old columns of the piazzetta, which seem to make a portal for it. (352)

Hyacinth's visit to Medley and his brief European tour, his introduction to that combination of luxury and aesthetic pleasure which is the special property of the truly rich and of tourists who play at being rich for limited periods, mark a turning point in his moral and political life, undermining his devotion to the anarchism of Hoffendahl and Poupin and replacing it with an uneasy, illogical dedication to "the splendid accumulations of the happier few, to which, doubtless, the miserable many have also in their degree contributed" (353). He is, in short, converted from some rather vague Jamesian version of left-wing materialism[42] to a form of aesthetic elitism that is clearly more compatible with James's own views and with the implicit views of privileged middle- and upper-class consumers of art and high culture. He has weighed material progress against aesthetic production and found himself unwilling to sacrifice "the monuments and treasures of art, the great palaces and properties, the conquests of learning and taste, the general fabric of civilisation as we know it" (353), whether for some abstract notion of equitable distribution of wealth or for the very concrete act of feeding the poor. Hoffendahl "would cut up the ceilings of the Veronese into strips, so that every one might have a little piece," he writes. "I don't want every one to have a little piece of anything" (354). "I think there can't be too many pictures and statues and works of art," he says later. "The more the better, whether people are hungry or not. In the way of ameliorating influences, are not those the most definite?" (371).

But Jamesian though his final position may be, Hyacinth's conversion by tourism remains problematic. Officially committed to "the people," sworn to carry out a terrorist act in their name, he no longer believes in his commitment. "I don't know what I believe, God help me!" he tells Paul Muniment but adds, "I don't want you to think I have ceased to care for the people. What am I but one of the poorest and meanest of them?" Paul answers Hyacinth's rhetorical question in two ways, first accounting for his friend's dilemma in the conventional naturalistic terms of heredity, and then attributing his predicament to the effects of Jamesian tourism. "You, my boy?" he begins. "You're a duke in disguise." "As regards caring for the people," he goes on, "there's surely no obligation at all, . . . I wouldn't if I could help it—I promise you that. It all depends on what you see" (403–4). Muniment "sees" very simply "that present arrangements won't do." Hyacinth, however, has learned on his travels to "see" two contradictory things: "the immeasurable misery of the people" and "all that had been, as it were, rescued and redeemed from it: the treasures, the felicities, the splendours, the successes, of the world" (404). His experience as a tourist has cost him his democratic innocence; his cultivated vision and his widened consciousness have undermined his political will, and in the end he kills himself instead of carrying out the assassination to which he was sworn.

In other hands the plot of *The Princess Casamassima* might well have served simply to illustrate the seductive, negative effects of high culture and luxury on principled political commitment. The meaning of James's novel, however, is not so clear. James's "little bookbinder" acquires in the course of his story exactly that expanded aesthetic consciousness which James purveys in his fiction and his travel writing, and it destroys him. *The Princess Casamassima* is an awkward book, hard to credit, uncertain in tone, but it is also very bold in its philosophical and political ambitions, spanning the gap between the artist figures of Poe and Hawthorne on the one hand and Conrad's early-twentieth-century political operatives on the other. In it James uses the tourist experience he enjoyed, packaged, sold, and criticized as a vehicle for his main character's highly ambivalent—and ultimately fatal—acquisition of a Jamesian consciousness.

The experience of Europe is as disturbing and as fateful, if not ultimately so melodramatic, for the most fully developed tourist in all of James's oeuvre, Mr. Lewis Lambert Strether, of Woollett, Massachusetts. Like Robinson, James's ambassador is profoundly shaken by his exposure to the beauty, the luxury, and the moral standards of European life. Like the typical aspiring Jamesian tourist, his consciousness of art, and of the possibilities of life, is expanded by his experience; like Robinson, he is unfitted by this experience for the life he has been living and to which he feels bound to return.

Strether's story recapitulates several of the patterns that we have observed in nineteenth-century travel writing. It is seen first as a belated initiation rite, in which the inexperienced male sets out alone into the great threatening world to perform a heroic task, defend his own purity, and prove himself worthy of honorific reintegration into his own society. At fifty-five, Strether seems an unlikely Red Cross knight or "jeune homme de province," but James frames his story as a turn-of-the-century version of the classic masculine initiation rite. Although he has been to Europe before, Strether is still an innocent. His earlier trip had been the earnest "pilgrimage" of a "helplessly young" newlywed, which resulted in "a relation formed with the higher culture," but no sense of a challenge overcome or any consciousness of broader possibilities for living and feeling.[43] That journey had been a celebration of newly established domesticity rather than a test of individual mettle; this journey is very clearly a mission into enemy territory, with a task to perform and a prize to be won. The task, simply put, is to persuade Mrs. Newsome's son, Chad, to leave Paris and return to the family fold and the family business. Maria Gostrey sums it up this way:

> "I seem with this freedom, you see, to have guessed Mr. Chad. He's a young man on whose head high hopes are placed at Woollett; a young man a wicked woman has got hold of and whom his family over there have sent you out to rescue. You've accepted the mission of separating him from the wicked woman. Are you quite sure she's very bad for him?" (93)

The prize is both the conventional marriage with the princess, in this case a dowager princess, to be sure, and a very American pot of money. Strether's friend Waymarsh lays it all out:

> "Because if you get him you also get Mrs. Newsome?"
> Strether faced it. "Yes."
> "And if you don't get him you don't get her?"
> It might be merciless, but he continued not to flinch. "I think it might have some effect on our personal understanding. Chad's of real importance—or can easily become so if he will—to the business."
> "And the business is of real importance to his mother's husband?"

"Well, I naturally want what my wife wants. And the thing will be much better if we have our own man in it."

"If you have your own man in it, in other words," Waymarsh said, "you'll marry—you personally—more money." (134)

The sense of Europe as alien, even hostile, territory comes across first in Waymarsh's experience of the whole continent as an "ordeal" (71), and then in Strether's successive solitary Balzacian confrontations with urban scenes and social settings that he feels must be evil but whose specific moral features he has trouble pinning down. Strether's preconceived notion of the European scene is embodied in the play he sees with Miss Gostrey, in which "a bad woman in a yellow frock . . . made a pleasant weak good-looking young man in perpetual evening dress do the most dreadful things" (92). The actual scenes that face him in Paris prove harder to interpret. "Chad's very house" (124) is the first of these, a disturbingly fine bright apartment, whose "distinguished front, testified suddenly, for Strether's fancy, to something that was up and up" (125). A breakfast party held there in Chad's absence compounds his confusion: Strether wonders "if the occasion weren't in its essence the most baited, the most gilded of traps" (136), but has trouble associating its sumptuous details with any sinister design. At table, he assumes that Chad's friends are discussing matters deemed "too bad to be talked about" at Woollett, but he cannot bring himself to specify their badness: "He wondered what they meant, but there were things he scarce thought they could be supposed to mean, and 'Oh no—not *that!*'—was at the end of most of his ventures" (139). Since Chad is in a "bad" situation, he argues to himself, these charming people, their conversation, and everything about them must be part of the general sinister scene.

> It befell therefore that when poor Strether put it to himself that their badness was ultimately, or perhaps even insolently, what such a scene as the one before him was, so to speak, built upon, he could scarce shirk the dilemma of reading a roundabout echo of them into almost anything that came up. (139)

Once we begin to think of Strether as a modern Spenserian quester seeking to rescue an erring prince from thralldom to an evil woman in a fallen land, it becomes easy to identify the pitfalls and temptations that beset his path. Luxury is rife in Paris, and temptresses are legion. At that first breakfast party, Strether joins Miss Barrace in "a succession of excellent cigarettes," explaining to himself that the reason he had never smoked before "was that he had never had a lady to smoke with" (138). When he lunches much later with the elegant Mme de Vionnet at what can only be the Tour d'Argent, he feels that "in the matter of letting himself go, of diving deep, . . . he had touched bottom" (278). When later still he stands in the antechamber to her linear suite of elegant, Old World rooms, he feels drawn in but also excluded from the vortex of their retreating historical resonance.

> The whole thing made a vista, which he found high melancholy and sweet—full, once more, of dim historic shades, of the faint far-away cannon-roar of the great Empire. It was doubtless half the projection of his mind, but his mind was a thing that, among old waxed parquets, pale shades of pink and green, pseudo-classic candelabra, he had always needfully to reckon with. They could easily make him irrelevant. (361)

If these ladies embody the blandishments of luxury and history, which the man from Massachusetts finds nearly irresistible despite the fact that he has been taught all his life to resist them, Chad's indisputable "improvement," his polish, his elegance, and his physical, sensual vitality pose an even more formidable challenge to his Yankee standards. "Chad was brown and thick and strong, and of old Chad had been rough. Was all the difference therefore that he was actually smooth? Possibly; for that he *was* smooth was as marked as in the taste of a sauce or in the rub of a hand" (166). Strether first sees Chad as "an irreducible young Pagan," but soon finds "himself wondering now if he weren't by chance a gentleman" (170, 173). In the end, the ambassador from Woollett is so firmly won over by his attractive young friend that he finds himself urging him to stay in Europe rather than give up his unexpected elegance and refinement.

If Strether has his tempters, however, he also has his guides: Little Bilham initiates him (selectively, it is true) into Chad's particular world, and Maria Gostrey, a combination guide and temptress, spots him at the dock in Liverpool, picks him up at the hotel in Chester, and proposes herself to him as "a sort of superior 'courier-maid'" who "wait[s] for people . . . put[s] them through . . . pick[s] them up . . . set[s] them down" (65). She acts at first as the conventional guide in a conventional initiation rite, putting her charges through the required experiences and returning them to the homebound ship ready for reintegration into American society. "I'm an agent for repatriation," she says. "I send you back spent. So you stay back. Passed through my hands—" (78). Eventually, however, she falls in love with Strether and offers herself to him less conditionally, as the most earnest and ultimately the most seductive because the most immediate and realistic temptress of all.

> "There's nothing, you know, I wouldn't do for you."
> "Oh yes—I know."
> "There's nothing," she repeated, "in all the world."
> "I know. I know. But all the same I must go." (512)

Strether's story figures an initiation rite, then, but it also reflects two other familiar motives for European travel, the search for sensual and aesthetic stimulation unavailable in puritanical America and the seductions of personal freedom, the possibility of constructing a new, original self outside the constraints of a restrictive culture. "The failure of Woollett," James makes very clear, is "the failure to enjoy" (64). One of the attractions of Europe is the possibility of "giving oneself up" to enjoyment (67), of "letting [one]self recklessly go" in the hope of overcoming one's "odious ascetic suspicion of any form of beauty" (197; see also 338). Strether's first impulse on touching English soil is to "give his afternoon and evening to the immediate and the sensible" (56); the "delight" he takes in even the "qualified draught of Europe" provided by a "huddled English town and ordered English country" proves "too deep almost for words" (56, 64). In London he dines boldly at his hotel with Maria Gostrey, "face to face over a small table on which the lighted candles had rose-coloured shades," enjoying "the soft fragrance of the lady" (89) and the view of "shoulders and bosom" (90) provided by her fashionable décolletage ("Mrs. Newsome's dress was never in any degree 'cut down'" [90]). In Paris he relaxes at last on a penny chair in the Luxembourg Gardens and treats himself to a classic Parisian scene in which "terraces, alleys, vistas, fountains, little trees in green tubs, little women in white caps and shrill little girls at play all sunnily 'composed' together" and "the cup of his impressions seemed truly to overflow" (112).

Strether's enjoyment is not free of lingering guilt, however: he wonders if it is "possible . . . to like Paris enough without liking it too much" and justifies his pleasure with the reflection that "he luckily . . . hadn't promised Mrs. Newsome not to like it at all" (119). Indeed, the specter of Mrs. Newsome hovers heavily over all Strether's pleasures, and the dynamic of the text as a whole tends to confirm his early suggestion that he might be "literally running away from Mrs. Newsome" (75) under the pretense of serving as her ambassador. James tempts Strether and the reader alike with the pleasures of Paris: the gardens, the theaters, the restaurants; Chad's "lovely home" (143); Maria's charming little entresol, "compact and crowded" with precious artifacts (141); Mme de Vionnet's elegant apartment in the aristocratic faubourg; a great sculptor's exclusive garden party and the society of artists like Little Bilham and alluring if slightly disreputable women like the avidly smoking Miss Barrace. At the same time he never lets Strether forget that he "didn't come out," as he himself puts it, "for the pleasant" (226), that he has a job to do, and that he ultimately fails to do it.

If Strether's openness to enjoyment distinguishes him from his Massachusetts employer's puritanical asceticism, however, the refinement of his chosen pleasures distinguishes him even more clearly from the vulgar consequences of that asceticism as they manifest themselves in the totally egregious Jim Pocock, "small and fat and constantly facetious," with his "constant preference for light-grey-clothes, for white hats, for very big cigars and very little stories" (330), his hint-hint, nudge-nudge vulgarity, and his determination to enjoy Paris in his own way, and what he erroneously assumes to be Strether's.

> "I say, you know, this *is* about my shape, and if it hadn't been for *you*—!" so he broke out as the charming streets met his healthy appetite; and he wound up, after an expressive nudge, with a clap of his companion's knee and an "Oh you, you—you *are* doing it!" that was charged with rich meaning. (326)

Neither Strether's pleasures nor Chad's have much in common with either the vulgar sensuality of the male tourist's "Gay Paree" or the Woollett sensibility of which Jim and Mrs. Newsome are contrasting but related representatives, a sensibility that equates sex with lower-class women, sordid naughtiness, and even "evil." Strether's developing understanding of Parisian pleasures is both sensually and morally attractive: he has come to value the personal freedom and the aesthetic richness of Parisian life and to honor what he takes to be Chad's "virtuous" if unconventional "attachment" to Mme de Vionnet. Even the revelation, in two of the most subtly and intensely beautiful chapters James ever wrote, of the fact that "virtuous" and "chaste" are not in France the synonyms Strether has been taking them for (452–68) does not finally destroy the beauty of the couple's "intimacy." If they had had to "lie," it was because he in his blind New England puritanism "had made them." "Intimacy, at such a point, was *like* that," he reflects, "—and what in the world else would one have wished it to be like?" (468).

It is easy to read the first eleven books of *The Ambassadors* as, among many other things, a testament to and even an advertisement for the sensual and aesthetic advantages of Europe and its superior moral sophistication. Strether's sojourn would in this reading be the occasion for his delayed but still positive coming of age; the novel would be a celebration of the liberating effects of the European experience. It seems to me that the novel works in just this way for most of its length and most of its readers, that it represents in the memory and in the reading a glamorous, even a glittering Europe, attractive for its marvelous surfaces *and* its profound moral and aesthetic understanding, rare or nonexistent commodities on the Boston side of the Atlantic.

And yet *The Ambassadors* is no salvation narrative. Chad is unquestionably "improved" by his European experience, but he turns out to have been improved *for* Woollett rather than turned by his improvement against it. His morality is rather less sophisticated than Strether would have liked, and his relationship with Mme de Vionnet is in the end rather more exploitative. And Strether himself is anything but "saved," as he famously rejects Maria Gostrey's offer of faithful solace, rejects, in other words, the pleasures *and* the moral sophistication of Europe in order to reassert his own version of the equation of virtue and chastity.

> "I know. I know. But all the same I must go." He had got it at last. "To be right."
> She had echoed it in vague deprecation, but he felt it already clear for her. "That, you see, is my only logic. Not, out of the whole affair, to have got anything for myself." (512)

Cultivating distinction by traveling to Europe is risky business. The European experience as James describes it can be genuinely revelatory and deeply disconcerting, teaching travelers things they did not know and really did not want to know, subverting their sense of self and of place in the world. One of the governing paradoxes of *The Ambassadors* is that it presents itself as a highly polished work of art offering European experience and heightened consciousness to highbrow purchasers, and at the same time questioning the practical and the moral value of these wares and even, though this is more than James anywhere says, of highly polished works of art themselves.

Dean MacCannell argues that "'the tourist' is one of the best models available for modern-man-in-general" because "for moderns, reality and authenticity are thought to be elsewhere."[44] "Elsewhere" is a grammatical shifter; once attained it becomes "here," so for MacCannell's modern sensibility "reality and authenticity" are always out of reach. The experience of James's traveler characters—the Caroline Spencers, Hyacinth Robinsons, Winterbournes, Babcocks, Newmans, Strethers, and many more—confirms MacCannell's insight and reinforces James's position as a proto-modernist. Europe starts as a goal for many of these characters, but it becomes a moving target, representing an elusive satisfaction, a series of disappointments, a lesson learned in some cases, but never a treasure neatly recovered or a life clearly redeemed. James celebrated Europe, packaged it, and sold it. He loved Europe as he loved art, but he also understood the enervating, demoralizing effect both could have on his almost universally ill-prepared compatriots.

Jonathan Freedman argues that James anticipated what might be called a modernist aesthetic of moral(istic) formalism by combining "the injunction that art be moral with the injunction that morality be aesthetic."[45] It seems to me that James anticipated the irony of modernism as well as its redemptive aestheticism, that though his uneasy, persistently American consciousness was certainly influenced by Ruskin's and Pater's, it had at least as much in common with that of his old friend, the consummate traveler and ironist Henry Adams. *The Ambassadors* is no travelogue, but its description of Lambert Strether's sensual awakening in a lovingly depicted European setting certainly did nothing to diminish "the receipts of the American touring agencies." Similarly, *Mont-Saint-Michel and Chartres* is no guidebook, but despite its author's loud disclaimers, it has served as a highbrow tourist vademecum for nearly ninety years. James, and to a lesser degree the far more private Adams, helped establish the superstitious valuation of Europe, but both remained far more skeptical of its ultimate power than the thousands of pilgrims they helped to convert to the modern cult of tourist travel.

CHAPTER NINE

Henry Adams, Traveler

Henry Adams despised tourists but adored touring. "The tourist," he wrote, "is an animal of a nature that never aroused my sympathy,"[1] but he traveled widely and frequently throughout his life, relishing, especially in periods of depression and idleness, the peculiar kind of busyness travel creates, the illusion of productive work and of accomplishment which arises simply from getting oneself and one's baggage from one place to another. He was particularly attracted by the tourist's conventional and contradictory position as both outsider and authority and cultivated an attitude of detachment not only from the countries he visited, but from the activity of tourism. His desire to be at the same time passionately engaged in the imaginative experience of travel and ironically detached from its self-indulgence and dilettantism mirrors the contradictions between his lifelong contradictory affinity for margins and his desire for power. His accounts of his travels and the rhetoric of his travel writing provide a good index to the strengths and the weaknesses of his peculiar brand of marginality and suggest a clear line of descent for his use of Europe in *Mont-Saint-Michel and Chartres* and the rhetorical strategies he developed in that book and in *The Education.*

Travel has always been a seductive but also slightly irresponsible activity. In exchange for privileged positions as onlookers, appreciators, and critics, travelers give up their connection with the life around them, becoming passive spectators who neither claim credit nor accept responsibility for the scenes they observe. As we have seen, the consequences of this bargain were particularly striking for those genteel nineteenth-century American men who gave up the possibility of respectable, remunerative careers in the law firms and banking houses of State Street and Wall Street in order to cultivate their minds, their sensibilities, and their artistic skills in Europe. These men aligned themselves *against* the money-makers, the men who were everlastingly in business and at business, and *with* their female relatives, whose own cultural business was the consumption of physical goods and services and the production of such social goods as cultivation, civility, and aesthetic enjoyment. Some of them tried to compensate for their economic marginality by writing, an activity that paradoxically negated the very idleness that made it possible, asserting that the apparent idler was in fact a conscientious worker, an active, productive member of society. Travel writing embodied for them a double gesture, an admission of marginality and a claim of centrality. Willingly identifying with an ordinarily passive, nonremunerative and therefore idle activity, travel writers strove nonetheless both to make that activity pay and to claim an active role as orderers and mediators of impressions and producers of texts.

If this is true of nineteenth-century American travelers in general, it is doubly true of Henry Adams, passionate traveler, prolific writer, and marginal man par excellence. Adams's work as his ambassador father's private secretary, his journalism, his assistant professorship at Harvard, his noontime Washington power "breakfasts," his voluminous private correspondence, and his privately or anonymously published works of imagination and theory were all attempts to influence the course of public affairs and private judgments from the sidelines. His favorite means of self-marginalization, however, was travel, and his favorite method of centering his own traveler's marginality was travel writing. The *traveler's* role as a detached, critical, and slightly superior observer with some claim to authority appealed to his sense of himself as a member of a disinherited republican aristocracy; the *narrator's* position as a central, privileged purveyor and interpreter of culture coupled with the double vicariousness inherent in the act of re-creating for a reader one's experiences as an observer appealed to his sense of himself as a writer and an artist.

Adams adopted the role of travel writer at three important junctures of his long career. At the end of his first, disappointing stay in Europe he dropped his studies and took off on a young man's toot through southern Germany, Austria, and Italy, overspending his allowance and composing the travel letters that he hoped would help him break into the world of political journalism on his return.[2] Five years after his wife's death, having left directions with Saint-Gaudens for her monument in Rock Creek Park and finished his great *History*, he tried marginalization with a vengeance by setting off with John La Farge for the South Seas. Much as he enjoyed this trip, and healing as he found it, Adams was not really content on a margin that had no chance of being a center; the volume of local history that the trip inspired is among the most esoteric and least successful of his writings. In early 1892 he returned to his Washington breakfast table, where he found even his old marginal influence on the wane, and soon developed the habit of spending a good part of every year in France, reading medieval history and literature and guiding his friends and their families around Normandy. One product of these trips was *Mont-Saint-Michel and Chartres*, in which Adams combined his own set of temperamental and intellectual positions with the generic and rhetorical possibilities of travel writing and history writing to produce a unique hybrid and a fitting culmination for the nineteenth-century American writer's romance with Europe.

ADAMS IN EUROPE, 1858–1860

Henry Adams was only twenty years old when he first touched foreign soil in the autumn of 1858. He had planned to study law in Berlin, but his German was not up to the task, so he enrolled in a secondary school instead, determined not to let the failure of his legal studies deprive him of his two years in Europe. When his brother Charles suggested that he turn his European tour to journalistic rather than legal purposes, however, he could hardly have been more outraged. "Now, my dear fellow," he wrote in reply, "my mind may be pretty but it's not original and never will be, and I shall never get any good out of it if I allow it to sprinkle all its little vigor away in newspapers and magazines. . . . [T]he law must be my ladder; without it, you might as well at once press me out into so many pages of the Atlantic Monthly" (*Letters* 1:15). And in a later letter he went on: "Of Atlantic Monthly and Putnam and Harper and the men who write for money in them, my opinion is short. . . . Gott bewahr mich from funny Lyceum lectures and rainbow articles in Atlantic Monthlys with a proof of scholarship as exhibited by a line here or there from 'the charming old Epicurean Horace.' . . . If I was born to be the admiration of girls and Tupperian philosophers, I'll cheat fate and quietly do nothing all my life" (*Letters* 1:23, 24).

Before long, however, Adams's desire to cut a public figure overcame his disdain for the public media, and by the spring of 1860 he was contemplating a series of letters from Italy and at the same time adopting the travel writer's conventional (false?) modesty.

Now, you will understand, I do *not* propose to write with the wish to publish at all hazards; on the contrary I mean to write private letters to you, as an exercise for myself, and it would be of all things my last wish to force myself into newspapers with a failure for my first attempt. On the other hand if you like the letters and think it would be in my interest to print

them, I'm all ready. . . . But if, under any absurd idea that I wish to print,
you dodge the responsibility of a decision, and a possible hurting of my
feelings; [*sic*] by showing me up to the public's amusement without any
guarantee against my making a slump, you'll make a very great mistake.
(*Letters* 1:106)[3]

The spectacle of the future writer of the *History*, *The Education*, and
Mont-Saint-Michel and Chartres backing so unwillingly into the profession of authorship is perhaps comic but also rather poignant. At the age
of twenty-two Adams was not yet ready to give up the potential centrality
of public life, but he was already clearly drawn to the marginal role of the
philosophical spectator. "In America," he had written to his brother, "the
man that can't guide had better sit still and look on" (*Letters* 1:67). In the
letters from Europe that he did eventually send home to the Boston *Courier*, he took up the position of spectator and began at the same time his
lifelong resistance to its marginality, his often frustrated attempt to assert
that one can guide precisely by sitting still and looking on.

These letters retain some interest as historical documents as well as
models for Adams's future relation to the world. He traveled from Vienna
to Venice to Florence to Rome to Naples and finally to Palermo at a time
of military uncertainty in the Austrian Empire and political upheaval in
Italy. He visited the former papal state of the Romagna and the former
grand duchy of Tuscany just weeks after they had been united under the
Piedmontese crown, witnessed the repressive governments of papal Rome
and royal Naples, and sailed to Palermo on a ship of the royal navy just
as that city's enormous garrison was surrendering to Garibaldi's redshirts.
During his brief stay in Palermo he moved between camps, delivering a
message to a Neapolitan officer and conversing with Garibaldi himself in
an informal after-dinner audience.

His reports of all these events partake of the same complicated tone
that he sets in the first paragraph of the very first letter, in which he
describes a concert he attended on his last evening in Dresden. He knew
that he should be impressed by the music but was unable to muster the
appropriate enthusiasm.

To a real lover of classical music who has never been in Germany, I suppose
the idea of listening to a concert like this, leaves about the same impression,
as to the real lover of art who has never been in Italy, the idea of seeing
Florence. To me it felt considerably like reading Homer with a very small
knowledge of Greek and no dictionary. All Pumpernickel was there however to listen. The miserable-looking old King sat with his daughters in the

royal box, and the daughters used their royal lorgnettes very condescendingly. Altogether it was a very successful concert and I was very glad to have
heard it. (*Letters* 1:110)

The irony, the simultaneous self-deprecation and self-congratulation, and
the sideways rhetorical leaps in this passage are remarkable. Adams begins
with the distance of a spectator and immediately increases that distance
by describing his lack of engagement in the musical performance. Because
of his musical inadequacy, he is in a sense excluded from this German
gathering, but this very exclusion puts him in the privileged position of
an outsider, an audience of the audience, an observer of the observers. In
this role he asserts his natural superiority: he may be musically illiterate,
but he is still capable of describing the rapt crowd as "all Pumpernickel"
and of condescending to the "miserable-looking old King" and his archly
gazing daughters. The "success" of the concert for Adams consisted at
least as much in his own successful transformation of marginality into
superiority as in the musicians' brilliant interpretation of Mozart and
Beethoven.

Adams maintains this double role all through his letters: he is always
the ironic observer, the critic rather than the participant, the tourist out
for larks, with no illusion as to the seriousness of his occupation and no
pretensions to romantic sensitivity in his reports. He does the sights with
casual American acquaintances and takes an idle critic's pleasure in the
cafés and promenades.

At two o'clock there was music on the Piazza and I came back to sit in the
sun, and drink chocolate, and smoke cigarettes, and look at the people. . . .
There was a pleasant variety about all this. The officiers [*sic*] were wandering up and down, looking their very prettiest; the beggars were as dirty and
as interesting as ever; the ladies' dresses were more or less pretty, and the
faces, many of them, considerably more so than less. (*Letters* 1:122)

He avoids above all things the conventional tourist's rapture, preferring
matter-of-fact details about the discomforts of the way to purple descriptions of already-familiar experiences. His treatment of one of the classic
moments of European travel, the arrival at Venice by sea, is a case in
point.

As for the seven hours of passage, I know little about them. After a short
conversation with the Captain . . . , I stretched myself out in the cabin, with
my boots in an Austrian Lieutenant's face, and a Hungarian Hussar's spurs
very near my nose, and there I went to sleep. I have an idea that it was

rather rough, but don't think it amounted to much. It had been some time
light when the Hussar kicked me on the head which woke me up and as
everyone seemed to be going on deck I followed them. Venice was right
before us and we were bringing to just opposite the Place of St Marc [*sic*].
(*Letters* 1:118)[4]

The pose Adams adopts in passages like this is self-consciously casual and
superior. He is a young man enjoying his own mock indifference to conventional pleasures: he eats his cake and has it, too, arriving in Venice by
sea and at the same time deprecating both that arrival and the usual reaction to it.

Unlike conventional tourists (but like Fuller and his own grandfather,
John Quincy Adams, whose *Letters on Silesia* served as a model for his
Italian letters), Adams pays attention to the political and military scene,
commenting on conditions in the Romagna and the state of the Piedmontese army, but always sideways, and a little diffidently. He describes
"queer old men and women on still queerer old donkey-carts" and wonders that Cavour should "trust the right of voteing [*sic*]" to them (*Letters*
1:125). He writes of the fortifications of Bologna and then disclaims access
to any authority but that of his own eyes (*Letters* 1:126). In Rome at last,
at the very center of political excitement, Adams remains interested but
marginal. "Here I am directly in the centre of it all, and what good do I
get of it?" (*Letters* 1:153). "If you are curious as to Roman politics, I'm
sorry that I can tell you next to nothing" (*Letters* 1:145). "Politics are out
of place here for a mere visitor. Here one lives in history and in art, and
needs nothing more" (*Letters* 1:146).

The closer Adams is drawn to the center of excitement, the more devices he deploys to distance himself. He refers to his trip to Palermo as "a
glorious lark" and then adds the following in a postscript to his brother:

Old moozer
    . . . Ye Gods what an escapade and won't the parients [*sic*] howl. Don't
let them know unless you think they can stand the news. It's perfectly safe.
Don't be afraid.

                                          My eye
                                          What a guy
                                          Ever your
                                          Henrye   (*Letters* 1:161–62)

Adams is clearly no partisan on a mission, but a political tourist taking
advantage of an opportunity to observe the center of action from a convenient, safe sideline. He plays the triumphant Sicilians for laughs, mock-

ing their "cutlasses and dirks" and ill-assorted firearms "suggestive of stagecoaches and highway robberies two centuries ago" (*Letters* 1:165). Although Adams's real hero in Italian politics is Cavour, on whom he gazed with pleasure at the Florence opera (*Letters* 1:130), he finds Garibaldi magnetic in his informality. The Europeans, he observes, "are fond of calling him the Washington of Italy, principally because they know nothing about Washington. Catch Washington invading a foreign country on his own hook, in a fireman's shirt" (*Letters* 1:167). Adams admires, without making any commitment. He reaches "the height of my ambition as a traveller, face to face with one of the great events of our day," and he withdraws into humor and superiority.

> And there was the Great Dictator, who, when your and my little hopes and ambitions shall have lain in our graves a few centuries with us, will still be honored as a hero, and perhaps half worshipped, who knows! for a God. (*Letters* 1:168)

Adams has taken himself to the center of the fray and then written an ironic, marginal piece about his excursion. Although the *Letters* are not remarkable for their maturity of tone or of vision—they border at times on the smugly sophomoric—they do begin to carve out a rhetorical position that Adams will occupy with ever greater aplomb and effect. He guides his readers from city to city, shows them the life that he observes, invites them to participate in his ironic superiority to much of what he sees, and treats them to a few political obiter dicta along the way.[5] He uses the experience of European travel to play the role of unassuming genial guide when in fact he is claiming the position of reliable critic and commentator. He will take up variations of this double persona throughout his life and use it most brilliantly in *Mont-Saint-Michel and Chartres*.

Travels/Tahiti

In the years that followed his first European tour, Henry Adams practiced marginality as a private secretary, a journalist, an assistant professor, and a Washington host. He seems also to have experienced a gratifying and invigorating, if not always comfortable, kind of centeredness in his marriage with Clover Hooper and his work on the great *History*.[6] Clover's suicide in late 1885 famously undid Henry; the following summer he took a restorative trip to Japan with the painter John La Farge, visiting temples with resident Americans (including Ernest Fenellosa, Pound's teacher) and buying carloads of silk and bric-à-brac.[7] But he had his *History* to write, and he returned to write it, working on through his father's death and his mother's long last illness, with the distraction, too, of his own growing fondness for his neighbor, Elizabeth Cameron. All this activity and responsibility kept Adams anchored if not comfortably centered until midsummer 1890, when the *History* was complete, his parents were buried, and his feelings for Elizabeth Cameron had become perhaps as disturbing to him as they had once been consoling.[8] For whatever reason—William Dusinberre believes it was "to disguise his nervous interest in the response to [the *History's*] publication,"[9] Samuels suggests that Elizabeth Cameron sent him away;[10] mental and emotional exhaustion seem to me equally likely motivations—Adams chose this moment to weigh anchor at last for the very edge of the world. There is surely no place more marginal than a South Sea island, a bit of territory practically all margin itself, where none of Adams's relatives came from or had ever been, where there was nothing to study and no society to break into, a restorative haven for the sick and the jaded, like Robert Louis Stevenson, and the deathly weary, like Henry Adams.

For the first few months of the trip the margin seemed just the place for Adams to be; his private letters from this time fairly glow with the traveler's keen, irresponsible pleasure. At the first stop, in Hawaii, he reveled in the inconsequentiality of everything he did and described it as the occupation of women and children. "My own water-color diversions . . . look like young ladies' embroidery of the last generation. . . . [My painting] has the charm that I felt as a boy about going fishing: I recognise that I am catching no fish on this particular day, but I feel always as though I might get a bite tomorrow" (*Letters* 3:270–71). The letters that followed were certainly the work of a man in love with images, colors, and words, but they were also the record of a desultory, detached tourist's experience of a foreign culture. One of the most striking begins with a vivid, slightly ironic picture of the fifty-two-year-old Adams gone native: "Since then, for elegance and comfort, I have adopted the native lava-lava, with a shirt, as my boating-costume; and the village applauds me every afternoon as I stalk across the green in a flaming red waist-cloth, and legs as bare as a Scotch Highlander's" (*Letters* 3:388). There follows a self-consciously literary passage comparing the tropical sunset to "the toilet of the loveliest girl in Parisian outfit," after which Adams comments on the fraudulent nature of photography and moves on to recount, with the tourist's typical detachment, an island murder (*Letters* 3:389). In this letter Adams is the very model of the cosmopolitan tourist in paradise and the self-consciously aesthetic dilettante. By the time he has reached Tahiti, however, he can stand his detachment no longer. "Never have I known what it was to be so bored before, even in the worst wilds of Beacon Street or the dreariest dinner-tables of Belgravia. My mind has given way. I have horrors" (*Letters* 3:445). He cannot paint; he has read all the books; there is no one to talk to; and writing chronicle letters is no substitute for more rigorous intellectual activity.

The solution that presents itself is to transcribe the memoirs of an old "chiefess," an activity enough like history writing to permit Adams to declare with some pride: "Positively I have worked. I am not quite so brazen-faced as to claim to have done real work; but I have been quite as busy as I should be at home. I have untangled two centuries of family history, and have got it wound up nicely" (*Letters* 3:479). What Adams has done is the basic research for the most curious of his works, the volume commonly known as *Tahiti* but actually entitled first *Memoirs of Marau Taaroa, Last Queen of Tahiti* (1893 edition) and then *Memoirs of Arii Taimai E . . .* (1901 edition), with the half-title *Travels/Tahiti.*

The subject matter of this book would seem most congenial for the author of a detailed history of the United States under Jefferson and Madison and future chronicler of the soldiers of William the Conqueror at eleventh-century Mont Saint-Michel, the court of Mary, Queen of Heaven, in Chartres, and the relentless entropic decline of Western civilization from "Twelfth-Century Unity" to "Twentieth-Century Multiplicity." It includes first a historical and genealogical study of Tahiti's ruling family, not very much like the Adams family history in detail, to be sure, but quite similar in outcome, since both families move from the center to the margins of political power. It describes the power of women in the island and especially that of the dowager queen, Arii Taimai. Finally, it outlines the inexorably downward course of Tahitian history, from before the arrival of white people to the present.

The project provided Adams with welcome intellectual activity and authentic, purposeful contact with his Tahitian hosts. For all that, however, it remained an exercise in self-distancing. Tahiti is a long way from the centers of nineteenth-century worldly power, and the Tahiti Adams chronicles is very different from the Tahiti he experienced. As John Carlos Rowe puts it, "For Adams at the turn of the century, the exotic Tahiti of Arii Taimai is already as remote as thirteenth-century France. Adams may have referred to the work as 'his *Tahiti*,' but both he and the old queen's daughter, Marau Taaroa, must have recognized that they were recording the fragments of a lost world."[11]

If the subject of Adams's little book is remote in time and space, the rhetoric of its various titles and its evasive narrative voice lay claim to an ambiguous anonymity. Why, in the first place, label it "Travels"? It is not a travel book in any conventional way, yet it takes up a position with regard to Tahitian history and culture that is similar to the position of the *Courier* letters with regard to Italian history and the private letters from Japan, Hawaii, and Samoa with regard to their people and customs. By half-titling the book *Travels/Tahiti*, its producer designates himself an outsider, limits his involvement with the book's content, and distances himself from its narrative voice. His editorial posturing makes it clear that this is a mere visit to history rather than an engaged and extended historical study like the ones he had written in the past.

The changes Adams made in the book's principal title also emphasize his distance from it. Marau Taaroa corresponded with Adams after he left Tahiti and translated the Tahitian material for him. His actual informant, however, was her mother, Arii Taimai. The change in title from *Memoirs of Marau Taaroa* to *Memoirs of Arii Taimai* would therefore seem reasonable but for the fact that both titles, and both title pages, ignore Adams's role in the book altogether. Furthermore, the conjunction of the 1901 half-title with the 1901 title page is doubly misleading: these are certainly not Arii Taimai's "Travels" in Tahiti, but she is the only author named anywhere in the volume. All an innocent reader can tell from the conflicting information contained on the cover and title pages of the book is that its authorship is ambiguous. Its traveler-author remains anonymous but prefaces the book with a broad gesture indicating that it has some source other than a royal Tahitian memoirist.

Rhetorically, too, the book's anonymity is at best ambivalent. The word *memoirs* in the title suggests a first-person account of the author's memories, and the text's first sentence supports this suggestion: "If the Papara family and people had any name, in European fashion, I suppose it would be Teva, for *we* are a clan, and Teva is *our* clan name."[12] The sentence claims to have been composed by a real speaker, a Tahitian, a member of the clan called Teva, and the source of the narrative. From that ostensible source proceeds an outline of Tahitian history going back to legendary times, emerging into European time "eight generations ago, about the middle of the seventeenth century," and continuing to the present. This outline relies heavily on European sources; its images and turns of phrase are often European; and it assumes a European superiority to these charming but "primitive" islanders.

The use of European sources would not in itself rule out a Tahitian author. A reader who did not know that Arii Taimai was illiterate and spoke only Tahitian might well assume that she had read Cook's *Voyages*, Diderot's "Supplément au *Voyage* de Bougainville," the writings of Johnson, Boswell, and Cowper, and the many other Europeans cited in the text. The attitudes the text conveys, however, are harder to reconcile with a Tahitian speaker. Substitute Quincy or Tunbridge for Papara, and the following sentence would be quite at home in any genteel volume of Anglo-American local history; as the putative utterance of Arii Taimai, however, it is implausible:

> Even a Papara school-girl, if she reads in her history-book the story of Appius Claudius or of Tarquin, would be a little surprised to find that she knew all about it, and that Papara had a Brutus and a Virginius of its own quite as good as the Roman. (20)

More striking even than this sort of anomaly is the Eurocentrism conveyed in other passages, which clearly imply a European or a highly Europeanized speaker:

> Men have in all times been ingenious in their reasons for deserting women when tired of them, but, even in the South Seas and at that early day, this pretext must have been though at least unusual, since it was preserved in legend. (13)

> Primitive people seem to have kept certain stock-stories, as one keeps pincushions to stick with pins, which represent the sharp points of their history and the names of their heroes. (21)

Travels/Tahiti is thus multiply marginal. From the edge of a society that is at the edge of the "civilized" world, Adams anonymously transcribes a family chronicle that is also an oblique comment on the trajectory of Western civilization and its moral and political influence in the world. The formally acknowledged author of the work is a Tahitian queen, but the actual voice of the narrative is Adams's cultivated Anglo-American academic, waxing melancholy over days gone by.

Adams described the project to Mrs. Cameron as the quintessential marginal activity, "a sort of excuse for doing nothing" (*Letters* 3:477). The mere act of traveling, it seems, represented total blankness to Adams; the marginality he aspired to was replete with text, which he saw as a kind of running gloss, a privileged commentary on the center-page narrative of history and civilization. In *Travels/Tahiti* and the activities that surrounded it he was teaching himself a new version of centered marginality, claiming a position parallel to but not identical with that of the anonymous author of *Democracy* and *Esther*, the nameless London correspondent for the *New York Times*, the officeless Washington host, and the eventual third-person narrator of the *Education*.

A position is not a voice, however, and one of the problems with *Travels/Tahiti* is the vagueness of its narrative mode, its lack of a speaking persona. If he was to be marginal in an effective way, Adams had to find a fictional source for his discourse, a credible figure to hide behind, a mouthpiece for his pronouncements. In fact, Adams was developing just such a persona even as he worked on the Tahitian "Memoir."[13] His letters from the South Seas to Mrs. Cameron and his nieces were not serious enough to satisfy his need for work, but they did provide a stage on which he could cast himself as the disarmingly modest old gentleman whose voice we hear again in *Mont-Saint-Michel and Chartres*.

> An idler man than your dear Uncle Henry during the last month, you would not find in Cambridgeport, I don't feel sure that you would find one even in Cambridge. I have done as near nothing as possible. . . . Did I send you any photograph with a native canoe in it? If not, I will stick into this envelope a sad attempt I made to paint one, after a small photograph; but don't you show my colored things! If you let them be seen by anyone, outside of you shrimps and your papa, I will never write you another line. I let you have my pictures because you children show me yours, which is fair exchange; but other people would think I was seriously intending to paint, and I don't want other people to think anything about it.[14]

The self-deprecation and childishly simple syntax here are cloying—the audience is an actual little girl—but the kindly uncle of the later work is adumbrated by Adams's pose.

In the "Memoirs," Adams played at history writing; in his letters to his nieces he played at "uncle-ing." Neither of these activities left him satisfied, but both prepared the way for one that would: his confrontation with European history and art and the composition of his great commentary on faith, architecture, gender, and the shape of history, a work that masqueraded as a travel book for actual nieces and for intellectual and aesthetic "tourists," *Mont-Saint-Michel and Chartres*.

MONT-SAINT-MICHEL AND CHARTRES

By the time Henry Adams began his regular visits to France in the mid-nineties, he had been using the experience of travel and the literary opportunities that travel writing afforded to cultivate the art of public marginality for more than thirty years. In *Mont-Saint-Michel and Chartres* he brought this project to brilliant fruition by exploiting the unique relation of Europe and European history to U.S. culture and re-creating in his text the complex experience of the American tourist and scholar confronting the familiar otherness of the European Middle Ages. Ordinary travel writers were content to describe *their* experiences in Europe; in *Mont-Saint-Michel and Chartres* Adams helps *his readers* experience not only the monuments it purports to describe, but the process of coming to understand their significance for their own time and for the dawning twentieth century as well.

Travels/France (the book's half-title) shares and modifies the doubleness of *Travels/Tahiti*, but it transcends its apparent genre even more thoroughly and claims a more centered marginality than its modest predecessor. The public reception and scholarly criticism of the work have predictably reflected its generic ambiguity. The anonymous reviewer in the general-interest *Booklist* asserted that *Mont-Saint-Michel and Chartres* was "a work by a scholar, primarily for scholars";[15] the historian Henry Osborn Taylor, writing in the *American Historical Review*, saw it as a more personal document, wondering "whether we have gone the round of the twelfth and thirteenth centuries, or the round of the mind of Henry Adams."[16] Adams's most sympathetic reviewer, the medievalist Frederick Bliss Luquiens, made a virtue of the book's doubleness, praising its ability to "appeal with equal force to layman and expert."[17]

Adams anticipated this confusion. His attitude toward travel writing was always ambivalent, from the time of the *Courier* letters to his rejection of Richard Watson Gilder's suggestion that he do a series of South Sea letters for the *Century*[18] to his at least half-serious invitation to John Hay to collaborate on a volume of French travels.

> I will come home, and immediately, if you will join me in writing, under any assumed name or character you please, a volume or two of Travels which will permit me to express my opinion of life in general, and especially of the French, their literature, and their art. . . . I have said and stick to it, that I will never again appear as an author, but I don't mind writing anonymously as one does in the newspapers, and Travels that say anything are nowadays read. . . . My notion of Travels is a sort of ragbag of everything; scenery, psychology, history, literature, poetry, art; anything in short, that is worth throwing in.[19]

This passage suggests that Adams could see travel writing as a vehicle for ideas and opinions and a way of gaining access to an audience, a possible means of fulfilling his writerly desires to express himself in print and to be read. It would be most convenient if he had also seen *Mont-Saint-Michel and Chartres* the way sympathetic critics and readers have, as the culmination of at least one aspect of his career, an artful expression of his ideas, a successful aesthetic structure in its own right, and an effective intervention—from the margin—in American intellectual and cultural history. Judicious quotation can make it seem that he held just this opinion.

> The only book I ever wrote that was worth writing was the first volume of the Series—the *Mont-Saint-Michel.* (*Letters* 1938, 542)

> My real comfort in life has been my volume on *Chartres.* (*Letters* 1938, 594)

The history of the book's publication, however, and Adams's other comments on it tell a different story.

Adams had been thinking about and working on the book in one way or another since the mid-nineties, but when the manuscript was finished, in February 1903, he adopted the superior tone of a Jamesian dilettante, refused to vulgarize it by publication, and even hesitated to print it at all, since the money he would have had to spend for a suitable private edition could be better spent on porcelain. "A private edition of fifty copies would cost at least fifteen hundred dollars, and I prefer Ming potiches. Think of giving up twenty Ming potiches for the vanity of a twentieth volume!" (*Letters* 1938, 396). The gesture these lines embody is multiply self-protective. By reducing his book to the status of a bibelot, Adams avoids the vulgar appearance of taking his work too seriously and sets up a perfect excuse in case it should be found defective. By refusing to publish it in the usual way, he is protecting it from the eyes of the mob and the criticism of the unsympathetic and the unworthy. "If you asked me to find out five hundred persons in the world to whom you would like to give the volume," he wrote to his brother Brooks, "I could say only that, as far as you and I know, five hundred do not exist,—nor half that number—nor a quarter of it" (*Letters* 1938, 453).

When Adams did print the volume he was almost true to this snobbish pronouncement. He printed a hundred copies in 1904 and distributed them to a selection of friends, real and honorary nieces, . . . and libraries. "I have not cared to make the *Chartres* a mercantile affair," he wrote with characteristic hauteur. "Yet it is, strictly, published, since all the chief libraries are supposed to have been presented with copies. No doubt the copies are now exhausted, and I've not thought the volume sufficiently interesting to reprint" (*Letters* 1938, 544). Not interesting enough to reprint but interesting enough to make sure that copies are preserved in the principal libraries. A mere trifle but one finally worth revising and reprinting in 1912, and publishing at last, with a seemly show of reluctance, in 1913. "Don't say I let 'em publish *Chartres*. I kicked so as to be a credit to my years" (*Letters* 1938, 623).

The narrative voice of *Mont-Saint-Michel and Chartres* reproduces both the diffidence and the pride evident in Adams's epistolary pronouncements and further develops the persona that had begun to emerge in his personal letters from the South Seas. A brief preface establishes the narrator's modesty and the marginality of his project. The ideal relationship between writer and reader is probably analogous to the relation between father and son, he begins, but such closeness is impossible nowadays. Failing a son, the next-best solution would be the regulated masculine intimacy of an uncle and a nephew. Nephews, however, being young and male, do not read: "The following pages, then, are written for nieces."[20] The narrator does not claim to be passing on essential knowledge to his heirs; he is simply producing a few pleasant pages for the amusement of young girls.

He is, in other words, marginal; his place is not in the main line of patriarchal succession, but off to the side, with the childless men and the marriageable young women. He emphasizes this marginality even more by identifying himself as a tourist, not a scholar or a philosopher, a seeker of mere feelings, rather than facts or technical understanding. In the early historical and architectural sections of the book Adams uses the role of tourist to renounce any claim to factual accuracy and scientific knowledge.

> Harold must have got great fame by saving life on the sands, to be remembered and recorded by the Normans themselves after they had killed him; but this is the affair of historians. Tourists only note that Harold and William come to the Mount: "Venerunt ad Montem." (20)

> The subject of vaulting is far too ambitious for summer travel. (35)

> Tourists want as few dates as possible; what they want is poetry. (36)

> We are not now seeking religion; indeed, true religion generally comes unsought. We are trying only to feel Gothic art. (108)

Later, too, in the philosophical sections, this pose serves to relieve Adams of the necessity of tackling thorny scholastic problems in his treatment of Aquinas.

For summer tourists to handle these intricate problems in a theological spirit would be altogether absurd; but, for us, these great theologians were also architects who undertook to build a Church Intellectual, corresponding bit by bit to the Church Administrative, both expressing—and expressed by—the Church Architectural. (349)

All these disclaimers are balanced by the serious content of the book and its clear intention to say something important. Earlier critics have variously praised Adams and taken him to task for his treatment of medieval history, art, and literature and for the general theory of history that he propounds, but no one has accepted the notion that *Mont-Saint-Michel and Chartres* is the trifling work of a dilettante, suitable for fancy binding, and so delicate as to need protection from the coarse eyes of the general reader. It has been understood, instead, as a private pronouncement on public matters, a view of the present from the past, a comment on the course of history, reason, belief, artistic expression, and gender relations from a man on the margins of all these things.

In its ambitions and its achievements, *Mont-Saint-Michel and Chartres* far outstrips its earlier nineteenth-century forebears, but it also betrays its relation to more conventional travel writings and its indebtedness to the cultural impulses that engendered them. Generically, *Mont-Saint-Michel and Chartres* is closely related to the traditional travel guide—a model Adams himself repudiated[21]—and the eclectic book of travel sketches, deriving ultimately from the eighteenth-century tradition of periodical essays and finding its nineteenth-century American pattern in Irving's *Sketch Book*. These books tend to be ragbags of one kind or another, combining travel narrative and folk tale with social, cultural, and political reportage to produce genial volumes of genteel chat and observation. Modest and marginal by definition (though as a genre extremely popular), they share one assumption: they implicitly claim at least temporary centrality for personal experience: they assume that the purposes of travel and the goals of travel writing include the search for, and the representation and the construction of, experiences.

Like thousands of Americans after him, Irving attributed magical qualities to the stones of Europe and was eager to open himself to the raptures they would certainly inspire.

I longed to wander over the scenes of renowned achievement—to tread as it were in the footsteps of antiquity—to loiter about the ruined castle—to meditate on the falling tower—to escape in short, from the commonplace realities of the present, and lose myself among the shadowy grandeurs of the past. (744)

Later travelers continue to value the sensations and the insights they gain from the experiences they arrange for themselves. Grace Greenwood makes the required stop at Westminster Abbey and is moved to the conventional O Altitudo!

> O, how the immortal genius of poet, and wit, and orator, and rare player seem to hover exultant on that solemn air! How the dead lords of mind seemed to rule us from their graves, to sway the wild pulses of our living hearts, and to bow our heads, borne high in the pride of life, low and sad before the mouldering, formless dust of theirs![22]

Longfellow has a similar reaction in Père La Chaise,[23] and even the superficial and dandified Nathaniel Parker Willis admits that a visit to the Parisian cemetery is likely to move the tourist to solemn contemplation.[24]

Adams shares these travelers' valuation of experience: he repeatedly claims that the goal of *Mont-Saint-Michel and Chartres* is to help the tourist/niece/reader experience the French Middle Ages and the monuments that they left behind. His understanding of the notion, however, is mediated by his own habitual detachment and his multiple ambitions as tour guide, medieval historian, and imaginative writer. His purpose is not to describe his own experience in the presence of the old and the beautiful, but to generate an experience for his reader that is both aesthetically satisfying and genuinely historical in its understanding of and imaginative contact with a bygone culture. His vehicle for this project is a rhetorically complicated text that holds readers at arm's length by commenting ironically on its own status as putative guidebook and theirs as tourists and uses the power of figurative language to develop a new mode of history writing.

Adams's introduction to Chartres Cathedral sounds as if it had been cribbed from a slightly precious guidebook.

> For a first visit to Chartres, choose some pleasant morning when the lights are soft, for one wants to be welcome, and the cathedral has moods, at times severe. At best, the Beauce is a country none too gay.
>
> The first glimpse that is caught, and the first that was meant to be caught, is that of the two spires. (62)

All is as it should be on a pleasant summer tour: the spires gleam in the distance, and the tourist finds the taller, newer tower the more impressive. This is natural, common—and wrong. "In want of a schoolmaster to lay down a law of taste," he writes, "you can admire the new flèche as much as you please" (67). "Of course," he continues, when you come closer you can see "that the lines of the new tower are not clean, like those of the old," and he goes on to guide the reader's eye over the comparative vulgarities of the newer structure, only to end with a metaphoric comparison whose intent is as much moral as it is aesthetic and historical.

> As a companion to the Virgin of Chartres, it recalls Diane de Poitiers. . . . It is self-conscious if not vain; its coiffure is elaborately arranged to cover the effects of age, and its neck and shoulders are covered with lace and jewels to hide a certain sharpness of skeleton. Yet it may be beautiful, still; the poets derided the wrinkles of Diane de Poitiers at the very moment when King Henry II idealized her with the homage of a Don Quixote; an atmosphere of physical beauty and decay hangs about the whole Renaissance. (67, 68)

From the conventional description and playful irony of the earlier passage, Adams moves here to intensify the niece/tourist/reader's experience of the towers by personalizing them. To see these monuments as two women, one old in years but ageless in appearance, the other younger but bedizened with decoration to hide her encroaching age, is to enter into an intimate imaginative relationship with them. The comparison evokes the reader's own experience of elderly ladies, the smell of clean, crisp linen and of powder and perfume, the recognition of chaste and ageless beauty beneath the simple religious habit of the one, and the uneasy awareness of the wrinkled skin beneath the lace and jewels of the other. It assumes as well a conventional, well-bred distaste for the showy woman and uses this distaste to reinforce Adams's low opinion of the later architectural style. Moreover, it simultaneously contracts and expands this judgment, from social types and architectural styles to individual women—the virgin queen of heaven and the worldly mistress of a worldly king—to the periods they epitomize. What might seem at first to be a simple lesson in aesthetics and a handy tourist-guide trick ("You don't see the difference? Well, imagine one's a nun and the other a strumpet. *Now* do you see?") has become a lesson in Adams's views of history and morality. The figurative language that began as a way of illustrating the difference between the two towers has been turned inside out: instead of objects to be illuminated, the spires become illuminating illustrations of a larger historical point. The female figures that began as devices to personalize and intensify the experience of Chartres Cathedral have become figures of a different kind, representations of times and places and systems that the contrasting styles of architecture can help us understand. The metaphorizing process has come full circle, and the spires that were to be figuratively explained have become themselves explanatory figures. In little more than a breath, Adams has combined his voices and his purposes in this text and created an experience for his readers that is like the tourist experience but far deeper in intensity and broader in significance.

Throughout *Mont-Saint-Michel and Chartres,* Adams asks the tourist to imagine and if possible to relive the experience of the medieval pilgrim while continuing to exercise her aesthetic taste and moral judgment. His rhetoric and his descriptions are personal: he addresses the reader directly as "you"; he describes the saints, queens, and soldiers of the past as human individuals as well as emblems for sets of beliefs and values.

The figure of Christ on the central portal, for example, welcomes the traveler, whether from nineteenth-century Quincy or twelfth-century Paris: "Never once are you regarded as a possible rebel, or traitor, or a stranger to be treated with suspicion, or as a child to be impressed by fear" (72). The figures of the Virgin are both queenly and homely, governed not by the rules of the churchmen, but by Mary's desire to communicate with her people: "In correct theology, the Virgin ought not to be represented in bed, for she could not suffer like ordinary women, but her palace at Chartres is not much troubled by theology, and to her, as empress-mother, the pain of child-birth was a pleasure she wanted her people to share" (73). The flanking statues—"the Eginetan marbles of French art" (76)—underscore the transcendent femininity of the whole ensemble, which Adams relates to the imagined humanity of the twelfth-century church and the concomitant strength of its appeal to peasants and crusaders alike.

> Not only the number of the female figures, and their beauty, but also the singularly youthful beauty of several of the males; the superb robes they wear; the expression of their faces and their figures; the details of hair, stuffs, ornaments, jewels; the refinement and feminine taste of the whole, are enough to startle our interest if we recognize what meaning they had to the twelfth century. (76)

> The whole charm lies for us in the twelfth-century humanity of Mary and her Court; not in the scriptural names under which it was made orthodox. Here, in this western portal, it stands as the crusaders of 1100–1150 imagined it. (77)

Adams's readers here approach the cathedral in their multiple roles of pilgrims, tourists, and scholars. He invites us to imagine the effect of the west portal on the twelfth-century faithful, take note of doc-

trinal irregularities, enjoy the classic grandeur of the sculpture, and relate the whole to the "feeling" of Christian Europe at the time of the
Crusades.

In his description of the north porch, Adams similarly guides the
reader/tourist's experience from aesthetic perception to emotional understanding, first pointing out a statue—in this case "the great figure of
Abraham about to sacrifice Isaac" (84)—then characterizing its subject—
"revolting . . . to a woman who typifies the Mother"—and finally describing the sculptor's successful attempt to reconcile the required biblical
subject with the tone of his great patroness.

> He has placed Abraham against the column in the correct harshness of atti-
> tude, with his face turned aside and up, listening for his orders; but the little
> Isaac, with hands and feet tied, leans like a bundle of sticks against his fa-
> ther's knee with an expression of perfect faith and confidence, while Abra-
> ham's left hand quiets him and caresses the boy's face, with a movement
> that must have gone straight to Mary's heart, for Isaac always prefigured
> Christ. (84)

This is the porch of the thirteenth-century Virgin, "no longer an Em-
press; she is Queen Mother, . . . too high to want, or suffer, or to revenge,
or to aspire, but not too high to pity, to punish, or to pardon" (84).

If the north porch (the Porche de France) is feminine and welcoming,
the south porch (the Porche de Dreux) is masculine and forbidding. The
sculpture here is exquisite, too, and Adams is quick to give it its due. He
cannot, however, stop there; Adams's tourist is no mere formalist art
critic but a seeker after feeling and, ultimately, understanding: questions
of relative formal merit may elude us, but those of feeling and meaning
demand to be answered.

> Which porch is the more beautiful is a question for artists to discuss and
> decide, if they can. Either is good enough for us, whose pose is ignorance,
> and whose pose is strictly correct; but apart from its beauty or its art, there
> is also the question of feeling, of motive, which puts the Porche de Dreux
> in contrast with the Porche de France, and this is wholly within our compe-
> tence. (85–86)

The feeling of the Porche de Dreux is to Adams "grand, . . . dignified,
impressive, and masculine" (86); its "theology" (88) is unimpeachable;
it represents the Virgin in her correctly exalted place, so exalted, in fact,
that she can be seen only from outside the porch, in the square, with
binoculars. The ensemble feels cold to Adams, however, and stern, and

unforgiving: it opens onto the later history of the church, away from the almost cozy "twelfth-century unity" that Adams imagines for his favorite era.

> The whole melodrama of Church terrors appears after the manner of the thirteenth century, on this church door, without regard to Mary's feelings; and below, against the trumeau, stands the great figure of Christ,—the whole Church,—trampling on the lion and the dragon. On either side of the doorway stand six great figures of the Apostles asserting themselves as the columns of the Church, and looking down at us with an expression no longer calculated to calm our fears or encourage extravagant hopes. No figure on this porch suggests a portrait or recalls a memory. (86)

So Adams the travel guide leads his group of tourist/readers from statue to statue, portal to portal, eliciting and imagining emotional and aesthetic responses and using these responses to develop a feeling for and an interpretation of the spirit and the life of the French Middle Ages. He structures his historical interpretation in classic hermeneutic fashion, moving from a perception of a part to a projection of the whole and back to interpretations of other parts in light of his understanding of the whole. The effect is to move generically from guidebook to narrative of personal experience to historical interpretation; Adams demands that his tourists give up passive list-checking and mere appreciation and think themselves into his version of the medieval mind-set in order to grasp his version of the shape of history and the fate of femininity and enjoy their experience of the past and the foreign.

While Adams is creating this intense personal experience for the reader, he is using figurative language to elaborate its historical significance and to create a complex textual experience. In the initial description of the spires at Chartres, he moved from metaphor (the towers are *like* women) to synecdoche (the women were *part of* historical periods) to a mutually explanatory combination of the two (thinking about the similarities and differences of these particular towers, women, and historical periods helps us understand them all). In the rest of the text he moves between synecdoche and metaphor to emphasize the continuities and discontinuities, the similarities and the radical differences between historical periods and modes of artistic and intellectual production.

His relation of the architectural details at Mont-Saint-Michel to the culture that produced them, for example, is synecdochic: instead of standing for or resulting from some quality of the whole, they share that quality with the whole. The sturdy rounded, "masculine" vaults of the early Romanesque do not symbolize a time and a place so much as they epitomize it, embodying in concentrated form qualities that pervade its culture. "The ['Chanson de Roland'] and the church are akin," he writes; "they go together, and explain each other. The common trait is their military character, peculiar to the eleventh century. The round arch is masculine. The 'Chanson' is . . . masculine" (22–23; see also 49).

Hayden White calls this kind of synecdochic representation "integrative" in strategy and relates it to a conservative view of the world, which suggests that a culture's institutions and ways of thinking form a consistent noncontradictory whole.[25] Adams was in many ways—temperamentally, for example—conservative, even reactionary, and devoted to the comforts of a synecdochic vision. His longing for the putative consistency of the Middle Ages (or the equally mythical eighteenth-century rationality of his great-grandfather's day) was tempered, however, by an admiration for the dynamism of other times and places. If he found the stolid consistency of the Romanesque appealing, he was at least as attracted by the monumentally balanced masses and forces of the Gothic. If his thinking and writing were anchored by synecdoche, they were energized by a bolder metaphoric vision.

The crowning chapter of his own Gothic edifice, entitled simply "Saint Thomas Aquinas," embodies the sort of contradiction that energizes the whole work. If Aquinas typifies one age as the Norman arch did another, his great work, the *Summa Theologiae*, stands in a metaphoric rather than a metonymic relation to the completed Gothic cathedrals of its time. The *Summa* and the cathedral are as fundamentally different as words and stone, systems and feelings: as artifacts they have almost nothing in common; it is impossible to conceive of one as a part of the other or an epitome of the other; they are freestanding entities, each obeying its own rules and embodying its own purposes. And yet, for Adams, they are alike. They are great structures of counterbalancing weights and ideas and great creations of human mind and human industry. They are firmly based in history, yet they transcend their historical origins to assert their monumental originality: "The immense structure [of the *Summa*] rested on Aristotle and Saint Augustine at the last, but as a work of art it stood alone, like Rheims or Amiens Cathedral, as though it had no antecedents" (350).

Once established, this basic metaphor becomes for Adams a bold heuristic device to generate new ways of thinking about both architecture and philosophy. The point is not to integrate one with the other or to juxtapose them as cause and effect, part and whole, or parts of the same whole, but to wrest comprehension from resemblance; it is not, in other words, to point out what is the case, but to create a new understanding by insisting on a metaphoric relationship. In the manner of a seventeenth-century poet, Adams extends his metaphor from general concept to detail, giving his readers new ways to think about both his subjects.

> Beginning with the foundation which is God and God's active presence in His Church, Thomas next built God into the walls and towers of His Church, in the Trinity and its creation of mind and matter in time and space. (350–51)

> He swept away the horizontal lines altogether, leaving them barely as a part of decoration. The whole weight of his arches fell, as in the latest Gothic, where the eye sees nothing to break the sheer spring of the nervures, from the rosette on the keystone a hundred feet above down to the church floor. (356)

St. Thomas is an architect; his systematic arguments are the vaults; his triumphant conclusions, the spires and towers; the weight of his great edifice is carried by the ineluctable logic of syllogistic elaboration from the height of his nave, arching toward salvation, to the bedrock of faith beneath the crypt. Similarly, the Gothic builders are theologians, embodying an idea of the cosmos in stone.[26] Adams's metaphor brings them together and offers their similarities as an aid and an inspiration for the reader's understanding.

Unlike synecdoche, however, metaphor insists on difference, on the nonidentity of the two figural elements: if two things are identical, it makes no sense to discuss their "resemblance"; if they are distinct, their similarities can be illuminating.[27] Metaphorical thinking therefore values differences and sees the world as a congeries of radically different entities that can be related only in the minds of their perceivers, who thus become heroic interpreters, dominating the anarchic world by the sheer bravado of their perceptions.[28]

This is close to Adams's view both of the world and of the power of human perception as he expressed them in *Mont-Saint-Michel and Chartres*. "It is," he wrote, "my declaration of principles as head of the Conservative Christian Anarchists; a party numbering one member. The Virgin and St. Thomas are my vehicles of anarchism. Nobody knows enough to see what they mean" (*Letters* 1938, 444). Despite the fact, then, that he liked to think of *Mont-Saint-Michel and Chartres* as "a Study of Thirteenth-Century Unity,"[29] he perceived its subjects as radically incomprehensible and the act of interpreting them as a heroic act of intellectual will, an act that galvanized natural "chaos and collision" into artful order for himself and his tourist/readers.

Making metaphors is by nature a transgressive activity, a wrenching mental juxtaposition of disparate elements and an insistence on their similarity. At the end of *Mont-Saint-Michel and Chartres* Adams repeats his bold, elaborate metaphor, in a manner that at the same time affirms his own power of synthesis and suggests its ultimate fragility as well as the fragility of the Gothic cathedral and the *Summa.* "The most vital and most perfect" symbol for the Gothic cathedral, he writes in the last paragraph of the book, "may be that the slender nervure, the springing motion of the broken arch, the leap downwards of the flying buttress,—the visible effort to throw off a visible strain,—never let us forget that Faith alone supports it, and that, if Faith fails, Heaven is lost" (383). St. Thomas had faith, and so did the Gothic builders, but faith has failed for Adams; the faithless, multiplicitous twentieth century has supervened, and the only way to experience unity, harmony, and perfect balance is to visit them, in the architecture, the literature, and even the philosophy of the past.

Because this contradiction between wholeness and anarchy, unity and multiplicity, control and chaos, embodies what Adams most deeply believes about history, his time, and himself, the pervasive tone of *Mont-Saint-Michel and Chartres* is neither comic nor romantic, neither conservative nor anarchic, but ironic. The distancing begins, as I have suggested, with Adams's rhetorical posturing in the preface and continues in his self-deprecation as mere tourist and uncle to nieces. The tone gently mocks Adams himself, his subject, his time, and his project.

> The great cathedrals after 1200 show economy, and sometimes worse. The world grew cheap, as worlds must. (9)

> We have got a happy summer before us, merely in looking for these church-towers. There is no livelier amusement for fine weather than in hunting them as though they were mushrooms. (48)

> To doubt the "Chanson" is to call the very roll of Battle Abbey in question. The whole fabric of society totters; the British peerage turns pale. (21)

We live in sorry times, Adams implies; our work is a mere summer's amusement; and our subject is important precisely *not* to the "whole fabric of society" but only to such social white elephants as "the British peerage." Self-deprecation is endemic to *Mont-Saint-Michel and Chartres*; it has been seen, indeed, as a symptom of the author's effete neurasthenia and the weakness of his writing. I would relate it instead to that "*aporia* or sense of contradiction*" that Hayden White finds "in *all* of the classic historians" and attributes to the fundamental opacity of language, its inability to serve as a transparent, undistorting medium for the transmission of facts.[30] I think that the "aporia" in Adams is even more basic. It is experience itself, rather than language, that has failed him; "first-hand," "authentic" experience is for Adams fundamentally contradictory, simultaneously central and marginal, concrete and ephemeral. Language, however, and particularly the suggestive, transgressive flash of metaphor, can redeem phenomenal experience by using it to create imaginative experience. This is what happens in *Mont-Saint-Michel and Chartres*, as Adams and his readers collaborate to produce a dynamic, critical experience not only of the Middle Ages but of their own time as well.

There is nothing wistful or nostalgic about Adams's view from the margin: his purpose in writing *Mont-Saint-Michel and Chartres* is not simply to display the remains of the past. Like the active tourist who quite consciously creates experience rather than simply exposing him/herself to it, and even more like the sophisticated historian who is aware that writing history is in a sense making history, travel writers who transcend the literal and remain readable despite the occasional banality of their subjects do so by developing complex strategies of representation and interpretation. Fuller does this, and so do Twain and James, but Adams outdoes them all (except, perhaps, the James of *The American Scene*) by combining the three rhetorical tropes of synecdoche, metaphor, and irony to produce a discourse that is both marginal and committed and an experience that is both critical and celebratory. For all the irony of its vision, *Mont-Saint-Michel and Chartres* affirms the power of the intellectual tourist—and the writer—to create meaningful experience from mere events and artifacts, to affirm and to transcend the aporia implicit in both history and narrative.

Adams occupied a marginal position in the society of his day and chose to enjoy the advantages of that position rather than simply suffer its handicaps. He used the leisure and the comfortable self-assurance that his class and gender afforded him to look at the past and the present with a tourist's detachment and an intellectual's critical acuity. He justified his privileges by opening his perspective to others, by writing a guidebook to history and sensibility, and by creating for the reader an intellectual, spiritual, and aesthetic journey. He makes, perhaps, the most original and the most productive use of Europe, its history, art, and culture, of any writer in this book. His achievement in *Mont-Saint-Michel and Chartres* is not, however, isolated and unique. If it foreshadows the rhetorical complexity and figurative density of *The Education* and its twentieth-century successors, it also depends on a pattern Adams developed in earlier travelogues, itself a variation on the conventions of nineteenth-century American travel writing.

Afterword

ON JUNE 13, 1965, boarding a student-chartered turboprop for the long flight to Gatwick, I felt that I was "bask[ing]," like Twain, "in the happiness of being for once in my life drifting with the tide of a great popular movement. Everybody was going to Europe—I, too, was going to Europe." That summer I ran into friends and classmates in London, Nîmes, Siena, Rome, and the Greek islands. My roommate was working as a summer intern in Hamburg; another friend was in Frankfurt; a third was in Vienna. All of us had studied European languages and history; many of us were interested in European art; and we all doubtless thought of ourselves as intrepid, independent young men of the world.

Although we would hardly have known or admitted it, we were the lineal descendants of such tourists and travelers as George Ticknor, David Dorr, Bayard Taylor, Mark Twain, and Henry James. We were in Europe for "the languages," the art, the exoticism of foreign cultures, and the adventure of travel. My own itinerary followed the classic nineteenth-century path from London to Paris to southern France and Italy. I had taken Art 101 and, like Benjamin Babcock, felt a kind of moral imperative to come to terms with the masterpieces of Western civilization (most of which had been mentioned by Murray as early as 1843). Like Taylor's, my trip was the fulfillment of years of dreaming and signified in a very important way the beginning of adult life: it was the first summer I spent away from my parents' home; I never spent more than a few weeks at a time there again. For me, and for many thousands of my peers, the summer in Europe represented a widely recognized, culturally sanctioned rite of passage.

Sometime between then and now—I don't remember the date—things changed. Western civilization lost its claim to universality; students came to recognize the importance of African and Asian cultures, of the native and postcolonial cultures of the Americas; jets began depositing eighteen-year-old Californians in Lima and Kathmandu; the Rough Guides to Southeast Asia joined *Let's Go! Europe* in the college bookstores; and satellite technology made it easy to call home for money from Lomé or Bangkok. Americans—especially young Americans—continued to use travel and the foreign as their nineteenth-century compatriots had done, for self-discovery and the discovery of art and of alien cultures. They even continued to go to Europe, but only as one destination among many possible others. Unlike James's Rimmle sisters and Caroline

Spencer, they would not immediately understand vague remarks about "going" or "having been" as references to the one thinkable destination, the dreamed-of, longed-for "Europe."

So the experiences and the texts on which this book is based may seem quaintly narrow today. American culture in the nineteenth century was unquestioningly Eurocentric; high culture was a valuable tool for social advancement; and history and civilization were understood to have originated in Mesopotamia and moved inexorably westward. Nowadays, culture, civilization, and history are global concepts that can be experienced at least as easily through social service projects, music, or sports as through tourism as it was understood at least as early as the 1830s and at least as late as the 1960s. Civilization no longer has one history, and what were once seen simply as progress and the spread of enlightenment by the advanced inhabitants of the North Atlantic Rim are now understood, in part, at least, as manifestations of self-serving economic and cultural imperialism.

Even admitting all this, however, and remembering that nineteenth-century Americans used Europe and European travel in ways that were determined by their particular place in culture and history, the patterns of experience and the modes of literary production that they established continue to inform the practices of travel and travel writing today. Americans still use travel as a way to shed the familiar constraints of their culture and place, to act out experimental roles and try out tentative personalities, to measure themselves against foreign customs and values, and to seek aesthetic or spiritual experience. They still use travel writing to shape their experiences, create attractive literary personas, hone their writing skills, and get published. Europe has lost its exclusive claim on their attention, and the tradition of high art, appropriated by if not originally created for the nineteenth-century bourgeoisie, now shares its prestige with the arts and the cultures of other classes and other places. A sequel to this book would need a wider focus—but it would still have to explore many of the patterns and practices that informed the uses of Europe for nineteenth-century American travelers.

Notes

PREFACE

1. James, *Complete Tales* 10:428.
2. See Pratt, *Imperial Eyes*; Mills, *Discourses of Difference*; and Blake, "A Woman's Trek."
3. Proust, *Remembrance of Things Past* 1:420.
4. Freud made a more theoretical case for the association between travel and desire, suggesting in "A Disturbance of Memory on the Acropolis" that there is an important connection between the longing for distant places and the guilty desire to escape from home and family. Dennis Porter developed this argument brilliantly (in a Lacanian direction) in *Haunted Journeys*.
5. There are a number of valuable things that this book is not, and it might be a good idea to list them here and let readers know where they can be found. First, this is not a major contribution to the exciting and relatively new field of travel theory, though I have been influenced in writing it by Dean MacCannell's *The Tourist* and by books and essays by Judith Adler, Roland Barthes, Michel Butor, Eric Cohen, Hans Magnus Enzensberger, John A. Jakle, Eric Leed, John Pemble, John Sears, and Georges Van Den Abbeele.

Second, this is not a history of American travel in Europe. Readers seeking an overview of this subject can look first at Foster Rhea Dulles's general study, *Americans Abroad*; Philip Rahv's interpretive anthology, *Discovery of Europe*; and Ernest Earnest's *Expatriates and Patriots*.

More detailed accounts of literary travelers can be found in the many works of Van Wyck Brooks, especially *New England Indian Summer, 1865-1915* and *The World of Washington Irving*, in O. W. Long's *Literary Pioneers*, Willard Thorp's "Pilgrims' Return," Ahmed Metwalli's "Americans Abroad," and Jeffrey Steinbrink's "Why the Innocents Went Abroad." Two bolder, theoretical approaches to this subject are William C. Spengemann's in *The Adventurous Muse* and Terry Caesar's in "'Counting the Cats in Zanzibar.'"

There are also many works on Americans in individual countries. For Great Britain the most notable of these are the works of Robert Spiller, Allison Lockwood, Benjamin Lease, and Christopher Mulvey. For Italy, the other most frequently treated country, there are books by Van Wyck Brooks, Paul R. Baker, Nathalia Wright, and William L. Vance as well as an excellent article by A. William Salamone.

Another very admirable and important project that I have not undertaken here is any rethinking of the notion of Americanness as it is influenced and evidenced by individual Americans' views of themselves and their relation to the Old World. William C. Spengemann deals with this subject, but the two most important works are Cushing Strout's *The American Image of the Old World* and Robert Weisbuch's brilliant *Atlantic Double-Cross.*

I am also not particularly interested here in the formal and thematic connections between travel writing and fiction, though the subject arises from time to time. Among the many writers who focus on this subject are William Spengemann, Percy G. Adams, and Jeffrey Rubin-Dorsky.

Finally, I do not offer here a major contribution to the history of sensibility. A very interesting book can be written on American travelers' evolving perception of place and space. Such a work would juxtapose American travel accounts, both at home and abroad, with the landscape aesthetics of Gilpin and Ruskin, the particularly American sense of the land explored by Annette Kolodny and Myra Jehlen, and the theoretical studies of Yi-Fu Tuan and Paul Shepard.

CHAPTER ONE
AMERICANS ABROAD

1. Tomes, "Americans on Their Travels," 57.

2. Sweetser, *Europe for $2 a Day*, 107.

3. Smith, *American Travellers Abroad.*

4. Schriber, "Julia Ward Howe and the Travel Book," 267, 269.

5. Metwalli, "Americans Abroad," 69–70.

6. As early as 1827, for example, the anonymous reviewer of N. H. Carter's *Letters from Europe* pointed out that the tomb of Petrarch's Laura had become "one of the assigned places for a sentimental rhapsody." "It may be," he went on, "that a special direction is given in the itineraries—'here you must exclaim and lament, but not exhaust yourself, as you may visit Vaucluse.'" "Our traveller," he concluded, "does not fail in the emergency." Indeed, Carter seemed to this reviewer rather consistently to repeat what he had read than to contribute anything new to his readers' understanding and appreciation of Europe. Review of *Letters from Europe . . . in the Years 1825, 1826, and 1827*, by N. H. Carter, *American Quarterly Review* 2 (December 1827): 562.

7. I am setting aside for the moment the very common practice of travel for health, since the real question here is not "Why travel?" but "Why Europe?" For further comment see the chapters on Emerson, James, and Adams.

8. James, *Literary Criticism . . . American Writers*, 351–52.

9. Pessen, *Jacksonian America*, 82.

10. Tomes, "Americans on Their Travels," 60.

11. "Going Abroad," 530.

12. The classic articulation of the relation between economic development and the development of the "leisure class," including both the idle and their busy but materially nonproductive hangers-on, is to be found in Veblen's *The Theory of the Leisure Class.*

13. Quoted in Long, *Literary Pioneers*, 14–15.

14. Ann Douglas, *Feminization*, 237.

15. See Bowen, *A Century of Atlantic Travel*, ch. 2.
16. See Dulles, *Americans Abroad*, 43–67, 102–15.
17. "Going Abroad," 530–31.
18. In Douglas's opinion this redefinition was a self-serving if not necessarily conscious act on the part of the dominant class of businessmen, whose purpose was both to channel the energies of the unproductive sector of respectable society and to pay lip service to a set of values that they nominally cherished but in practice preferred to ignore. "The minister and the lady were appointed by their society as the champions of sensibility. They were in the position of contestants in a fixed fight: they had agreed to put on a convincing show, and to lose" (*Feminization*, 12). Although this interpretation is doubtless valid at its own level of generalization, it does not seem to me to grant enough importance to the ministers' and the ladies' own sense of mission and to the dominant class's inability to control its results in every case. As Douglas demonstrates elsewhere, the act of writing made people feel empowered, even when they were being used. What is more important, the opening of the professions of journalism and sentimental writing to women made possible the influential writings of people like Harriet Beecher Stowe and Margaret Fuller.
19. Butler, *The American Gentleman*, 76.
20. Douglas, *Feminization*, 85.
21. James, *Literary Criticism . . . American Writers*, 473.
22. Hall, *Rambles in Europe*, v.
23. Sigourney, *Pleasant Memories*, iii–iv.
24. See Douglas, *Feminization*, 45–48.
25. Taylor, *Views A-foot*, 17.
26. "The nearest thing to writing a novel," writes Paul Theroux, "is traveling in a strange country" (*Sunrise with Seamonsters*, 140). Michel Butor agrees. "To travel, or at least to travel in a certain way," he believes, "is to write, and to write is to travel" ("Le voyage et l'écriture," 4).
27. Twain, *Innocents Abroad*, 205.
28. See Hillard, *Six Months*, 531.
29. Fuller, "Books of Travel," 1.
30. Tuckerman, "William Beckford," 9, 10.
31. James, *Literary Criticism . . . American Writers*, 475.
32. Butor, "Le voyage et l'écriture," 8.
33. Ibid., 17.

Chapter Two
Travel as Ritual

1. Putnam, *Tourist in Europe*, 11.
2. Morford, *Short-Trip Guide*, 140.
3. Putnam, *Tourist in Europe*, 12.
4. Siddons, *Norton's Hand-Book*, 25–26.

5. Morford, *Short-Trip Guide*, 154.

6. Dewey, *The Old World and the New*, 1:25.

7. Clarke, *Eleven Weeks in Europe*, 33.

8. Dewey, *The Old World and the New*, 1:88.

9. Clarke, *Eleven Weeks in Europe*, 47.

10. Sigourney, *Pleasant Memories of Pleasant Lands*, 372.

11. For example:

You cannot go to Europe without faith. You cannot go to Heaven without faith. If you would go to Europe, you must have faith in the word of others who have crossed the sea before you; you must have faith in the ship on which you sail; you must have faith in the machinery; you must have faith in the compass and chart; you must have faith in the captain and crew. If you would go to Heaven, you must have some degree of faith in Christian people and in the Christian Church; you must have implicit faith in the chart—the Bible—and in Jesus Christ, the great Captain of your Salvation. (Winchester, *Gospel of Foreign Travel*, 9)

12. Veblen, *Theory of the Leisure Class*, esp. 119–25, 370.

13. Lukes, "Political Ritual and Social Integration," 291.

14. The definition derives from Durkheim. See Graburn, "Tourism: The Sacred Journey," 24.

15. Turner, *From Ritual to Theatre*, 13.

16. Ibid., 24.

17. Ibid., 44–45.

18. Leed, *The Mind of the Traveler*, 217.

19. For a corroboration of this point see Mills, *Discourses of Difference*, and Pratt, *Imperial Eyes*.

20. Taylor, *Views A-foot*, 22.

21. "We soon attained the summit, and mounting a little mound of earth and stones, I saw the half of Scotland at a glance. The clouds hung just above the mountain tops, which rose all around like the waves of a mighty sea. On every side—near and far—stood their misty summits, but Ben Lomond was the monarch of them all" (*Views A-foot*, 49).

22. "On reaching the peak, the night was one of beauty and grandeur such as imagination never painted. You see around you no plain ground, but on every side constellations or groups of hills exquisitely dressed in the soft purple of the heather, amid which gleam the lakes, like eyes that tell the secrets of the earth and drink in those of the heavens" (Fuller, *These Sad but Glorious Days*, 74). Although I worked with the letters as they originally appeared in the *Tribune*, for the reader's convenience I provide page references to their recent republication by Reynolds and Smith. Further references to these texts are to this edition and are followed by the abbreviation *Dispatches* and page numbers in parentheses.

23. Beatty, *Bayard Taylor*, 1–12.

24. Taylor, *Views A-foot*, 17–18.

25. Blanchard, *Fuller*, 65, 69.

26. Fuller, *Letters of Margaret Fuller* 4:248, 1:243, 1:254.

27. "I do not look forward to seeing Europe now as so very important to me. My mind and character are too much formed. I shall not modify them much but only add to my stores of knowledge. Still, even in this sense, I wish much to go. It is important to me, almost needful in the career I am now engaged in. I feel that, if I persevere, there is nothing to hinder my having an important career even now. But it must be in the capacity of a journalist, and for that I need this new field of observation" (quoted in Blanchard, *Fuller*, 244).

28. See Blanchard, *Fuller*, 246.

29. Hansen-Taylor and Scudder, *Life and Letters*, 46.

30. Fuller, *Letters* 4:245.

31. Taylor, *Views A-foot*, 320.

32. Hansen-Taylor and Scudder, *Life and Letters*, 34.

33. Ibid., 43.

34. Fuller, *Memoirs* 2:268–69. Quoted in Blanchard, *Fuller*, 324.

35. Hansen-Taylor and Scudder, *Life and Letters*, 44.

36. See Blanchard, *Fuller*, 339.

37. Adler, "Travel as Performed Art," 1375.

38. Ibid., 1375–76.

Chapter Three
Guidebooks

1. Putnam, *Tourist in Europe*, 5.

2. For a generation-by-generation analysis of the place of Europe in the American imagination, see Strout, *American Image*.

3. Although a large percentage of nineteenth-century American tourists were women, guidebooks almost always assumed a male reader. Putnam assumes that his readers are "gentlemen" (10); Park includes two full pages of packing advice for men, adding a single sentence that "for ladies' baggage, the writer will not attempt to prescribe" (Park, *Hand-Book*, 15–16); Morford pays detailed attention to the problem of tobacco ("there is no decent tobacco in Europe") for "the men and citizens of that great nation which can certainly out-chew and out-expectorate the wide world!" (Morford, *Short-Trip Guide*, 71). Many guidebooks also suggest that their readers take special precautions if they should happen to be traveling with ladies. See, for example, Putnam: "Start early on your ascent, and reach Montanvert to see the Glaciers, which is a fatiguing operation; but, by the assistance of a guide, and if you are not a pedestrian, by a horse, part of the way, it may be well accomplished; indeed, if you go alone, two guides will be necessary, but each person must have one at 6fr. each, and 3fr. for a horse; and if ladies are of the party, it may be advisable to have a chaise à porteur, for which you pay 20fr."

4. Park, *Hand-Book*, 9–10.

5. Morford, *Short-Trip Guide*, 11.

6. James, *Novels, 1871–1880*, 573.

7. Hemstreet, *Economical European Tourist*, 2.

8. Nieriker, *Studying Art Abroad*, 6–7.

9. Jones, *European Travel for Women*, 16, 123.

10. Smith-Rosenberg, "The New Woman as Androgyne," in *Disorderly Conduct*, 245–96.

11. WRTA, *Summer in England*, 5.

12. Allen, *European Tour*, 9.

13. Sherburne, *Tourist's Guide*, 14.

14. Judith Adler traces the connection between travel and the acquisition of information back to the seventeenth century's elevation of experience over authority and of the eye over the ear as a source of knowledge. By the late eighteenth century, she argues, when the parts of the world frequented by ordinary travelers had been exhaustively described, a vaguer, more metaphysical—that is, a properly romantic—notion of the value of travel arose, which emphasized "the spiritual significance" of "experiences of beauty and sublimity" for individual travelers and understood improvement in terms of spiritual or aesthetic exaltation rather than mundane information. It seems to me that both of these justifications for travel persist throughout the nineteenth century, at least among the American travelers I have studied; it is certainly true that guidebooks throughout the period hold out the possibility of both kinds of improvement as lures for the prospective traveler. See Adler, "Origins of Sightseeing," 11–16, 22.

15. Murray, *Hand-Book for Travellers on the Continent*, 47–48.

16. See Boorstin, *The Image*, 87–88; Paul Fussell, *Abroad*, 37–50; Cohen, "Toward a Sociology."

17. Enzensberger, "Theorie des Tourismus," 156.

18. Murray, *Handbook for Central Italy*, 263.

19. Fetridge, *Harper's Hand-book*, v.

20. Pemble, *Mediterranean Passion*, 67, 142.

21. Vance, *America's Rome* 2:139–60.

22. Vance's chapter on Victorian Americans and Baroque Rome relates a fascinating high-culture version of this ethnocentric (and in this case specifically Protestant) snobbery. See *America's Rome* 2:77–102.

23. MacCannell, *The Tourist*, 57–76, esp. 64.

24. Ibid., 177–79.

25. Van Den Abbeele, "Montesquieu touriste," 67.

26. Adler, "Origins of Sightseeing," 14.

27. Ibid., 21, 24.

28. Vasi, *New Picture of Rome*, 381, 382, 383.

29. Murray, *Handbook for Central Italy*, 337.

30. Osgood, *Pocket-Guide*, 351.

31. See MacCannell on the place of "'experience' in the rhetoric of modernity" and the spurious connection between experience and understanding (68).

32. See Osgood, *Pocket-Guide*, 314; Starke, *Information*, 302; Fetridge,
Harper's Hand-book, 288.

33. Van Den Abbeele, "Montesquieu touriste," 65.

34. Ibid., 67.

35. *Satchel Guide*, 59.

36. Starke, *Information and Directions*, 305.

37. Fetridge, *Harper's Hand-book*, 347.

38. Hillard, *Six Months in Italy*, 181–82.

39. Adler, "Travel as Performed Art," 1368.

Chapter Four
Travel Chronicles

1. On the sentimental novel see Baym, *Women's Fiction*, ch. 2, and Brown,
The Sentimental Novel, ch. 4. On the slave narrative see Stepto, *From Behind the
Veil*, Gates, "Introduction" to *The Classic Slave Narratives*, and Andrews, *To Tell
a Free Story*.

2. Adler, "Travel as Performed Art," 1368.

3. Examples are from the *Providence Gazette*, September 1821.

4. *Hartford Courant*, January 4, 1842, reprinted from the *New York American*.

5. Silliman, *Journal* 1:90.

6. Rubin-Dorsky, "Washington Irving: Sketches of Anxiety," 499. Rubin-
Dorsky argues that this was a misperception and suggests that Crayon was in fact
the product and in some ways the representation of Irving's personal anxiety and
cultural insecurity. See also his *Adrift in the Old World*.

7. For an excellent discussion of the sketch as conventional genre, see Rubin-
Dorsky, "Washington Irving and the Genesis of the Fictional Sketch."

8. This tone is anticipated by the physical form of the 1844 edition that I am
using. This volume is slightly smaller (roughly 7″ × 4.5″) than the travel books
on my shelf that were published at about the same time; the edges of its pages are
gilded; it is bound in pink cloth, blind-stamped with a floral border, with the
title and more floral ornaments gold-stamped on the spine, and a gold cross
surrounded by an elaborate border in the center of both covers. It looks like a
keepsake and feels like a prayer book.

9. Andrews, *To Tell a Free Story*, 17.

10. Dorr, *Colored Man*, 12.

11. "I am going from the Custom house, where I have deposited my baggage"
(13); "Last night I arrived here, making the time from Liverpool to London in
five hours and a half" (19); "I am now all cap a pie for Paris" (25).

12. "Just then I saw Mr. Fellowes of the firm of Fellowes & Co., step up to this man and shake him warmly by the hand" (39); "I must now introduce the reader to an American 'merchant prince,' better known by his associates as the 'Prince of Good Fellows.' This is Cornelius Fellowes" (61).

13. "The Crystal Palace is the acquafortis of curiosity that gives the arcadial polish to London's greatness" (19).

14. Greenwood, *Haps and Mishaps*, 6.

15. Clarke, *Eleven Weeks in Europe*, 29.

16. [Fiske, S. W.], *Mr Dunn Browne's Experiences in Foreign Parts*, 9.

17. But see my discussion of Thomas Witmer's *Wild Oats Sown Abroad* in chapter 7.

18. Farrison, *William Wells Brown*, 114.

19. William Wells Brown, *American Fugitive*, 313, 314.

20. See Farrison, *William Wells Brown*, 207.

21. *The Liberator*, no. 1139 (November 19, 1852).

22. *The British Friend* 10 (July 1852): 187–88.

23. See, for example, Irving, *Sketch Book*, 896–97; Willard, *Journal and Letters*, 292–93; Taylor, *Views A-foot*, 82–83.

CHAPTER FIVE
RALPH WALDO EMERSON

1. Emerson, *Essays and Lectures*, 15. Further references to this volume are followed by an *E* and the page number in parentheses.

2. Weisbuch, *Atlantic Double-Cross*, xiv.

3. Emerson, *Letters* 1:369. Further references to this edition of the letters are followed by *L* and the volume and page number in parentheses.

4. Barish, *Roots of Prophecy*, 186.

5. Richardson, "Emerson's Italian Journey," 121.

6. For comments on this feature of Emerson's style as it manifests itself in *English Traits*, see Peacock, "Self-Reliance and Corporate Destiny," and Goluboff, "Emerson's *English Traits*."

7. Barish, *Emerson in Italy*. Photographs by Evelyn Hofer.

8. "Early in 1833, Emerson traveled to Malta, Sicily, Italy, and France. It was not until he reached Paris in late June that he began to think in earnest about the rest of his life" (Cayton, *Emerson's Emergence*, 138).

9. Barish, *Roots of Prophecy*, 182. The travel literature of the time abounds with accounts of recuperative journeys, as well as posthumously published journals of sufferers whose disease did not respond to sea air and a change of scene. Celebrated travelers-for-health include Richard Henry Dana, Jr., Francis Parkman, Alice James, and Henry Adams.

10. See, for example, Samuel Greene Wheeler Benjamin, *The World's Paradises; or, Sketches of Life, Scenery, and Climate in Noted Sanatoria* (New York:

Appleton, 1880); Robert Jefferson Breckinridge, *Memoranda of Foreign Travel* (Philadelphia: Joseph Whetham, 1839); and James Brooks, *Seven Months' Run, Up, and Down, and Around the World* (New York: Appleton, 1872).

11. Barish, *Roots of Prophecy*, 186.

12. Evelyn Barish agrees. See ibid., 231–42.

13. Emerson, *Journals.* Further references are followed by *J* and the volume and page numbers in parentheses.

14. Irving, *Sketch Book*, 747.

15. Eames, *Budget*, 5.

16. Hillard, *Six Months in Italy*, 72.

17. See *J* 4:168 n. 14. Fanny W. Hall quotes the same line in her *Rambles in Europe* 2:22.

18. It can also be seen as an indication of the Americans' lingering provincialism. Judith Adler points out in "Origins of Sightseeing" that the transition from travel as an occasion for conversation with foreign authorities to travel as a means of collecting objective facts and aesthetic impressions had occurred much earlier for European travelers.

19. Reviews and comments quoted in Burkholder, "The Contemporary Reception of *English Traits*," 159.

20. Review of *English Traits*, *Putnam's Monthly* 8 (October 1856): 407.

21. "The currents of thought are counter: contemplation and practical skill; active intellect and dead conservatism; world-wide enterprise, and devoted use and wont; aggressive freedom and hospitable law, with bitter class-legislation; a people scattered by their wars and affairs over the face of the whole earth, and homesick to a man; a country of extremes,—dukes and chartists, Bishops of Durham and naked heathen colliers;—nothing can be praised in it without damning exceptions, and nothing denounced without salvos of cordial praise" (*E* 793).

CHAPTER SIX
MARGARET FULLER AND THE DISCOURSES OF TRAVEL

1. Watson, *Margaret Fuller*, 115.

2. The best short account of these years may be found in Larry J. Reynolds and Susan Belasco Smith's introduction to their edition of Fuller's *Tribune* letters, *"These Sad but Glorious Days": Dispatches from Europe, 1846–1850*, 1–35.

3. Douglas, "Margaret Fuller and the Search for History," passim.

4. Blanchard, *From Transcendentalism to Revolution*, 340.

5. Chevigny, *The Woman and the Myth*, 451.

6. Stern, *Life*, 420.

7. Deiss, *Roman Years*, 7.

8. To be fair, I should add that the passion in Deiss's account is humanitarian and political as well as erotic.

9. Anthony, *Psychological Biography*, 210–11.

10. Wade, *Whetstone of Genius*, 216–17.

11. To the works of Douglas, Blanchard, and Chevigny already quoted I would add Welter, *Dimity Convictions*, and Allen, *The Achievement of Margaret Fuller*.

12. Douglas, "Search for History," 42.

13. Ibid., 73.

14. Allen, *Achievement*, III.

15. Reynolds, *European Revolutions*, 62.

16. Chevigny, "To the Edges of Ideology," 174.

17. Ibid., 188–89.

18. Chevigny, *The Woman and the Myth*, 369.

19. In "Julia Ward Howe and the Travel Book," Mary-Suzanne Schriber asserts that the travel book was "a predominantly masculine preserve" (264) and cites the impressive fact that "of the 691 books of travel published between 1800 and 1865, only 35 were by women" (269). What she does not tell us is how many of the 691 concerned travel to Europe and how many were examples of specifically masculine subgenres such as the sailor's account or the diplomatic memoir. I do not doubt that, like most aspects of public life, publishing a travel book was harder for a woman than it was for a man, but I do not believe that a public that had welcomed the travel books of Emma Willard, Lydia Sigourney, Catharine Maria Sedgwick, and Caroline Cushing and that would soon greet works by Grace Greenwood, Fanny Fern, Harriet Beecher Stowe, Julia Ward Howe—and Margaret Fuller—was "a masculine preserve."

20. Bakhtin, *Dialogic Imagination*, 262.

21. The difference between my reading of the *Sketch-Book* and that of Rubin-Dorsky in "Washington Irving and the Genesis of the Fictional Sketch" stems from the different generic traditions we are dealing with. He emphasizes the protonovelistic element, the development of the Crayon persona, and the genre of the individual fictional sketch. I emphasize the way in which the book as a whole served as a model for future travel writers and helped establish the conventions of a popular form of quasi-literary nineteenth-century nonfiction.

22. Zachariah Allen, *The Practical Tourist*, 6.

23. Willard, *Journal and Letters*, 53.

24. "Wherever we see it, the lines of the great buttress in the fragment of stone, the hues of the waterfall, copied in the flowers that star its bordering mosses, we are delighted; for all the lineaments become fluent, and we mould the scene in congenial thought with its genius" (Fuller, *Summer on the Lakes*, 7).

25. "I trust by reverent faith to woo the mighty meaning of the scene" (28).

26. "For the magnificence, the sublimity of [the Falls] I was prepared by descriptions and by paintings. When I arrived in sight of them I merely felt, 'ah yes, here is the fall, just as I have seen it in picture'" (11).

27. Christina Zwarg also notices the syncretism of style and content in *Summer* and shows it contributes to Fuller's feminist, antiracist purposes. See "Footnoting the Sublime."

28. Similarly, it seems to me that although Fuller's experience in her last years of political engagement, mutual heterosexual love, and motherhood certainly differentiate those years from previous periods of her life, they do not negate all her previous experience.

Chapter Seven
The Innocents in Europe

1. Fiedler, "An American Abroad," 89.
2. Hawthorne, *The Marble Faun*, 3.
3. James, *Literary Criticism . . . American Writers*, 351–52.
4. Women travelers and writers had to claim identities for themselves, too, but whereas their task was collectively more difficult, because of entrenched social opposition to their assuming public personas, and individually more challenging, because of the paucity of role models, it was simplified by the culture's assumption that there was a "natural" affinity between women and art, and that women were in their best, most characteristic state genteel. Sigourney, Fuller, and Willard did not have to justify their interest in art, history, scenery, and poetry or their "failure" to be productive members of a commercial society.
5. Leverenz, *Manhood and the American Renaissance*, 74.
6. Bell, *The Problem of American Realism*, 28. See also Charvat, *Profession of Authorship*, 116, 120, 122, 126, 134, 135 (cited by Bell).
7. Habegger makes the more general point that the grand ambitions of certain nineteenth-century male American writers—he is referring specifically to Howells and James, but the point is equally valid for earlier writers such as Emerson, Longfellow, and Taylor—helped them compensate for their sense of marginality without capitulating to the values of the society around them. "The idea of becoming a great man of letters," Habegger writes, "was attractive partly because it offered . . . an escape from both the threat of feminization and the pressures of normal masculinity" (*Gender, Fantasy, and Realism*, 62).
8. Baym, "Melodramas of Beset Manhood," 123.
9. Habegger, *Gender, Fantasy, and Realism*, 119.
10. See especially Rogers, *Mark Twain's Burlesque Patterns*; Cox, *The Fate of Humor*; Covici, *Mark Twain's Humor*; and Sloane, *Mark Twain as a Literary Comedian*.
11. Tenney, "Twain's Early Travels," 6.
12. See Leverenz, *Manhood and the American Renaissance*, ch. 4, 7.
13. See Douglas, *Feminization*, 236.
14. Brown, *American Fugitive*, 114.

15. Witmer, *Wild Oats*, 5.

16. Haliburton, *The Attaché*, 107–8.

17. Curtis, *Potiphar Papers*, 191–92.

18. Browne, *Artemus Ward in London*, 28.

19. Cf. Twain's effusions over an Etruscan "tear-jug" (*Innocents Abroad*, 197–98).

20. DeMille, *Dodge Club*, 6.

21. Anderson, ed., *Mark Twain: The Critical Heritage*, 25–26.

22. Ibid., 31.

23. Ibid., 33–34.

24. It sold seventy thousand copies the first year, and one hundred thousand in three years. See Lauber, *The Making of Mark Twain*, 256.

25. Canby, *Turn West, Turn East*, xi.

26. Fiedler, "An American Abroad," 77.

27. On this subject see Stoneley, *Mark Twain and the Feminine Aesthetic*, 51.

28. See Cox, *The Fate of Humor*, 38: "Yet what makes Mark Twain a powerful writer, and what makes *The Innocents Abroad* genuinely new, is not the attitudes [it expresses,] but their coordination into the character of his stance, the character of humor."

29. In *Mark Twain and the Feminine Aesthetic*, Stoneley suggests that Twain created in his depictions of women and in the women who surrounded him a lodging place for his own "feminine" impulses, so that he could both "own" and "disown" them. This view nicely complements my position on Twain's construction and deployment of a male persona for himself.

30. Regan, "Reprobate Elect."

31. See Rogers, *Mark Twain's Burlesque Patterns*.

32. On Twain's authorial slipperiness, see Robinson, "Patterns of Consciousness."

33. Twain, *Letters* 1:117.

34. As proof that he is no insensitive clod, Twain does in fact advance his response to landscape.

> If I did not so delight in the grand pictures that are spread before me every day of my life by that monarch of all the Old Masters, Nature, I should come to believe sometimes that I had in me no appreciation of the beautiful whatsoever. (188–89)

35. Robinson, "Patterns of Consciousness," 51.

36. See the sections on travel books (406–7, 422–23), on the tomb of Adam (451), and on the Sphinx (502–4) in *The Innocents Abroad* and the many satirical passages of the otherwise tedious *A Tramp Abroad* (chs. 1, 2, 8, 9, 10, 11, 20, and 24, of the first volume, for example, and chapter 19 of volume 2, which provides an excellent parody of art criticism).

CHAPTER EIGHT
HENRY JAMES, OR THE MERCHANT OF EUROPE

1. Ford, *Henry James*, 22.

2. Henry James, *The Ambassadors*, 504. Further references to this text are followed by page numbers in parentheses.

3. James, *Letters* 2:166. Further references are followed by the letter *L* and volume and page numbers in parentheses.

4. Veblen, *Theory of the Leisure Class*, esp. ch. 2.

5. And Weber. See *From Max Weber*, 181–94.

6. Bourdieu, *Distinction*, 7.

7. Or, as Jean Baudrillard puts it, to convert "economic exchange value (money) . . . into sign exchange value (prestige, etc.)," by mastering the vocabulary and the usage of a culturally privileged idiolect. See *For a Critique of the Political Economy of the Sign*, 115. See also Cox, "The Memoirs of Henry James," 236.

8. "I pursue my pilgrimage through these rather dull French towns and through a good deal of bad weather, and all my desire now is to bring it to a prompt conclusion. It is rather dreary work, for most of the places, I am sorry to say, are much less rich in the picturesque than I had supposed they would be" (Henry James, quoted in Leon Edel, *The Middle Years*, 53).

9. See Anesko, *"Friction with the Market,"* 167–97.

10. These are the others: "Travelling Companions" (1870); "A Passionate Pilgrim" (1871); "At Isella" (1871); "The Madonna of the Future" (1873); "The Sweetheart of M. Briseux" (1873); "The Last of the Valerii" (1874); "Mme de Mauves" (1874); "Adina" (1874); "Eugene Pickering" (1874); "Four Meetings" (1877); "Théodolinde" (1878); "An International Episode" (1878); "The Pension Beaurepas" (1879); "A Bundle of Letters" (1879); "The Point of View" (1882); "The Siege of London" (1883); "Lady Barberina" (1884); "The Author of Beltraffio" (1884); "Pandora" (1884); "Georgina's Reasons" (1884); and "A New England Winter" (1884).

11. James, *Autobiography*, 22, 110, 150, 161.

12. See, for example, Taylor's descent into Italy in *Views A-foot* (321–26), and Howells on Oxford in *Certain Delightful English Towns* (193–218).

13. Freud, *Character and Culture*, 319.

14. Porter, *Haunted Journeys*, 9.

15. For example, *L* 1:89–90, *L* 1:98, *L* 1:102, *L* 1:114–15.

16. James, *Italian Hours*, 26, 17, 64, 125. Further references to this text are followed by the abbreviation *IH* and the page number in parentheses.

17. "I go twice a week to dancing school and seldom have I seen a more hideous collection of females than I do on these occasions. . . . I learned to dance because at the parties here that is the sole amusement—they do not even have

supper but hand round little glasses of syrop [*sic*] and 'helpings' of ice-cream about twice as large as a peach pit!" (*L* 1:18).

18. "If . . . you had such an abundant stock of news to retail, that you did not know with which choice bit to commence, if *you* who have nothing but the gossip of a *little country village* to relate find yourself in such case, how much more perplexed must I be, I who can speak of the most hallowed spots of time-honoured historic Europe!!!!!!" (*L* 1:22).

19. For example:

> The window at which I write is in the fifth storey and looks down on part of the Palais Royal and up at the New Louvre. Underneath is a wide open place upon which there is a ceaseless swarming movement. On one side there is a cab station. The drivers are snoozing with their bloated heads reclining on the tops of their square boxy fiacres, and the little low rats of horses are wearily stamping and whisking their feet and tails. Now, there is a group of warriors of the line receding across the place, little squat, brown men in blue and red who move with a gait formed of a mixture of a waddle and a swagger (*L* 1:35).

20. James, *A Little Tour*, 209. Further references are followed by the abbreviation "*LT*" and page numbers in parentheses.

21. James, *Literary Criticism: French Writers*, 1042–43. Further references to the prefaces are drawn from this edition and are followed by page numbers in parentheses.

22. Agnew, "The Consuming Vision," 74.

23. James, *Autobiography*, 571.

24. Ibid., 17.

25. Edwin Fussell, *The French Side of Henry James*, 8.

26. Quoted in ibid., 9.

27. Brodhead, *Cultures of Letters*, 123, 125, 158.

28. James, *Art of Travel*, 53, 55, 62.

29. James, *Transatlantic Sketches*, 7. Further references to this text are followed by the abbreviation "*TS*" and the page number in parentheses.

30. "Compose" is one of the most characteristic of Jamesian verbs. Jamesian scenes and settings "compose" by arranging themselves in perfect, as it were artistic, order. Jamesian writers and painters "compose" both imagined scenes—"pictures"—and artistic creations—texts and paintings. Jamesian travelers, finally, "compose" experience, organize it in such a way as to produce aesthetic response, treat it, in other words, as the raw material of art.

31. MacCannell, *Tourist*, 43.

32. Culler, "Semiotics of Tourism," passim.

33. Pratt, *Imperial Eyes*, 52.

34. Frow, "Tourism and the Semiotics of Nostalgia," 150.

35. Pratt, *Imperial Eyes*, 201–5.

36. James, "Americans Abroad," 208, 209.

37. James, *Complete Tales* 4:362.

38. James, *Daisy Miller and Other Stories*, 233.

39. Ibid., 15.

40. "I think you managed him very nicely," says Maud Van Vechten to Barbara Atchison in Champney's *Three Vassar Girls Abroad.* "I suppose he thought all American girls were like *Daisy Miller*, and had never heard the proverb,— There are two kinds of girls, girls who flirt, and girls who go to Vassar College" (40).

41. James, *Novels, 1886–1890*, 119.

42. For an illuminating account of the sources of James's knowledge of left-wing movements, see Tilley, *The Background of "The Princess Casamassima."*

43. James, *The Ambassadors*, 116.

44. MacCannell, *The Tourist*, 1, 3,

45. Freedman, *Professions of Taste*, 242.

Chapter Nine
Henry Adams, Traveler

1. Adams, *Letters*, ed. Levenson et al., 3:196. References to this edition are followed by the abbreviation "*Letters*" and the volume and page number in parentheses. See also *Letters of Henry Adams (1892–1918)*, ed. W. C. Ford, p. 87: "To be a tourist is to lose self-respect and invite insult." References to this edition are followed by the abbreviation "*Letters* 1938" and the page number in parentheses.

2. Chalfant, *Both Sides of the Ocean*, 141.

3. Cf.: "Its presentation in book form was not then thought of by the author; but so numerous and apparently sincere were the solicitations that it should be reprinted in book form, that he could not, without ingratitude, allow them to pass unheeded" (Scripps, *Five Months Abroad*, v); "No one can realize more fully than the writer the absence of literary merit in these Letters. . . . For the habitual readers of The Tribune especially were these Letters written, and their original purpose has already been accomplished. Here they would have rested, but for the unsolicited offer of the publishers" (Greeley, *Glances at Europe*, iii, iv).

4. Compare Hillard, *Six Months in Italy*, 22–23.

5. For example: "We all, of course, wish luck to the 'rissorgimento' and I would if I were an Italian, hang tight to the coat-tails of Count Cavour, but that is really no reason why the Pope or the King of Naples should allow his people to riot or rebel" (*Letters* 1:145); "these European popular elections have a little too much demonstration in them; they are a sort of continental squatter sovereignty, and very like a satire on our theories" (*Letters* 1:173).

6. See Dusinberre, *The Myth of Failure*, chs. 3 and 4.

7. On purchases, see *Letters* 3:24. Adams claimed to be seeking nirvana in

Japan, but Levenson remarks, "The closest he came to Nirvana was to regard the world as show, and the best use he could make of this attitude was to sharpen his skill as a spectator" (*Mind and Art*, 206).

8. Dusinberre, *The Myth of Failure*, 187–90, and see Samuels, *The Major Phase*, ch. 1.

9. Dusinberre, *The Myth of Failure*, 200.

10. Samuels, *The Major Phase*, 3.

11. Rowe, *Henry Adams and Henry James*, 81–82.

12. Adams, *Tahiti*, 1 (emphasis mine).

13. See Levenson, *Mind and Art*, 217: "The South Sea letters and the volume of memoirs, taken together, point the way to Adams's extremely personal expression of an historical subject in *Mont-Saint-Michel and Chartres*; but as they stand, they mark the disparity between his epistolary and his formal writing, between his vision and his capacity for rendering it, during the interval between his two careers."

14. Adams, *Letters to a Niece*, 34–35.

15. Review of *Mont-Saint-Michel and Chartres*, by Henry Adams, *Booklist* 10 (February 1913), 215.

16. Henry Osborn Taylor, review of *Mont-Saint-Michel and Chartres*, by Henry Adams, *American Historical Review* 19 (April 1914): 593, 592. Later scholars have tended to finesse the issue of genre, focusing instead on the work's meaning and value and either taking the debunking position of Yvor Winters, that *Mont-Saint-Michel and Chartres* could serve as evidence of "the radical disintegration of a mind" (*In Defense of Reason*, 414) (see also Dusinberre, who describes *Mont-Saint-Michel and Chartres* as "dilettante" [2] in comparison with the *History*, and Harvey Gross, "Henry Adams' Broken Neck"), or following the lead of Oscar Cargill and Richard P. Blackmur in recognizing *Mont-Saint-Michel and Chartres* as a successful artistic representation of Adams's understanding of the medieval and modern worlds (Cargill, "Medievalism"; Blackmur, "Harmony of True Liberalism").

17. Frederick Bliss Luquiens, review of *Mont-Saint-Michel and Chartres*, by Henry Adams, *Yale Review*, n.s., 3 (July 1914): 826, 827.

18. Samuels, *Major Phase*, 25.

19. Adams, *Henry Adams and His Friends*, 262–63.

20. Adams, *Mont-Saint-Michel and Chartres*, xiii.

21. When he decided to reprint the volume privately, he was determined not to let it be turned into "a text-book and a guide-book." "I'll burn Chartres itself before I degrade it to such a fate" (Samuels, *Major Phase*, 519).

22. Greenwood, *Haps and Mishaps*, 29–30.

23. Longfellow, *Outre-Mer*, 86–93.

24. Willis, *Pencillings by the Way*, 55–56. See also Howells, *Venetian Life* 1:47, and Hay, *Castilian Days*, 271.

25. See White, *Metahistory*, 34–36, and the following passage: "The reader is

left to contemplate the coherence of the historical field, considered as a *completed* structure of "Ideas" (i.e., institutions and values), and with the kind of feeling engendered in the audience of a drama that has achieved a definitively Comic resolution of all the *apparently* tragic conflicts within it. The tone of voice is accommodationist, the mood is optimistic, and the ideological implications are Conservative" (28).

26. This idea is a commonplace. What is original with Adams is the elaboration of the *Summa* as architecture.

27. See White, *Metahistory*, 34.

28. See ibid., 8–9.

29. Adams, *Education*, 435.

30. White, "Fictions," 36.

Works Cited

Adams, Henry. *The Education of Henry Adams*. Edited by Ernest Samuels. Boston: Houghton Mifflin, 1973.

————. *Henry Adams and His Friends: A Collection of His Unpublished Letters*. Compiled by Harold Dean Cater. Boston: Houghton Mifflin, 1947.

————. *Letters*. 6 vols. Edited by J. C. Levenson, et al. Cambridge, Mass.: Harvard University Press, 1982–88.

————. *Letters of Henry Adams (1892–1918)*. Edited by Worthington Chauncey Ford. Boston: Houghton Mifflin, 1938.

————. *Letters to a Niece*. Boston: Houghton Mifflin, 1920.

————. *Mont-Saint-Michel and Chartres*. Princeton, N.J.: Princeton University Press, 1981.

————. *Tahiti*. Edited by Robert E. Spiller. New York: Scholars' Facsimiles and Reprints, 1947.

Adams, Percy G. *Travel Literature and the Evolution of the Novel*. Lexington: University Press of Kentucky, 1983.

Adler, Judith. "Origins of Sightseeing." *Annals of Tourism Research* 16 (1989): 7–29.

————. "Travel as Performed Art." *American Journal of Sociology* 94 (1989): 1366–91.

Agnew, Jean-Christophe. "The Consuming Vision of Henry James." In *The Culture of Consumption*, edited by Richard Wightman Fox and T. J. Jackson Lears. New York: Pantheon, 1983.

Allen, Grant. *The European Tour*. New York: Dodd Mead, 1900.

Allen, Margaret Vanderhaar. *The Achievement of Margaret Fuller*. University Park: Pennsylvania State University Press, 1979.

Allen, Zachariah. *The Practical Tourist*. Providence, R.I.: A. S. Beckwith, 1832.

Anderson, Frederick, ed. *Mark Twain: The Critical Heritage*. New York: Barnes and Noble, 1971.

Andrews, William L. *To Tell a Free Story: The First Century of Afro-American Autobiography, 1760–1865*. Urbana: University of Illinois Press, 1986.

Anesko, Michael. *"Friction with the Market": Henry James and the Profession of Authorship*. New York: Oxford University Press, 1986.

Anthony, Katharine. *Margaret Fuller: A Psychological Biography*. Darby, Penn.: Darby Books, 1920.

Baker, Paul R. *The Fortunate Pilgrims: Americans in Italy, 1800–1860*. Cambridge, Mass.: Harvard University Press, 1964.

Bakhtin, M. M. *The Dialogic Imagination*. Edited by Michael Holquist. Translated by Michael Holquist and Caryl Emerson. Austin: University of Texas Press, 1981.

Barish, Evelyn. *Emerson in Italy.* Photographs by Evelyn Hofer. New York: Holt, 1989.

————. *Emerson: The Roots of Prophecy.* Princeton, N.J.: Princeton University Press, 1989.

Barthes, Roland. *L'Empire des Signes.* Geneva: Skira, Les Sentiers de la création, 1970.

Baudrillard, Jean. *For a Critique of the Political Economy of the Sign.* Trans. Charles Levin. St. Louis: Telos, 1981.

Baym, Nina. "Melodramas of Beset Manhood." *American Quarterly* 33 (1981): 123–39.

————. *Women's Fiction: A Guide to Novels by and about Women in America, 1820–1870.* Ithaca, N.Y.: Cornell University Press, 1978.

Beatty, Richmond Croom. *Bayard Taylor: Laureate of the Gilded Age.* Norman: University of Oklahoma Press, 1936.

Bell, Michael Davitt. *The Problem of American Realism: Studies in the Cultural History of a Literary Idea.* Chicago: University of Chicago Press, 1993.

Blackmur, Richard P. "The Harmony of True Liberalism: Henry Adams' *Mont-Saint-Michel and Chartres.*" *Sewanee Review* 60 (1952): 1–27.

————. *Henry Adams.* Edited by Veronica A. Makowsky. New York: Harcourt Brace Jovanovich, 1980.

Blake, Susan L. "A Woman's Trek: What Difference Does Gender Make?" In *Western Women and Imperialism: Complicity and Resistance,* edited by Nupur Chaudhuri and Margaret Strobel. Bloomington: Indiana University Press, 1992.

Blanchard, Paula. *Margaret Fuller: From Transcendentalism to Revolution.* Radcliffe Biography Series. Reading, Mass.: Addison-Wesley, 1987.

Boorstin, Daniel. *The Image: A Guide to Pseudo-Events in America.* New York: Harper and Row, 1961.

Bourdieu, Pierre. *Distinction: A Social Critique of the Judgment of Taste.* Translated by Richard Nice. Cambridge, Mass.: Harvard University Press, 1984.

Bowen, Frank C. *A Century of Atlantic Travel: 1830–1930.* Boston: Little, Brown, 1930.

Bridgman, Richard. *Traveling in Mark Twain.* Berkeley: University of California Press, 1987.

Brodhead, Richard H. *Cultures of Letters: Scenes of Reading and Writing in Nineteenth-Century America.* Chicago: University of Chicago Press, 1993.

Brooks, Van Wyck. *The Dream of Arcadia: American Writers and Artists in Italy, 1760–1915.* New York: Dutton, 1958.

————. *New England Indian Summer, 1865–1915.* New York: Dutton, 1940.

————. *The World of Washington Irving.* New York: Dutton, 1944.

Brown, Herbert Ross. *The Sentimental Novel in America, 1789–1860.* Durham, N.C.: Duke University Press, 1940.

Brown, William Wells. *The American Fugitive in Europe: Sketches of Places and People Abroad.* Boston: John P. Jewett, 1855.

[Browne, Charles Farrar.] *Artemus Ward in London and other papers.* New York: G. W. Carleton, 1867.

Burkholder, Robert E. "The Contemporary Reception of *English Traits.*" In *Emerson Centenary Essays,* edited by Joel Myerson. Carbondale: Southern Illinois University Press, 1982.

Butler, Charles. *The American Gentleman.* Philadelphia: Hogan and Thompson, 1836.

Butor, Michel. "Le voyage et l'écriture." *Romantisme* 4 (1972): 4–19.

Buzard, James. *The Beaten Track: European Tourism, Literature, and the Ways to "Culture," 1800–1918.* Oxford: Oxford University Press, 1993.

Caesar, Terry. "'Counting the Cats in Zanzibar': American Travel Abroad in American Travel Writing to 1914." *Prospects* 13 (1989): 95–134.

Canby, Henry Seidel. *Turn West, Turn East: Mark Twain and Henry James.* Boston, Houghton Mifflin, 1951.

Cargill, Oscar. "The Medievalism of Henry Adams." In *Essays and Studies in Honor of Carleton Brown.* New York: New York University Press, 1940.

Cayton, Mary Kupiec. *Emerson's Emergence: Self and Society in the Transformation of New England, 1800–1845.* Chapel Hill: University of North Carolina Press, 1989.

Chalfant, Edward. *Both Sides of the Ocean: A Biography of Henry Adams: His First Life, 1838–1862.* Hamden, Conn.: Archon, 1982.

Champney, Lizzie W. *Three Vassar Girls Abroad.* Boston: Estes and Lauriat, 1883.

Charvat, William. *The Profession of Authorship in America, 1800–1870.* Edited by Matthew Bruccoli. Columbus: Ohio State University Press, 1968.

Chevigny, Bell Gale. "To the Edges of Ideology: Margaret Fuller's Centrifugal Evolution." *American Quarterly* 38 (1986): 173–201.

———. *The Woman and the Myth: Margaret Fuller's Life and Writings.* Old Westbury, N.Y.: Feminist Press, 1976.

Clarke, James Freeman. *Eleven Weeks in Europe, and What May be Seen in that Time.* Boston: Ticknor, Reed, and Fields, 1852.

Cohen, Eric. "A Phenomenology of Tourist Experience." *Sociology* 13 (1979): 179–201.

———. "Rethinking the Sociology of Tourism." *Annals of Tourism Research* 6 (1979): 18–35.

———. "Toward a Sociology of International Tourism." *Social Research* 39 (1972): 164–82.

———. "Who Is a Tourist?" *Sociological Review,* n.s. 22 (1974): 527–55.

Conder, John J. *A Formula of His Own.* Chicago: University of Chicago Press, 1970.

Covici, Pascal, Jr. *Mark Twain's Humor.* Dallas, Tex.: Southern Methodist University Press, 1962.

Cox, James M. *Mark Twain: The Fate of Humor.* Princeton, N.J.: Princeton University Press, 1966.

————. "The Memoirs of Henry James: Self-Interest as Autobiography." *Southern Review,* n.s. 22 (1986): 231–51.

Culler, Jonathan. "Semiotics of Tourism." *American Journal of Semiotics* 1 (1981): 127–40.

Curtis, George William. *The Potiphar Papers.* New York: Harper and Brothers, 1869.

Deiss, Joseph Jay. *The Roman Years of Margaret Fuller.* New York: Thomas Y. Crowell, 1969.

De Mille, James B. *The Dodge Club; or, Italy in 1859.* New York: Harper & Brothers, 1869.

Dewey, Orville. *The Old World and the New.* 2 vols. New York: Harper and Brothers, 1836.

Dorr, David F. *A Colored Man Round the World.* Cleveland, 1858.

Douglas, Ann. *The Feminization of American Culture.* New York: Doubleday Anchor, 1988.

————. "Margaret Fuller and the Search for History: A Biographical Study." *Women's Studies* 4 (1976): 37–86.

Dulles, Foster Rhea. *Americans Abroad: Two Centuries of European Travel.* Ann Arbor: University of Michigan Press, 1964.

Dusinberre, William. *Henry Adams: The Myth of Failure.* Charlottesville: University Press of Virginia, 1980.

Eames, Jane. *A Budget of Letters; or, Things Which I Saw Abroad.* Boston: Ticknor, 1847.

Earnest, Ernest. *Expatriates and Patriots: American Artists, Scholars, and Writers in Europe.* Durham, N.C.: Duke University Press, 1968.

Edel, Leon. *Henry James. Vol. 3, 1882–1895, The Middle Years.* Philadelphia: Lippincott, 1962.

Emerson, Ralph Waldo. *Essays and Lectures.* New York: Library of America, 1983.

————. *The Journals and Miscellaneous Notebooks of Ralph Waldo Emerson.* 17 vols. Edited by William H. Gilman et al. Cambridge, Mass.: Harvard University Press, 1960–82.

————. *The Letters of Ralph Waldo Emerson.* 6 vols. Edited by Ralph L. Rusk. New York: Columbia University Press, 1939.

Emerson, Ralph Waldo, and Thomas Carlyle. *The Correspondence of Emerson and Carlyle.* Edited by Joseph Slater. New York: Columbia University Press, 1964.

Enzensberger, Hans Magnus. "Eine Theorie des Tourismus." In *Einzelheiten.* Frankfurt/Main: Suhrkamp, 1962.

Farrison, William Edward. *William Wells Brown: Author and Reformer.* Chicago: University of Chicago Press, 1969.

Fetridge, W. Pembroke. *Harper's Hand-book for Travellers in Europe and the East.* Fifth Year. New York: Harper and Brothers, 1866.

Fiedler, Leslie. "An American Abroad." *Partisan Review* 33 (1966): 77–91.

[Fiske, S. W.] *Mr Dunn Browne's Experiences in Foreign Parts.* Boston: John P. Jewett and Company, 1857.

Ford, Ford Madox [Ford Madox Hueffer]. *Henry James: A Critical Study.* New York: Albert and Charles Boni, 1915.

Freedman, Jonathan. *Professions of Taste: Henry James, British Aestheticism, and Commodity Culture.* Stanford, Calif.: Stanford University Press, 1990.

Freud, Sigmund. *Character and Culture.* Edited by Philip Rieff. New York: Collier, 1963.

Frow, John. "Tourism and the Semiotics of Nostalgia." *October* 57 (1991): 123–51.

[Fuller, Margaret.] "Books of Travel." *New-York Tribune,* 18 December 1845.

Fuller, Margaret. *The Letters of Margaret Fuller.* 4 vols. Edited by Robert N. Hudspeth. Ithaca, N.Y.: Cornell University Press, 1983–87.

————. *The Memoirs of Margaret Fuller Ossoli.* 2 vols. Edited by Ralph Waldo Emerson, William Henry Channing, and James Freeman Clarke. Boston: Phillips Sampson, 1852.

————. *Summer on the Lakes.* Boston: Little, Brown, 1844.

————. *"These Sad but Glorious Days": Dispatches from Europe, 1846–1850.* Edited by Larry J. Reynolds and Susan Belasco Smith. New Haven, Conn.: Yale University Press, 1991.

Fussell, Edwin. *The French Side of Henry James.* New York: Columbia University Press, 1990.

Fussell, Paul. *Abroad: British Literary Traveling between the Wars.* New York: Oxford University Press, 1980.

Ganzel, Dewey. *Mark Twain Abroad: The Cruise of the "Quaker City."* Chicago: University of Chicago Press, 1968.

Gates, Henry Louis, Jr. Introduction to *The Classic Slave Narratives.* New York: New American Library, 1987.

"Going Abroad." *Putnam's Magazine,* n.s. 1 (1868): 530–38.

Goluboff, Benjamin. "Emerson's *English Traits*: 'The Mechanics of Conversation.'" *ATQ,* n.s. 3 (1989): 153–67.

Graburn, Nelson H. H. "Tourism: The Sacred Journey." In *Hosts and Guests: The Anthropology of Tourism.* 2d ed., edited by Valene L. Smith. Philadelphia: University of Pennsylvania Press, 1989.

Greeley, Horace. *Glances at Europe.* New York: Dewitt and Davenport, 1851.

Greenwood, Grace [Sara Jane Lippincott]. *Haps and Mishaps of a Tour in Europe.* Boston: Ticknor, Reed, and Fields, 1853.

Gross, Harvey. "Henry Adams' Broken Neck." *Centennial Review* 12 (1968): 169–80.

Habegger, Alfred. *Gender, Fantasy, and Realism in American Literature.* New York: Columbia University Press, 1982.

[Haliburton, Thomas Chandler.] *The Attaché, or Sam Slick in England.* 2 vols. London: Richard Bentley, 1843–44.

Hall, Fanny W. *Rambles in Europe . . . in 1836.* New York: E. French, 1839.

Hansen-Taylor, Marie, and Horace E. Scudder. *The Life and Letters of Bayard Taylor*. Boston: Houghton Mifflin, 1884.

Hawthorne, Nathaniel. *The Marble Faun*. New York: Penguin, 1990.

Hay, John. *Castilian Days*. Boston: Houghton Mifflin, 1901.

Hemstreet, William. *The Economical European Tourist: A Journalist Three Months Abroad for $430*. New York: S. W. Green, 1875.

Hillard, George Stillman. *Six Months in Italy*. Boston: Houghton Mifflin, 1881.

Howells, William Dean. *Certain Delightful English Towns*. New York: Harper and Brothers, 1906.

———. *Venetian Life*. Boston: Houghton Mifflin, 1892.

Irving, Washington. *History, Tales, and Sketches*. New York: Library of America, 1983.

Jakle, John A. *The Tourist: Travel in Twentieth-Century North America*. Lincoln: University of Nebraska Press, 1985.

James, Henry. *The Ambassadors*. New York: Penguin, 1986.

[———.] "Americans Abroad." *Nation* 692 (3 October 1878): 208–9.

———. *The Art of Travel: Scenes and Journeys in America, England, France, and Italy, from the Travel Writings of Henry James*. Edited by Morton Dauwen Zabel. Freeport, N.Y.: Books for Libraries, 1970.

———. *Autobiography*. Edited by Frederick W. Dupee. Princeton, N.J.: Princeton University Press, 1983.

———. *The Complete Tales of Henry James*. 12 vols. Edited by Leon Edel. Philadelphia: J. P. Lippincott, 1964.

———. *Daisy Miller and Other Stories*. Edited by Jean Gooder. New York: Oxford University Press, 1985.

———. *Italian Hours*. New York: Grove Press, 1979.

———. *Letters*. 4 vols. Edited by Leon Edel. Cambridge, Mass.: Harvard University Press, 1974–84.

———. *Literary Criticism: Essays on Literature; American Writers; English Writers*. Selected by Leon Edel with the assistance of Mark Wilson. New York: Library of America, 1984.

———. *Literary Criticism: French Writers; Other European Writers; The Prefaces to the New York Edition*. Selected by Leon Edel and Mark Wilson. New York: Library of America, 1984.

———. *A Little Tour in France*. London: Home and Van Thal, 1949.

———. *Novels, 1871–1880*. New York: Library of America, 1983.

———. *Novels, 1886–1890*. New York: Library of America, 1989.

———. *Transatlantic Sketches*. Boston: Houghton Mifflin, 1893.

Jehlen, Myra. *American Incarnation*. Cambridge, Mass.: Harvard University Press, 1986.

Jones, Mary Cadwalader. *European Travel for Women: Notes and Suggestions*. New York: Macmillan, 1900.

Kolodny, Annette. *The Land Before Her*. Chapel Hill: University of North Carolina Press, 1984.

Lauber, John. *The Making of Mark Twain.* New York: American Heritage, 1985.

Lease, Benjamin. *Anglo-American Encounters: England and the Rise of American Literature.* Cambridge: Cambridge University Press, 1981.

Leed, Eric. *The Mind of the Traveler: From Gilgamesh to Global Tourism.* New York: Basic Books, 1991.

Levenson, H. C. *The Mind and Art of Henry Adams.* Boston: Houghton Mifflin, 1957.

Leverenz, David. *Manhood and the American Renaissance.* Ithaca, N.Y.: Cornell University Press, 1989.

Lockwood, Allison. *Passionate Pilgrims: The American Traveler in Great Britain, 1800–1914.* New York: Cornwall Books, 1981.

Long, Orie William. *Literary Pioneers: Early American Explorers of European Culture.* Cambridge, Mass.: Harvard University Press, 1935.

Longfellow, Henry Wadsworth. *Outre-Mer.* Philadelphia: David McKay, 1890.

Lukes, Steven. "Political Ritual and Social Integration." *Sociology* 9 (1975): 289–308.

MacCannell, Dean. *The Tourist: A New Theory of the Leisure Class.* New York: Schocken, 1976.

McKeithan, Daniel Morley. *Traveling with the Innocents Abroad: Mark Twain's Original Reports from Europe and the Holy Land.* Norman: University of Oklahoma Press, 1958.

Mane, Robert. *Henry Adams on the Road to Chartres.* Cambridge, Mass.: Harvard University Press, 1971.

Metwalli, Ahmed M. "Americans Abroad: The Popular Art of Travel Writing in the Nineteenth Century." In *America: Exploration and Travel.* Bowling Green, Ohio: Bowling Green University Popular Press, 1979.

Mills, Sara. *Discourses of Difference: An Analysis of Women's Travel Writing and Colonialism.* New York: Routledge, 1991.

Morford, Henry. *Morford's Short-Trip Guide to Europe.* New York: Lee, Shepard, and Dillingham, 1874.

Mulvey, Christopher. *Anglo-American Landscapes: A Study of Nineteenth-Century Anglo-American Travel Literature.* Cambridge: Cambridge University Press, 1983.

———. *Transatlantic Manners: Social Patterns in Nineteenth-Century Anglo-American Travel Literature.* Cambridge: Cambridge University Press, 1990.

Murray, John. *Handbook for Travellers in Central Italy and Rome.* London: J. Murray, 1843.

———. *Hand-Book for Travellers on the Continent.* London: J. Murray, 1843.

Nieriker, May Alcott. *Studying Art Abroad: How to Do It Cheaply.* Boston: Roberts, 1879.

Osgood, James R. *Osgood's Complete Pocket-Guide to Europe.* Boston: James R. Osgood, 1883.

Park, Roswell. *A Hand-Book for American Travellers in Europe.* New York: G. P. Putnam, 1853.

Peacock, John. "Self-Reliance and Corporate Destiny: Emerson's Dialectic of Culture." *ESQ* 29 (1983): 59–72.

Pemble, John. *The Mediterranean Passion: Victorians and Edwardians in the South.* New York: Oxford University Press, 1988.

Pessen, Edward. *Jacksonian America: Society, Personality, and Politics.* Rev. ed. Homewood, Ill.: Dorsey Press, 1978.

Porter, Dennis. *Haunted Journeys: Desire and Transgression in European Travel Writing.* Princeton, N.J.: Princeton University Press, 1991.

Pratt, Mary Louise. *Imperial Eyes: Travel Writing and Transculturation.* New York: Routledge, 1992.

Proust, Marcel. *Remembrance of Things Past.* 3 vols. Translated by C. K. Scott Moncrieff and Terence Kilmartin. New York: Vintage, 1982.

Putnam, George Palmer. *The Tourist in Europe.* New York: Wiley and Putnam, 1838.

Rahv, Philip. *Discovery of Europe: The Story of American Experience in the Old World.* Boston: Houghton Mifflin, 1947.

Regan, Robert. "The Reprobate Elect in *The Innocents Abroad.*" *American Literature* 54 (1982): 240–57.

Reynolds, Larry J. *European Revolutions and the American Renaissance.* New Haven, Conn.: Yale University Press, 1988.

Richardson, Robert D., Jr. "Emerson's Italian Journey." *ESQ* 34 (1988): 121–31.

Robinson, Forrest G. "Patterns of Consciousness in *The Innocents Abroad.*" *American Literature* 58 (1986): 46–63.

Rogers, Franklin R. *Mark Twain's Burlesque Patterns: As Seen in the Novels and Narratives, 1855–1885.* Dallas, Tex.: Southern Methodist University Press, 1960.

Rowe, John Carlos. *Henry Adams and Henry James.* Ithaca, N.Y.: Cornell University Press, 1976.

Rubin-Dorsky, Jeffrey. *Adrift in the Old World: The Psychological Pilgrimage of Washington Irving.* Chicago: University of Chicago Press, 1988.

————. "Washington Irving and the Genesis of the Fictional Sketch." *Early American Literature* 21 (1987): 226–47.

————. "Washington Irving: Sketches of Anxiety." *American Literature* 58 (1986): 499–522.

Salamone, A. William. "The Nineteenth-Century Discovery of Italy: An Essay in American Cultural History. Prolegomena to a Historiographical Problem." *The American Historical Review* 73 (1968): 1359–91.

Samuels, Ernest. *Henry Adams: The Major Phase.* Cambridge, Mass.: Harvard University Press, 1964.

————. *Henry Adams: The Middle Years.* Cambridge, Mass.: Harvard University Press, 1958.

————. *The Young Henry Adams.* Cambridge, Mass.: Harvard University Press, 1948.

The Satchel Guide for the Vacation Tourist in Europe. New York: Hurd and Houghton, 1872.

Schriber, Mary-Suzanne. "Julia Ward Howe and the Travel Book." *New England Quarterly* 62 (1989): 264–79.

Scripps, James E. *Five Months Abroad.* Detroit: F. B. Dickerson, 1882.

Sears, John. *Sacred Places: American Tourist Attractions in the Nineteenth Century.* New York: Oxford University Press, 1989.

Shepard, Paul. *Man in the Landscape.* New York: Knopf, 1967.

Sherburne, John Henry. *The Tourist's Guide.* Philadelphia: G. B. Zieber, 1847.

Siddons, Joachim Heyward. *Norton's Hand-Book to Europe.* New York: C. B. Norton, 1860.

Sigourney, Lydia H. *Pleasant Memories of Pleasant Lands.* Boston: James Munroe, 1842.

Silliman, Benjamin. *A Journal of Travel in England, Holland, and Scotland.* 3 vols. New Haven, Conn.: S. Converse, 1820.

Sloane, David E. E. *Mark Twain as a Literary Comedian.* Baton Rouge: Louisiana State University Press, 1979.

Smith, Harold F. *American Travellers Abroad: A Bibliography of Accounts Published Before 1900.* Carbondale-Edwardsville: Library of Southern Illinois University, 1969.

Smith, Henry Nash. *Mark Twain: The Development of a Writer.* Cambridge, Mass.: Harvard University Press, 1962.

Smith-Rosenberg, Carroll. *Disorderly Conduct: Visions of Gender in Victorian America.* New York: Oxford University Press, 1985.

Spengemann, William C. *The Adventurous Muse: The Poetics of American Fiction, 1789–1900.* New Haven, Conn.: Yale University Press, 1977.

Spiller, Robert. *The American in England.* New York: Henry Holt, 1926.

Starke, Mariana. *Information and Directions for Travellers on the Continent.* Paris: Galignani, 1829.

Steinbrink, Jeffrey. "Why the Innocents Went Abroad." *American Literary Realism* 16 (1983): 278–86.

Stepto, Robert B. *From Behind the Veil: A Study of Afro-American Narrative.* Urbana: University of Illinois Press, 1979.

Stern, Madeleine. *The Life of Margaret Fuller.* New York: E. P. Dutton, 1942.

Stoneley, Peter. *Mark Twain and the Feminine Aesthetic.* Cambridge: Cambridge University Press, 1992.

Strout, Cushing. *The American Image of the Old World.* New York: Harper and Row, 1963.

Sweetser, M. F. *Europe for $2 a Day.* Boston: Osgood, 1975.

Taylor, Bayard. *Views A-foot.* Rev. ed. New York: G. P. Putnam and Son, 1855.

Tenney, Thomas A. "Mark Twain's Early Travels and the Travel Tradition in Literature." Ph.D. diss., University of Pennsylvania, 1971.

Theroux, Paul. *Sunrise with Seamonsters.* Boston: Houghton Mifflin, 1985.

Thorp, Willard. "Pilgrims' Return." In *Literary History of the United States*. Edited by Robert E. Spiller et al. 4th ed. New York: Macmillan, 1974.

Tilley, W. H. *The Background of "The Princess Casamassima."* University of Florida Monographs. Humanities no. 52. Gainesville: University of Florida Press, 1960.

[Tomes, Robert.] "The Americans on Their Travels." *Harper's New Monthly Magazine* 31 (1865): 57.

Tuan, Yi-Fu. *Topophilia*. Englewood Cliffs, N.J.: Prentice-Hall, 1974.

Tuckerman, Henry T. "William Beckford and the Literature of Travel." *Southern Literary Messenger* 16 (1850): 7–14.

Turner, Victor. *From Ritual to Theatre: The Human Seriousness of Play*. New York: Performing Arts Journal Publications, 1982.

Twain, Mark. *The Innocents Abroad and Roughing It*. New York: Library of America, 1984.

———. *Mark Twain's Letters*. Edited by Edgar Marquess Branch, Michael B. Frank, and Kenneth M. Sanderson. Berkeley: University of California Press, 1988.

———. *A Tramp Abroad*. 2 vols. New York: Harper and Brothers, 1919.

Van Den Abbeele, Georges. "Montesquieu touriste; or, a View from the Top." *L'Esprit créateur* 25 (1985): 64–73.

———. "Sightseers: The Tourist as Theorist." *diacritics* 10 (1980): 2–14.

———. *Travel as Metaphor from Montaigne to Rousseau*. Minneapolis: University of Minnesota Press, 1992.

Vance, William L. *America's Rome*. 2 vols. New Haven, Conn.: Yale University Press, 1989.

Vasi, Marien. *A New Picture of Rome and Its Environs in the Form of an Itinerary*. London: Samuel Leigh, 1818.

Veblen, Thorstein. *The Theory of the Leisure Class: An Economic Study of Institutions*. New York: Modern Library, 1934.

Wade, Mason. *Margaret Fuller: Whetstone of Genius*. New York: Viking Press, 1940.

Watson, David. *Margaret Fuller: An American Romantic*. New York: Oxford University Press, 1988.

Weber, Max. *From Max Weber: Essays in Sociology*. Translated and edited by H. H. Gerth and C. Wright Mills. New York: Oxford University Press, 1946.

Weisbuch, Robert. *Atlantic Double-Cross: American Literature and British Influence in the Age of Emerson*. Chicago: University of Chicago Press, 1986.

Welter, Barbara. *Dimity Convictions*. Athens: Ohio University Press, 1976.

White, Hayden. "The Fictions of Factual Representation." In *The Literature of Fact*. Selected Papers from the English Institute, edited by Angus Fletcher. New York: Columbia University Press, 1976.

———. *Metahistory: The Historical Imagination in the Nineteenth Century*. Baltimore: Johns Hopkins University Press, 1973.

Willard, Emma. *Journal and Letters.* Troy, N.Y.: Tuttle, 1833.

Willis, Nathaniel P. *Pencillings by the Way.* New York: Charles Scribner, 1852.

Winchester, C. W. *The Gospel of Foreign Travel.* Rochester, 1891.

Winters, Yvor. *In Defense of Reason.* New York: Swallow Press and William Morrow, 1947.

[Witmer, Theodore.] *Wild Oats Sown Abroad; or, On and Off Soundings, Being Leaves from a Private Journal By a Gentleman of Leisure.* Philadelphia: T. B. Peterson, 1853.

Women's Rest Tour Association. *A Summer in England, with a continental supplement: A Hand-Book for the Use of American Women.* Boston: Alfred Mudge, 1894.

Wright, Nathalia. *American Novelists in Italy: The Discoverers, Allston to James.* Philadelphia: University of Pennsylvania Press, 1965.

Zwarg, Christina, "Footnoting the Sublime: Margaret Fuller on Black Hawk's Trail." *American Literary History* 5 (1993): 616–42.

Index